CHARLES WHEELER

WITNESS TO THE TWENTIETH CENTURY

CHARLES WHEELER

WITNESS TO THE TWENTIETH CENTURY

SHIRIN WHEELER
With a foreword by Christiane Amanpour

MANILLA PRESS

First published in the UK in 2023
This paperback edition published in the UK in 2025 by
MANILLA PRESS
An imprint of Bonnier Books UK
5th Floor, HYLO, 105 Bunhill Row,
London, EC1Y 8LZ

Copyright © Shirin Wheeler, 2023
Foreword copyright © Christiane Amanpour, 2023

All rights reserved. No part of the publication may be reproduced, stored in a retrieval system, transmitted or circulated in any form or by any means, electronic, mechanical, photocopying, recording or otherwise, without prior permission in writing of the publisher.

The right of Shirin Wheeler to be identified as the Author of this work has been asserted by her in accordance with the Copyright, Designs and Patents Act, 1988.

Every reasonable effort has been made to trace copyright holders of material reproduced in this book, but if any have been inadvertently overlooked the publishers would be glad to hear from them.

A CIP catalogue record for this book is available from the British Library.

Paperback ISBN: 978-1-78658-178-5

Also available as an ebook and an audiobook

Typeset by Envy Design Ltd
Printed and bound by Clays Ltd, Elcograf S.p.A

1 3 5 7 9 10 8 6 4 2

The authorised representative in the EEA is
Bonnier Books UK (Ireland) Limited.
Registered office address: Floor 3, Block 3, Miesian Plaza,
Dublin 2, D02 Y754, Ireland
compliance@bonnierbooks.ie
www.bonnierbooks.co.uk

To Ma and Fa, with love
And to my darling godfather Jack

CONTENTS

Foreword by Christiane Amanpour	ix
1. Beginnings: Shaping the Man	1
2. Cold War Warrior	41
3. One Cheer for Democracy	73
4. Berlin Revisited: In the Shadow of the Wall	123
5. Protest and Uprising in 1960s America	153
6. Conspiracy and Cover-Ups: The Undoing of American Presidents	185
7. Remaking Europe: The Brussels Years	231
8. Home Front: Friends and Neighbours	261
9. Voices from the Edge	309
10. New Horizons	347
Acknowledgements	369
Bibliography	375
Notes	379

FOREWORD BY CHRISTIANE AMANPOUR

I first fell into Charles's orbit in the summer of 1981. I was twenty-three and at university in the US, but had managed to get a paid internship with BBC Radio 4's *World Tonight* programme at Broadcasting House. Charles was doing some shifts as one of a rotating group of presenters on the show. At the end of my internship I was allowed to help put out a programme he was presenting. He had the confidence (in us both!) to let that happen, which was amazing. It also meant that at the end of the show he mentioned my name as one of the producers. I was staying with my family in London for the summer, having left Iran the previous year because of the revolution. My parents and sisters were sitting in the apartment in this rather emotional, post-revolution refugee status, and there was a hush as they heard Charles – Charles Wheeler – read out my name. They were so proud. I was so proud.

That moment tied me to him in a lasting way. He became a kind of mentor as well as a friend, and it was to be a mentorship that continued from that first summer when I met him, on through my career at CNN, until his death in 2008. Charles paid a lot of attention to my work over the years. We would meet when I was in London, usually for dinner or lunch but, if there wasn't the time, even just a coffee. We sometimes exchanged letters and postcards and he would comment on my field reports.

He was the first 'elder', if I might call him that, who saw something in me and who thought that I might be good at this profession. But even though he was a hugely senior figure, an authority in the business, somebody who obviously had decades on me in terms of experience and life, I never thought of him as being old. He was very young at heart and had so much vitality, so much enthusiasm for the job, an endless curiosity and willingness to learn new things. You sensed he really delighted in it. And there was that shock of white hair, of course, the chiselled features, a swashbuckling air about him. He not only looked the part – he was the part.

I loved that Charles was married to an Indian woman, Dip. Having an Iranian Muslim father and an English Catholic mother myself, I always felt a cultural affinity to him. I felt that he, in his own life, understood what it was to be close to people who are from another culture, from different backgrounds, or outside the main discourses of the powerful. I think his experience informed his approach, about giving a voice to those who don't have one. It is an incredibly important goal for a journalist. I considered Charles a teacher and an ally in that regard, and in holding accountable the powerful.

I was aware from early on that Charles did the kind of journalism I wanted to do, and he was someone who showed me the right path from the beginning. He never put himself at the centre of his story. I think in his way, although he wasn't specifically an interviewer, everything he did was a form of interviewing. With a lot of encouragement from him, I became a foreign correspondent and was proud of it. Being in the field as a reporter is the heart and soul of journalism. And I remember when I got my own studio-based programme on CNN in 2009, my aim was to bring that reporting into the studio. I wanted to interview the big players on the world stage as if I was in the field getting the news, going to the source all the time. That's a Charles thing – that's what he did.

Most of all, I always felt that Charles had so much integrity. That's something on which he never compromised. I think he believed that there was no alternative to going to wherever the story demanded you go, witnessing it for yourself, and then reporting that story. You were doing something essential because you were reporting the truth, and you are the eyes and ears of the viewers at home . . . It's always inconvenient for those in authority and doesn't always make you popular with politicians or military commanders or even, sometimes, with your own editors and managers. But it's an approach that has been fundamental for me.

In some ways, Charles's generation of journalists was lucky, a luck that just about extended to my own, because for younger journalists now the idea of what constitutes objective truth is so much more compromised. Charles passed away just before the explosive effect of smartphones transformed the way news is consumed. The assault on truth mounted exponentially from that point and it is now under sustained attack by a whole range of vested interests. But I believe that for Charles, as for me, there is absolutely an empirical truth, based on collecting the facts and evidence, and it's up to journalists to say to readers, viewers and listeners, we are going to report that truth and you must make a judgement based on that. That's why for all of us, Charles's work doesn't just represent an important record of events of the last 100 years as told by one reporter, but a reminder of enduring values that we must all actively uphold.

Christiane Amanpour
London, January 2023

1.
BEGINNINGS: SHAPING THE MAN

Any amount of dash and power of command.

Patrick Dalzel-Job on Captain Charles Wheeler RM,
from his book *From Arctic Snow to Dust of Normandy*

The two boys are standing with their father in the lobby of the Atlantic Hotel in Hamburg when the head porter asks them to move to one side. An ordinary-looking man wearing a mackintosh comes through the revolving door. The boys' father, moustached and straight-backed, leans down and whispers to them, 'We're so close we could shoot the bugger.' Charles and his older brother John watch as Adolf Hitler brushes past them and walks up the staircase.

The year is 1932. Selwyn Charles Cornelius-Wheeler (he drops the Selwyn from his name as soon as he can; Cornelius will be jettisoned a couple of decades later) is nine years old. As will happen so often throughout his life, he finds himself at the epicentre of upheaval, face turned towards the turbulent churn of history, witness to a framing moment. Here, what he has just seen is as yet only partially understood. But he knows that, for his father to say such a thing about him, the man walking into the hotel cannot be anything other than bad. With hearts beating a little faster, the boys and their father return to the lakeside house on the outskirts of the city where their mother is waiting.

Hitler is visiting Hamburg to give a speech at the Viktoria-Sportplatz ahead of an election that will make the Nazis the biggest single party in the Reichstag. There is menace in the air. Nerves are frayed. This is a cosmopolitan and outward-facing city, a trading port with a thriving jazz scene. But that's all changing. Life will never again be so free and easy.

It was one of those chance outcomes that followed in the wake of the First World War that meant Charles Wheeler, the quintessential BBC TV news correspondent of his generation, should experience this very particular and dramatic German childhood. Charles senior (as Charles's father was always referred to in the family) met my grandmother, Winifred Rees, in Canada, on Vancouver Island shortly before the First World War. Winifred and her sister Dorothy had left England in 1910 to travel halfway around the world on their own and take up jobs as ladies' companions. Charles senior had also gone to Canada to find work, following in the footsteps of his older brother, Selwyn. He was working as a gardener when he met Winifred. They married in 1913 and were so poor in their first year together that they survived largely on the tomatoes from their garden. But when the war began, Charles senior joined the Canadian Territorial Army and was then posted to France. It was here that he transferred to the Royal Flying

Corps, where he became a pilot, flew rickety RE8 bi-planes, and reached the rank of flight commander.

The main role of an RE8 pilot was in reconnaissance – that is, spotting and photographing enemy artillery positions at the Somme and Arras for the Allies to target. In spite of some hair-raising moments, including crashing his plane into a tree (a photo of the wreck was on permanent display in our sitting room), Charles senior survived the war. He remained in the military as an RAF commander in the Army of Occupation in Germany and considered making it his career. But anticipating the impending financial cuts by the government, in what would become known as the Geddes Axe, he left to take up a post at an engineering company. This took him to Bremen in Germany, where he ran a huge logistical operation involving the repair and refit of thousands of surplus lorries and cars left after the war.

His two sons were born in Bremen – John in 1921 and Charles on 26 March 1923. When the job came to an end, Charles senior moved the family to Hamburg, where he took up a position at the Weber, Smith & Hoare shipping company. Their move happened just as Germany's political system was about to plunge into turmoil following the Great Crash and the rise of the Nazi state.

Charles's first 'political memory', as he would later put it, was of street fighting in Hamburg between Nazis and Communists. The local baker went missing only to come back later with his head permanently tilted to one side. 'He's been in a concentration camp,' Charles's mother told him. 'And you mustn't say anything in case they send him back again.' Then, one day, Charles and John came home from their *Grundschule* with an account of how the Jewish children were being harried by the other pupils. One boy was surrounded. '*Jude, Jude*', they'd jeered, and spat at him.

Winifred made her own quiet stand. She refused to join the others in what was becoming the customary '*Heil Hitler*' greeting at her local butcher's. They lived on the edge of the city in Reinbek, and she made discreet trips with the boys, carrying bags of bread and cheese into the woods for Jewish families hiding from the Nazis. She was also close to other dissident members of the community, such as the Anglo-Irish writer Christabel Bielenberg, married to a German lawyer, Peter Bielenberg, who later became a leading member of the Kreisau Circle, the internal resistance to Nazism, and was sent to Ravensbrück concentration camp following the assassination attempt on Hitler on 20 July 1944.

These ugly displays of bigotry and bullying – and of quiet resistance – seeded themselves in the young Charles, making and shaping the man who would for many become the greatest TV journalist of his age. He recounted these stories to me decades later, and they took their place among my earliest memories too. These childhood glimpses of anti-Semitic violence and persecution were important in driving his wish as a journalist to tell the stories of the victims and the voiceless. I think growing up at this time, in this place, instilled in him an almost instinctive sense of history as well as an awareness of injustice.

Increasingly worried about the boys' safety and their education, Charles senior and Winifred sent them away to boarding school in Northumberland, where the headmaster was a distant cousin known as Uncle Lance. For a while, they returned regularly to Hamburg to see their parents for school holidays, boarding the ferry at Tynemouth and, on arrival, always being treated by their mother to their favourite 'special tea' at the Alsterpavillon, overlooking the lake in the centre of Hamburg. Despite the increasingly tense atmosphere in the city, holidays in Hamburg were a relief for the boys, especially as their minor English boarding school was a far more present and brutal regime in their lives. Uncle Lance, who called John and Charles 'Wheeler 1 and 2', deployed the strap, the ruler and the belt as his instruments of choice to enforce discipline and punishment.

'He was a sadist,' Charles told us, his appalled daughters. And it seems that Wheeler 2, mischievous and already a natural disrespecter of authority, was frequently the object of Uncle Lance's chastisement. But for all that, it was more the prospect of a Geordie accent than the thought of his sons' beatings at the hands of Uncle Lance that finally led Charles senior to move the boys south to Cranbrook School in Kent instead. This was, in any case, easier to reach from Antwerp, the Belgian port to which they relocated in 1938 when the situation in Hamburg had become too intolerable for them to carry on living there.

Life at Cranbrook was better than with Uncle Lance. Charles, always full of energy, played rugby for his House XV. He was also an active member of Cranbrook's flourishing OTC – Officer Training Corps – a useful preparation for the great conflict about to commence.

'Selwyn had quite a good birthday . . . he is buying a 7/6 dart board with some of the birthday money you sent and I am giving him darts. It is a good game.' John, an assiduous letter writer, unlike his younger brother Charles, kept his parents up to date, thanking them for money on behalf of his younger sibling and wishing them a good silver wedding anniversary. Charles's school reports are, on the whole, positive and complimentary, though there is the occasional blip – '. . . he has done little,' his geography master bluntly commented in the final report before he left the school in 1940.

At the end of the boys' last summer vacation in their parents' new home of Antwerp, they heard the news that Britain had declared war on Germany. As they approached the English coast that early September day in 1939 on the crossing back, Charles took photographs of the white cliffs of Dover on his father's camera – a German-made Leica. He must have felt a great sense of relief at seeing the famous cliffs, but the atmosphere had already darkened. The film was confiscated by the authorities as a security risk in case it fell into enemy hands. Charles senior stayed on in Antwerp to wind up his affairs there and, the following month, locked up the house and handed the key to their neighbours, asking them to keep an eye on things. Their new home was in Surrey – they would never live outside England again. Remarkably, when Charles's parents returned to Antwerp after the war to collect their belongings, the neighbour gave them back the key and told them everything was still there and intact.

In an England now at war, Charles senior re-enlisted in the RAF, earning the rank of wing commander and going on to serve as technical director (in effect, an intelligence liaison officer between the different branches of the military) in the

WITNESS TO THE TWENTIETH CENTURY

RAF's Field Information Agency throughout the war. The boys wanted to follow his example and join up. At just sixteen years old, Charles was too young and returned to Cranbrook. But some months later, he was inspired by Secretary of State for War Anthony Eden's broadcast on 14 May 1940 calling for people to join the newly created Local Defence Volunteers force. The key part of Eden's speech for Charles was that the LDV was open to men from the age of seventeen. He pedalled off immediately to the local police station to sign up, only to find that the local bobby on duty hadn't heard the broadcast and didn't know what he was on about. Within two months, more than one and a half million had volunteered and the LDV had been rechristened the Home Guard. One of Charles's strongest memories of that time was serving alongside veterans of the Boer War, whose feet were so misshapen that they had to wear carpet slippers rather than boots when they went on parade. It's hard to imagine Charles as the young Private Pike of his platoon, but certainly *Dad's Army* became his favourite family comedy when the programme appeared on BBC TV in the 1970s, and he would always insist how true to his life in the Home Guard it was.

John, being Charles's elder by two years, joined up earlier. He followed his father into the Royal Air Force and, in 1941, wrote to him from the RAF College Cranwell in Lincolnshire to tell him he'd been commissioned into the RAF Volunteer Reserve with the initial rank of pilot officer on probation. Winifred must have had mixed feelings. Her brother Arthur, in whose honour John's middle name had been given, had died in the previous war, in 1916 in France, a member of the Canadian Scottish. And young Charles was champing at the bit to volunteer.

John was posted to RAF Andover in early 1941 and his letters home are vivid, excited. He was flying long-nosed Blenheims, he informed his father. 'One day I was up for over six hours,' he wrote. 'When I was climbing from the Bristol Channel through the clouds I came to a clear patch and saw a cable with a balloon fifty feet above it in front of me. I avoided it quite easily by putting the nose down and doing a diving turn.' But John also describes darker moments: the sight of bodies blown to pieces after an attack and enemy aircraft coming perilously near and machine-gunning the base. 'We all went to the windows and saw the plane, a JU88. We went outside and watched it until it got unpleasantly close when we all crowded in again. He then did three or four more circuits going just over our heads. Each time we crouched low expecting the bombs.' A week later, on 7 April, the enemy returned to attack the airfield with terrible consequences.

John's roommate wrote to Charles senior and described what happened. He'd returned from leave one night to find John already asleep in their hut. He went to the bathroom. 'Immediately the bombs started falling. There was no time to move and it was all over in a few seconds.' A bomb, dropped from a low level, had probably hit the ground and bounced into the hut via the bedroom window. The only solace he could offer was that 'John was sound asleep and knew nothing about it'. It was barely two months after he'd arrived at Andover. He was just nineteen years old.

With the death of his beloved older brother, Charles's own

plans to enlist were temporarily put on hold. From as far back as I can remember, Charles told us stories about his brother. My sister and I were conscious of an 'Uncle John' who had died in the war, and I mused over the idea of children he never had, cousins we would never know. But publicly, Charles rarely spoke about John, until later in his life when for the BBC he sought out the stories of servicemen on both sides of the conflict in a series of radio documentaries. In these projects, John was very much in his mind. 'I remember the shock of his being killed, but it was something that one almost expected,' he said. 'I began to miss him much more as I got older.'

His mother Winifred also kept her grief to herself but poured it out in pages and pages of letters addressed to her dead son, which, as a teenager, I found many years after her death in a trunk in a tin shed at the bottom of Charles's garden. I spent some hours reading them, then and there on the wooden floor of the shed, unsure at first if this was an intrusion into my grandmother's private suffering. Charles did not want to read them when I told him what I had found. Winifred's heartbreak, her deep religious faith and conviction that she would be reunited with John are all equally striking. So is her fear for her younger son, who she knew would inevitably also soon join up.

Until he was able to do so, Charles, who'd left school early in anticipation of joining the army, had to find work. It seems that the cut and thrust of a newsroom already appealed to him as he took a job at the popular tabloid the *Daily Sketch* as a copy boy. He would credit this interest to a film he'd seen while still at school, *This Man is News*, a low-budget British movie made in 1938 in which a journalist is accused of a crime that he ends up having to solve himself. It was about 'reporters in dirty macs and trilbys with Press cards stuck in their hat-bands', Charles recalled. He loved the film and thought, 'that's for me'. He told his teacher at school, who coincidentally had just received a circular from Kemsley Newspapers, who were looking for copy boys at the *Daily Sketch*. As a copy boy, his main job was rather more mundane – taking articles for editing from one sub's desk to another – though it might also involve doing anything to help get the paper out, including making the tea. Charles certainly did his fair share of brewing-up, as well as slipping out to the pub to buy boozy sub-editors bottles of whisky, but he liked the work and the atmosphere of a newsroom. As he remarked later, his experiences there made him feel that journalists as a whole were more interesting than most of the people he had met up to that point. His year in the newsroom made a clear impression on his future ambitions: when he volunteered for military service and was asked on the application form what trade he had come from, and what he intended to do in the future, Charles wrote 'journalist'.

Charles joined the Royal Marines' 3rd Battalion, an elite amphibious light infantry brigade, in early 1943 and was sent to the Royal Marines training camp at Lympstone in Devon. He and his fellow volunteers were viewed as somewhat wet behind the ears by the regular Marines and were a part of the regiment merely for the duration of the war, being given the general name of HOs – 'Hostilities Only' – with a perceptible stress on 'only', according to Charles. After six weeks of basic training, he was ready to start as a cadet officer. One of the perks was the location: the Marines had cannily taken over the beautifully situated Thurlestone Hotel, overlooking a rocky cove on the English Channel, as their Officer Cadet Training Corps headquarters. Here, Charles and his cohort of fellow cadets were put through their paces as potential officers who would be expected to lead Marine Commandos from the front in the invasion of German-occupied Europe that everyone knew must, at some point, take place.

There was a lot of physical work – hours spent on the assault course set up in the field opposite the Village Inn, weapons training, and plenty of landing-craft training as well in preparation for the type of frontline seaward attack that would be vital in any future assault on the European mainland. The Marines certainly spiced up life in this quiet corner of Devon and were generally very popular with villagers, young and old – though maybe not with the owners of the Thurlestone Hotel. The dining room curtains, which had cost a whopping £1,000, were later traced to the Marines' base in Devonport, where they'd been cut up and used as dusters, and the roof was structurally damaged due to the weight of the anti-aircraft gun the Marines had put up there. To add insult to injury, the War Office compensation was so low that the owners had to sell off part of the property to pay for the repairs.

As it turned out, Charles would never take up the role of a 3rd Battalion Royal Marine officer when D-Day finally came. He was destined for a different type of war, due in large part to his exceptional childhood experiences. His fluency in German, along with his keen intellect and independence of spirit, meant that he had come to the attention of NID – the Naval Intelligence Division. In 1943, Charles attended the Army

School of Intelligence and qualified as a brigade intelligence officer. In January 1944, he was summoned to NID's lair in the Old Admiralty Building overlooking Horse Guards Parade for an interview to assess his suitability for a very specialised and highly secret role – one of Naval Intelligence's small band of officers in the Combined Services Detailed Interrogation Centre, or CSDIC, as it was known. He was indeed, it seems, made of the right stuff, and was brought on board.

CSDIC combined all branches of the military in conjunction with British intelligence agencies MI5, MI6 and MI9 for the purpose of interrogating captured German personnel, such as prisoners of war and defectors. They had a small number of interrogation centres in and around London – Charles was based at Latimer House, a grand nineteenth-century mansion, now a hotel, in Amersham, Buckinghamshire. This was euphemistically referred to as 'No 1 Distribution Centre', and a very small number of people, not even Members of Parliament beyond a select few, knew anything of its existence.

Someone in NID who had given a lot of thought to the most effective method of extracting information from a prisoner was Lt Commander Ian Fleming, later famous as the creator of James Bond, but during the war the influential personal assistant to the Director of Naval Intelligence. What Fleming sought in the department's interrogators wasn't just fluency in the language but a background in Germany itself and the ability to connect with those being interrogated. It was believed that an interrogator should be able to, as an NID report put it, 'assert his personality' over the prisoner: 'the first necessity was that the interrogator . . . should give the impression that

[he] knew the full details of the information which he was in fact trying to obtain.' To this end, a grasp of the nuances and subtleties of the POW's own language meant that the prisoner had no linguistic barriers to hide behind.

This often meant recruiting officers without conventional British military backgrounds. One of Charles's colleagues in CSDIC was the *Daily Mail* journalist Ralph Izzard, who had lived in Berlin for most of the 1930s and was married to a German woman with connections to Berlin's high society. Izzard was personally recruited into Naval Intelligence by Ian Fleming. Another was Brian Connell, a foreign correspondent and, later, an ITN newscaster. Intriguingly, sifting through documents at the National Archives at Kew, I came across a top-secret Naval Intelligence Division report about CSDIC and what makes a good interrogator. It was written just after the end of the war by a friend of Charles, Lt Commander Colin McFadyean (another Ian Fleming recruit). He commented that while it was initially thought that, because of their courtroom experience, lawyers were a natural fit for the job, it seemed 'the only civilian occupation which could be taken as pointing to a likely capacity for interrogation was that of journalism'.

As a Naval Intelligence member of CSDIC, Charles would have been primarily involved in the interrogation of rescued German U-boat crewmen. As much as seeking technical information about the German navy, Charles's task was to elicit details of the day-to-day life of U-boat crew on board ship and at their naval bases in western France. This micro-level information would be fed into the Atlantiksender propaganda radio broadcasts (created by yet another journalist, the BBC's

Sefton Delmer) transmitted to U-boats on active duty. The aim was to undermine German morale by conveying the idea that British intelligence was all-knowing and that they were constantly being watched.

Ahead of D-Day, the heads of the Naval Intelligence Division saw the importance of having some of its agents moving through Europe with the forward lines of the invading Allied armies. As such, its top interrogators at CSDIC, including the recently promoted Captain Wheeler, were formed into the free-flowing Royal Navy Forward Interrogation Unit (FIU). This had just five members and a remit to locate and interrogate German naval officers, scientists and technicians before they were lost into the general mix of POWs.

Charles was about to be pitched into a life as an FIU officer that would be intense and demanding, but also full of daring and sheer bravado. According to Donald McLachlan, one of Fleming's NID colleagues based in London and a future foreign editor of the *Economist*, 'never, probably, have intelligence officers been given such a free hand and such a front seat'.

Sixth of June 1944. D-Day. Charles arrived at the Normandy coast to be confronted by a scene of apocalyptic proportions. The noise of the naval bombardment by Allied battleships was continuous and deafening. The smoke from their guns blotted out the sun, turning noon into dusk. Incoming shells from the enemy batteries up on the heights to the east whooshed and splashed into the sea around him. Like many there that day, it was the first time he'd been under fire, encountering the real heat of war. Charles was on a landing craft mothership – a large ship transporting the landing craft needed for getting troops onto the beach.

As his ship arrived at its destination at Sword Beach, on the extreme – and highly exposed – left flank of the anchorage opposite the tiny fishing port of Ouistreham, Charles saw a lone enemy fighter in the sky above him. Within seconds, it seemed to him that every battleship, cruiser and destroyer in the fleet turned their guns on it and opened fire. The plane careered off to the west before crashing in flames into the sea. Charles thought it was a spectacular example of Allied firepower, prompting him to wonder if the landing they'd all trained for might turn out to be a walkover.

That, of course, was not going to be the case.

On the morning of D-Day, the first wave of the great armada of 7,000 ships and 150,000 troops had taken part in an audacious assault on Nazi-occupied Europe, landing at low tide on five beaches in Normandy, codenamed, from west to east, Utah, Omaha, Gold, Juno and Sword. At Sword Beach, the British 3rd Division spearhead began disembarking at 7.25 a.m. To begin with, there was fairly strong resistance from the German defenders, but by 9.30 the beach was secure enough to begin moving troops inland. But later that afternoon, the Germans regrouped sufficiently to launch a counterattack and troops of the 192nd Panzergrenadier Regiment reached the edge of Sword Beach itself. They were rapidly rebuffed, mainly due to the blistering shellfire from the Royal Navy just off the coast, witnessed by Charles from his ship in anchorage.

Charles always emphasised that, although he was there on D-Day, he was not an active part of the invasion force carrying out the assault. However, it wasn't enough for him to simply watch events unfold from his ship; he wanted to get onto the beach himself. A close friend of his from Marine training days in Devon, Lt Peter Haynes, was the skipper of a landing craft – and so Charles simply hitched a ride. As would become rather typical of this particular officer throughout his career, he was acting entirely independently and had received no official order to be there at all. When I went back with him to Sword Beach for the sixtieth anniversary of D-Day in 2004. I asked him why he took such a risk. His answer was typically short and to the point, 'I wanted to take a look.'

As it turned out, he was immediately ordered back off the beach again by the harassed beachmaster, the Royal Navy officer in charge of keeping the traffic flowing, who clearly didn't see why this young Marine captain should be adding to his problems. But Charles was there long enough to observe that Sword Beach was one enormous jam. High winds had created a tide that reduced the width of the beach from thirty yards to just thirty feet, and in this narrow space it was extremely difficult to manoeuvre the vast quantity of heavy equipment coming off the ships. Fortunately, the 3rd Division's infantrymen had landed at dawn and moved inland. But the plan for a lightning attack on Caen, nearly ten miles away, depended on them being carried on the tanks, trucks and other vehicles that were now bogged down in the chaotic pile-up.

Charles returned to his ship but the next day Peter Haynes offered to take him to Sword Beach again. This time he faced no opposition from the beachmaster and was alone as he walked into Ouistreham, armed only with a pistol. It felt more secure than the day before. After a scout around town, he returned to the beach and hopped onto Peter's boat on its way back to the mothership. (Peter Haynes would be killed before the end of the month, his landing craft taking a direct hit from a German shell; he was a friend Charles would never forget.) It was already clear that the timetable had slipped. Those traffic jams on the beach Charles had witnessed on D-Day would prove extremely costly – for many, deadly – over the following six weeks.

In this new and dangerous environment, one of Charles's first encounters after moving inland from Sword Beach was with someone very familiar. His position as a special intelligence officer gave him a remarkable freedom to go where he pleased, so he immediately equipped himself with a motorbike and was able to travel at will around the Normandy countryside. On 8 June, just two days after D-Day, Charles was riding along a road not far from the coast when he noticed an RAF support unit camped in an orchard. Aware that his father was being posted to France as a wing commander with Air Technical Intelligence, he pulled up on the off chance that they might have news of him. 'And there he was, having a shave,' Charles later recalled. 'I got off my motorcycle and saluted him.' There was little time for much more than this between them. That chance meeting would be the last time he would see a member of his family for another two years.

In the weeks following D-Day, the Royal Navy continued to guard the Normandy beaches, where troops and supplies were still being landed in vast quantities from England. With the Allies having complete air superiority, the Germans were resorting to more extreme ways of attacking the supply ships, including with the use of Neger and Biber human torpedoes. The basic idea was that they would conduct night-time raids on Allied shipping. For greater accuracy, the pilot sat in a tiny cockpit on the front of the torpedo directing it towards its target and, in theory, would jump off just before impact. In reality, the casualty rate was extremely high. Although they were unable to stop the flow of Allied resources into Normandy, the human torpedoes were nonetheless dangerous and had achieved some successes in sinking Allied ships, including two British minesweepers at the beginning of July 1944.

As a Naval Forward Interrogation Unit officer, Charles was sent for by Vice-Admiral Philip Vian, Commander of the Royal Navy's Eastern Task Force and, in Charles's opinion, a 'terrifying man'. Vian told him several Allied ships had been sunk with many men lost that night. They'd managed to pick up one of the human torpedo operatives from the sea but he'd refused to give any information as to the location of the base from where the attacks were being launched. It was imperative that the base should be found and destroyed, and Vian demanded Charles extract the necessary information. He was given two hours in which to do it. The pressure was on.

Charles found that the torpedo pilot was extremely resistant to the usual methods of interrogation. Time was running out. He had to make a quick decision. He took the man out on deck and made him stand on the edge of the stern with his back to the water. There was a long drop to the sea below. 'I told him that if he didn't tell me where the torpedo unit was based by the count of ten, I'd push him in the drink,' Charles recalled some decades later. For such a threat to work, of course, the man had to believe his interrogator was entirely capable of carrying it out – and evidently Charles's prisoner did. 'I got as far as seven when he gave me the name of a seaside resort twenty miles up the coast. They bombed it the next day.' This incident stayed with Charles throughout his life. He later said that it was not his finest hour as 'it was a kind of mental torture' – but it had to be done and he knew he had to be the man to do it.

'I remember one evening early in July, lying on my back in an orchard, watching the sky, which was black with hundreds of low-flying Allied bombers.'

It was now one month after D-Day and yet Charles was still only six or seven miles from Sword Beach. The planes he was watching were heading to Caen, a few miles to the south. Caen had been a key objective on D-Day itself but the advance had been woefully slow and, frustrated by their inability to dislodge the Germans from their formidable defences in front of the city, the Allies resorted to employing massive aerial bombardment. Charles would later write that, 'As a military operation the bombing was futile. It left the Germans untouched. All it achieved was to complete the destruction of Caen and the deaths of countless civilians.'

It was around this time that Charles first met Lieutenant-Commander Patrick Dalzel-Job, a charismatic commander in another special forces naval unit created by Ian Fleming –30 Assault Unit, or 30AU. Whereas Charles's FIU unit was charged with the grinding job of locating and interrogating German naval personnel, 30AU was a free-ranging intelligence-gathering commando unit whose prime purpose was to capture documents, equipment and other materiel – often behind enemy lines – that would be transported back to London for analysis. There was a natural symbiosis between the two units and they would at times almost merge into each other, with Charles for a time effectively becoming a member of 30AU.

Their ultimate aims were the same: both units were on the hunt for general naval intelligence but were especially focused on finding out as much as they could about V1 and, later, V2 rocket sites, as well as the latest Walter hydrogen-peroxide-propelled U-boats and torpedo-boats. Just days after D-Day, now on the defensive, the Germans had begun hitting London with the winged V1 cruise missiles in what became known as the second Blitz, causing huge loss of life. The Allies were keen to stop the attacks but also wanted to get their hands on this cutting-edge rocket technology.

Charles and Patrick Dalzel-Job hit it off immediately. In his autobiography, *From Arctic Snow to Dust of Normandy*, Dalzel-Job recounts that, 'I was joined by a lively young officer who was to be with me on most of my searches in Normandy and Brittany. He was supposed to be an interpreter and interrogator, but was a splendid second-in-command for my [30AU] reconnaissance team as well as being a very pleasant and amusing companion [and with] any amount of dash and power of command.' The admiration was mutual. Charles found Dalzel-Job 'marvellously well-equipped both mentally and mechanically to do his own thing', always a highly prized attribute in Charles's book. Dalzel-Job's reputation preceded him, though, and he'd already achieved a semi-legendary reputation in military circles. Earlier in the war, as a naval officer, he was in Norway prior to the German invasion. Instructed to withdraw, he explicitly disobeyed orders and mounted a daring rescue of thousands of civilians in Narvik by evacuating them on fishing boats. He expected a court martial – but instead received the Knight's Cross of the Order of St Olav from King Haakon VII.

Life in 30AU suited Charles down to the ground. The unit, which at its largest only numbered around 300 men split into small sections, allowed huge amounts of independent action in the company of an intriguing group of individuals: 'It was a pretty undisciplined freelance outfit, rather glamorous people. It was great fun rushing around in an armoured car capturing a few Germans here and there, finding little radar stations, getting hold of a few documents,' as he typically downplayed it. Members of 30AU had received training in everything from street fighting and handling of weapons to lock-picking and safe-breaking – the great American general George Patton would honour them with the name of 'that bunch of Limey pirates'.

Unsurprisingly, it has been said that Fleming based his swashbuckling hero James Bond on the men of 30AU, especially Patrick Dalzel-Job. Some have even said he was based on Charles. But all the men in the unit seemed to possess a certain irreverent streak – disciplined and brave but undisposed to playing by the book. In fact, in creating this composite character, Charles surmised that the Eton-educated, desk-bound Fleming was indulging fantasies born out of frustration and jealousy of his own men. Indeed, Charles was generally quite withering about Fleming, whom he and his fellow Marines and naval officers thought of as a dilettante who spent far too much time in nightclubs and having expensive lunches within a short walk of his base at the Admiralty.

On 12 July, almost as soon as he'd met up with Dalzel-Job's unit, Charles was already in action. Just outside Caen, at the old Chantiers Navals at Blainville-sur-Orne, a half-sunk German patrol boat was lying in the *bassin* that ran along the Caen canal. It was well worth checking out, they thought. Charles found a small cork raft and, using planks of wood for paddles, he and Dalzel-Job went across and clambered onto the boat. It proved to be full of the sort of loot 30AU were looking for. Inside, they found a number of safety boxes containing technical equipment and papers, and they got on with the job of sifting through it all. What they didn't know, though, was that a company of German gunners, positioned on a ridge about 1,000 yards away, had spotted them.

As the first shells fell on the *bassin*, the two commandos suddenly realised the danger they were in. They'd found a good-sized dinghy on board and, under continuous shellfire, emptied the contents of the boat into it, while debris from a nearby building blown up by the shells rained down on them. With the dinghy piled up with pilfered treasure, Charles and Patrick paddled furiously back to their jeep and safety. As 30AU's own official history records, they had shown considerable enterprise and gallantry, although it also notes that they came in for some criticism from British Army authorities 'largely on account of the boisterous manner of their blowing open safes'. But it was a sign of things to come:

whenever Charles was with Patrick Dalzel-Job, there would always be the chance that something exciting – for which read, dangerous – would happen.

The reconnaissance team's tactical headquarters was on the coast in a house called the Villa Belle Vue, surrounded by pines and sand dunes. The area was full of US tanks from the armoured divisions. At this point, 30AU, and specifically Patrick Dalzel-Job and Charles's small reconnaissance team, was the only British unit active in the American sector. Members of 30AU were expected to be tight-lipped when it came to what they were doing, even to senior officers. It was hardly surprising that these renegade outliers sniffing around on the Americans' patch frequently met with a frosty reception. London had to intervene at the highest level asking her allies to give the unit as much freedom as possible.

As a result, the supreme commander of the Allied Forces in north-west Europe, General Eisenhower himself, sent word to senior US commanders that 30AU should be supported in the capture of targets of important naval intelligence interest. Charles and Dalzel-Job were duly given one of the greatest gifts available to an Allied soldier in Europe in 1944, and one coveted, but rarely owned, by even the highest-ranking officers: a *laissez-passer* signed by Supreme Allied Commander Dwight D. Eisenhower that entitled them to go where they wanted.

At about this time, Charles makes a touching appearance in the vivid war diary of Lt Commander Tony Hugill, a 30AU stalwart. Hugill recorded that he wished he had more leisure time to write of the many notable things he saw each day, including, 'the antics of Ginette de St Sauveur, Charles Wheeler's minute black kitten who sleeps all day in Charles's jacket and spent last night climbing an apple tree . . . and jumping onto our sleeping forms'.

30AU's next target was Granville, on the Normandy coast west of Caen. On 30 July, Dalzel-Job got wind of news that the US 6th Armored Division was heading there. He obtained permission for 30AU to join the assault. The US troops, prepared for battle, were jumpy and that made some trigger-happy. It was just outside the town of Bréhal on the road to Granville that Charles stopped to speak to a Frenchman in the garden of a chateau. He wanted to know if German troops had been sighted and, more importantly for 30AU, if there had been any sign of them moving equipment. They were mid-conversation when an American soldier in a passing truck picked up his rifle, took aim and shot at the Frenchman. The bullet might as easily have hit Charles. The Frenchman died in Charles's arms.

Patrick remonstrated with the Americans and Charles tried to comfort the man's family, who were hysterical with shock. The team concluded that in this febrile atmosphere anything seen through the trees was liable to be shot with questions asked later. After a tense night the unit set off for Granville, with Dalzel-Job and three Marines leading in the jeep, and Charles following close behind in his scout car. When they arrived at the edge of the city, they were met with a wonderful sight: the road was covered in flowers, arranged in all kinds of shapes: diamonds, crosses and circles. Flags hung out of every window of the town's distinctive white granite buildings. Bouquets landed on the unit's jeep and Charles's scout car. The crowds cheered, roared and wept and girls rushed to embrace the young commandos. The Germans had left – and 30AU were treated as Granville's liberators. A treasured photo on my mantelpiece comes from this time: Charles and Patrick stand by the jeep with a couple of the local friends they've made. Charles is cradling a tiny figure in one hand – it's Ginette de St Sauveur, his little black cat.

As a result of their searches through Normandy and Brittany, members of 30AU were providing a regular stream of information to Fleming back at NID, often based on tip-offs from the locals and members of the Resistance. 'It was because Charles gleaned so much information from German prisoners and civilians that we were able so often to get into our targets before any other Allied troops had reached the area,' reflects Patrick Dalzel-Job in his account of the time. 'In the first shock of seeing us arrive the Germans were very ready to talk; men never refused information, and we even had cases of women or children coming out of their shelters to volunteer information about their own troops. Prisoners too were seldom unwilling to talk to Charles.' And they scarcely moved a step in France, Charles recalled, without finding out from a farmer how to avoid unwelcome encounters with German troops.

But despite their successes, it was a fraught time. They drove on the edge of their nerves for hours on end along ominously silent roads, often behind enemy lines, 'expecting at any moment to face the harsh rattle of a machine-gun or the devastating burst of a road mine'. Charles described the sight of the small, mobile 30AU unit out on a mission: Patrick Dalzel-Job with two Marines in a jeep, its trailer jam-packed with kit – a folding airborne forces motorbike lashed to the front bumper, a captured German machine-gun mounted on a tripod bolted to the bonnet, jerrycans of petrol and plastic explosives jammed into any remaining space; himself following in the scout car, his gun trained and ready. Charles mainly credited Dalzel-Job's competence as leader for the fact that his reconnaissance team didn't lose one man throughout the whole war: 'I slowly discovered that despite his impetuous sorties into enemy territory his companions were in safe and capable hands.'

In August, Dalzel-Job's 30AU troop moved south into Brittany. Their target was the seventeenth-century Château de la Massaye at Pont-Réan, fifteen miles south of Rennes. They'd received intelligence that this was the German control centre for the bombardment of Allied convoys in the Atlantic and, as ever, wanted to seize anything useful before it could be taken by the retreating enemy. The problem was the chateau was beyond the most forward Allied position. This was held by the American 8th Division, and, when Patrick and Charles came through the line, the Americans told them they knew nothing of what lay ahead. They pushed on.

The roads and villages were empty. They spotted two Frenchmen and called out, asking if they knew where the Germans were. '*Ils sont partout, partout*,' they shouted, and ran off. At any turn in the road, they might have been hit by fire from German 88-millimetre guns, but they arrived at the chateau intact to find the enemy had just left, their field kitchens still alight. Dalzel-Job sent his men back to the Allied positions, ordering them to return the next day with reinforcements, but he and Charles elected to remain there to guard the assets. It was to be a tense night. Tony Hugill, one of the 30AU officers who was sent back from the chateau, wrote that the following day Charles told him they really had been scared, as they'd heard groups of German soldiers moving past them for the entire night and it was just good luck that none came into the chateau to have a look. Hugill recorded the permanent 'tenseness which comes from living in a no man's land as one of a party of fifty only six miles away from 5,000 SS troops'.

It was in Charles's nature to downplay the exploits he was involved in. 'We had little encounters here and there,' he said. 'We took some prisoners in Brittany, really just by shouting at them and letting them think we were a much larger force than we were.' He'd also become aware that the Germans were now more fearful of the Maquis – the tough guerrilla fighters of the French Resistance – than they were of the British or Americans. And it was for a reason that troubled him. One summer evening several decades later, as we sat in the quiet of his beloved garden in Sussex, Charles suddenly began telling me about his personal encounter with the Maquis in Brittany, a story that to me summed up the brutality and the arbitrary nature of what went on there.

He was in a 30AU convoy of six or seven jeeps when they were radioed that a German troop truck with a heavy machine-gun was headed their way. They soon heard the rumble of the truck as it approached. The 30AU jeeps carried on, with Patrick Dalzel-Job's in front. When the Germans came into sight, Dalzel-Job veered leftwards into a ditch, leaving Charles in front. Charles told his Bren gunner to wait. The German truck came nearer. Then he gave the order: 'Fire three rounds, not in rapid fire.' But the Bren gun jammed. With the German truck coming ever closer, Charles aimed his sub-machine gun and fired – but it too jammed. He then pulled a Luger pistol from the map-case he kept it in and let off three rounds. He missed each time but it had the desired effect. It was so loud that the truck halted, Charles said, and the four German soldiers inside jumped out and surrendered. The highly mobile 30AU team couldn't hold the prisoners, of course, and they were handed over to the French Resistance to look after.

Some time later, Charles was out on a patrol with his sergeant when he spotted a German soldier walking along the road carrying a rifle. Charles crept up on him and leapt onto his back, bringing him down. The soldier, terrified, gave up immediately. He was about thirty-five years old (an old man in the eyes of twenty-one-year-old Captain Wheeler) and, it turned out, a pastry chef from Vienna. Charles told him he'd have to hand him over to the French Resistance. The pastry chef looked horrified. 'I've heard they are killing German prisoners of war,' he said. Charles searched out the same French Resistance officer they'd dealt with before and handed him over, asking what happened to the other four soldiers. 'Oh, we shot them,' the officer replied matter-of-factly. 'Can you make sure this one is OK?' Charles asked. 'He's just a pastry chef.'

'Really,' said the Frenchman. 'A pastry chef, eh . . .' A month later, when Charles returned to the area, he found the pastry chef still alive and working as their cook.

Historians of 30AU have suggested that Patrick, Charles and their 30AU colleagues were passing on valuable captured information to Commander Fleming in London, which was helping to contain the threat from the V-bombs falling on the capital and the south-east. But their barely concealed dismissiveness towards the Admiralty and Fleming himself was offending military sensibilities. After one incident when the team apparently forgot to send on some captured equipment from Cherbourg specifically requested by Fleming, the irate commander sent this threatening message: 'I urge you not to continue questioning the decisions of the Director of Naval Intelligence . . . under whose orders you operated. One thing is certain and unless the unit obeys its orders without question during the future stages of the campaign, it will be impossible for me to prevent higher authority intervening drastically.'

At the end of August, Charles parted company with Dalzel-Job's unit for the rest of 1944, something he later said left him feeling 'devastated'. But whereas 30AU were soon sent back to England for rest and retraining, Charles was heading to the centre of the action once again.

Back under the command of Ralph Izzard in the Forward Interrogation Unit, Charles was 'lent', as Izzard put it in a report, to another rather exotic and, in this case, short-lived intelligence group, the Mobile Port Reconnaissance Party. Charles spent two weeks in September with this very ad hoc unit, mainly focused on Operation Wellhit, General Spry's 3rd Canadian Infantry Division's assault on Boulogne. In a rapid manoeuvre to seize the radar installation at Rupembert, just outside the port, before it could be destroyed, the Reconnaissance Party swept in with the Canadian 8th Brigade. The entire installation was captured intact and Charles and the unit spent almost two weeks there assessing the materiel they'd found.

All too typically, Charles managed to 'capture' an Opel car as well, in which he enjoyed zipping up and down the north French coast until, as one of his colleagues put it, he was forced 'to surrender it to the authorities on our return to base'.

The operation – and the unit itself – was wound up in late September. Charles, back with Lt Commander Ralph Izzard and the FIU, now crossed into Belgium, where the search for German personnel of significance took him to Ostend and Antwerp. Izzard's report to Naval Intelligence in London gives an idea of the difficulties the changing circumstances of the war were bringing. Whereas they had dealt with half a dozen prisoners a week in the first period after D-Day, by early November they were confronted with 10,000 in a single day. Trying to filter out the ones with useful information was becoming increasingly challenging.

But it wasn't all hard grind. Charles spent an agreeable sojourn in the small town of Pulle, east of Antwerp. He and other members of the FIU were quartering at the Castle Krabbelshof, which belonged to a friendly Belgian aristocrat called Gaëtan van de Werve d'Immerseel. The viscount invited the officers to join him and his family for tea. Decades later, Nadine d'Oultremont, his by then middle-aged daughter, was asked if she remembered the soldiers being there. Yes, she said. *'Mais Capitaine Charles Wheeler, bien sûr!'* Clearly, for some, Charles already had a star quality about him.

The FIU team would remain at Pulle till the end of the year, though, as the castle was hit by a V1 rocket soon after they arrived, they 'lived in the viscount's barn, eating oysters we bought by the barrel and drinking whisky to keep out the cold', as Charles recalled. But with the advent of 1945, the biggest step of all was about to be taken – crossing the Rhine into the Third Reich itself.

'It was when we crossed the Dutch frontier at Venlo that we knew Hitler had lost his war,' Charles wrote nearly half a century later. The villages of the German countryside he was now advancing through were awash with pillowcases, featherbed covers, towels – anything that could pass for a white flag was hanging from the upstairs windows of every house. Germany's civil population, he added wryly, was 'giving up on the Fuehrer, opting to capitulate, using free choice for the first time since 1933'.

In April 1945 30AU had regrouped and Charles was with Dalzel-Job's unit once again for the approach to the German port of Bremen – the city of his birth.

The endgame for the Reich was approaching. On a single day, 10 April, the US Army captured Hanover and Essen, British warships sank the German U-boat submarine U-878 in the Bay of Biscay and Allied aircraft shot down thirty highly prized Messerschmidt fighter planes, severely hobbling the German Luftwaffe, as a result of which the defence of Berlin was abandoned.

Three days later, acting on information from NID in London, 30AU set off for what they believed was an important target in Bakum, south-west of Bremen. They drove through a desolate landscape of bombed-out farmhouses and roads pockmarked by shellfire. Charles questioned farmers where he could find them and they were directed onto various backroads. At one point, they were told that German troops held the two farms ahead. After a brief skirmish, one German soldier was killed and thirteen captured. They seemed relatively sanguine to be honourably captured by such a group as 30AU, according to Dalzel-Job's account. But it is easy to forget that, living in the moment, Charles and his comrades didn't know at any given point whether they might confront a more motivated or heavily armed force than they did that day, and had regularly to face the prospect of injury or death. To cap it all, when they arrived in Bakum they discovered that the target had vanished.

A fortnight later, on 1 May, Charles, who'd received orders to separate from Dalzel-Job's team again and head towards Hamburg, spent the evening in an improvised prisoner-of-war camp on open farmland and enclosed by coils of barbed wire. It was in these bleak surroundings that he heard the BBC announce the death of Adolf Hitler. He was the one to break the news to the POWs. The reaction of the troops was striking:

'It had rained for three days; there was a biting wind; and some 3,000 prisoners were up to their ankles in mud, soaked to the skin. I suggested telling the Germans the news. "They're probably too miserable to care," said the major in charge, "but go ahead." So, from the top of a truck, its headlights on to get them to listen, I called for quiet. "*Ruhe!*" And, still in German: "Some news from London. Your Führer is dead. It was suicide." For several seconds, dead silence. Just below me, a single POW started clapping. Slowly it spread, a chorus of applause, all across that sodden field,' Charles recalled.

Once the German collapse really began to get going, the pressure was on, with a new concern to make sure that valuable intelligence stayed in British hands and especially did not end up with their ostensible allies, the Russians. 'There was a huge flurry of activity. There were so many targets. Everyone was rushing around in all directions, securing stuff, looking for stuff, finding stuff, failing to find stuff. Denying or trying to deny as much as possible to the Russians.'

Things were becoming increasingly fraught and free-wheeling. One of Charles's drivers, Marine Ron Knight, recalled that their many journeys around western Germany, in a trusty 4x4 Humber 'Box' vehicle, took them to places such as Tambach Castle in Bavaria, where 30AU had discovered the entire German naval archive and struggled to protect it from being incinerated by fanatical members of the Kriegsmarine Helferinnen – the women's naval auxiliary. They drove east via Magdeburg, into Helle and even beyond Leipzig, where they came into contact with the Red Army. Strictly speaking, this search for German officers and scientists beyond the agreed line of demarcation between the Soviet Union and the Allies meant that 30AU were breaching the Yalta agreement, the wartime conference between the Soviet Union, United Kingdom and United States that had established the future zones of influence in post-war Europe.

In the ten days between Hitler's death and VE Day, it wasn't always clear whether hostilities had actually ended and the enemy had been instructed to lay down their weapons or not. During this twilight period in early May, Charles would have a personal, and highly unusual, encounter with the German military. At the Hamburg HQ one day, he received a report from NID in London that a major target – Admiral Heye, the officer in charge of Nazi Germany's special naval operations – was at the naval base in Brunsbüttel at the southern end of the Kiel Canal. Without giving it a second thought, Charles set off with one soldier, Marine John 'Doc' Livingstone, to get the admiral.

When he arrived at the port he was taken on board a U-boat to see the captain. The captain was drunk.

'You are my prisoner,' he told Charles.

'Listen,' Charles said, 'you've lost the war. Hitler is dead. That's why you're drunk. And you are *my* prisoner.'

The U-boat officer's resolve wilted. 'I believe Admiral Heye is here,' Charles continued.

But it seems that the intel from London had been wrong. It was the admiral's cousin, also called Heye, who was in charge of the base. Charles was taken to meet him. 'I have orders for you to carry out,' Charles told him coolly. Heye seemed relieved to surrender.

'How many men do you have under your command here?' Charles asked.

Seven thousand was the answer. And so, however extraordinary it might seem, at the age of twenty-two, Captain Charles Wheeler single-handedly took the surrender of seven thousand German soldiers.

The Germans were giving up in droves and generally the German prisoners seemed to want to cooperate with their British and American captors rather than risk being caught by the

Russians further east. With the Reich crumbling, the Russians were now fast becoming the main bogeymen. Charles thought the threat of the Russians might prove an effective interrogation technique in the case of one chief petty officer, who had served on the Russian front and who was suspected of knowing a lot more about the torpedo programme than he was letting on. With the help of his friend and colleague from the US Forward Intelligence Unit, Angus MacLean Thuermer – and some amateur dramatics – he tried the good cop/bad cop tactic. In this case, the bad cop was Angus, masquerading as a Red Fleet lieutenant on attachment. Charles – the good cop – told the German that if he didn't give him the information he wanted he would turn him over to the Russian. Angus came in at this point, his US Navy bridge-coat, complete with shoulder boards and stars, doubling as a Red Fleet officer's uniform. Angus gave Charles what he thought was a suitably Soviet clenched fist salute. The questioning began. Then the phone went. Angus picked it up and began speaking English, forgetting he was meant to be a Russian. That pretty much put an end to the interrogation as the German was now laughing along with his two interrogators. 'Oh, to hell with him, Wheeler,' Angus said. 'I don't think he knows much about torpedoes anyway.'

Hamburg formally surrendered to the British Army on 3 May. A number of officers were allowed to requisition properties to be used as accommodation. The majority grabbed the most prominent houses in the city centre. But when Charles arrived in Hamburg he directed his driver west from the centre, through side streets where he had spent so much of his childhood, to a house in the smart Altona district. It was the one that he and John, his brother, had admired when they were boys and had promised themselves they would own one day.

Charles immediately ordered the inhabitants to leave and requisitioned it for himself. It turned out that it had been occupied by the local Hitler Youth leader, who had absconded some time earlier. Charles had a look around his new home. In the garage, he found a red BMW soft-top roadster with white seats, the key in the ignition, but the clutch burnt out. He looked through the telephone book and found the number of a garage. Amazingly, a car mechanic answered. 'You will come here tomorrow at nine; you will be paid in cigarettes,' Charles told him. Even more unusually, the mechanic turned up when he said he would and carried out the job successfully. Charles loved his car. He used to drive up to Copenhagen in it for a spot of R&R whenever he had leave, and later, when he was posted briefly to Flensburg on the German/Danish border, took the BMW with him.

Hamburg became the new regional HQ for the Forward Interrogation Unit and 30AU. This part of northern Germany had suddenly become a key focus of attention for Allied intelligence agencies. At Yalta, Roosevelt, Churchill and Stalin had agreed that the Elbe River, running out from Hamburg to the North Sea, would be the line to mark the border between the Red Army and the Western forces, where the two sides should not encroach on the other. But now Operation Eclipse was designed to stop the Russians breaching that agreement and to prevent the USSR's occupation of Kiel and planned takeover of Denmark. As part of that, the race was on to quickly secure high-grade information from senior German naval officers and scientists before the Russians could get their hands on them.

As the war in Europe came to an end, Charles assumed that he would be sent next to the Far East, where the war with Japan was still raging. But with the dropping of atomic bombs on Hiroshima and Nagasaki and Japan's subsequent unconditional surrender announced by Emperor Hirohito on 15 August, that threat came to an end. He would remain in Germany for another year.

Until the spring of 1946, Charles was the Forward Intelligence Unit's commanding officer in Hamburg, Interrogation former U-boat commanders and naval officers coming through the port city – though he also made regular trips to Berlin, where FIU's senior officer Ralph Izzard was now stationed. There, in July 1945, he went to see Hitler's bunker, where the German dictator had shot himself just over two months earlier. It was, Charles wrote, a 'subterranean shambles . . . of rubbish and rubble, with an awe-inspiring smell of decay.' This was the ultimate symbol of the end of Nazi Germany. But he was now sifting through the intelligence gained in the light of a new world order, assessing the value of information for Western interests and whether assets needed to be prevented from reaching the Soviet Union, still nominally an ally but fast dissolving into something else, something murkier.

Lt Commander George Blake, his replacement in Hamburg, recorded hobnobbing with what he called Charles's 'personal friends, many of whom were members of the high German aristocracy'. Blake – who would achieve notoriety as a Russian double agent twenty years later – wrote in his autobiography of the frequent parties that lasted through the night, with 'beautiful women and champagne, in high-ceilinged rooms stuffed with antique furniture and portraits of ancestors'. Charles admitted that he'd enjoyed 'a few weeks of dizzy social life that are best covered by the Official Secrets Act', in Hamburg, and confided to me once that a more intimate acquaintance was the daughter of a former SS general. The naval hierarchy did not approve of the liaison and he was told it would be marked on his war record. But Charles never lost focus on his role as an intelligence officer and one is left wondering how much this really was play and how much work.

In April 1946, he moved east to Berlin. It was already a divided city, split into four occupation zones and jointly administered by the Allied Powers. One part of his work was to reunite captured German scientists with their families before relocating them to Britain. They were being offered asylum to ensure that the rocket and submarine technology, which men like Hellmuth Walter and Wernher von Braun were working on, stayed with the British and Americans rather than fall into Soviet hands. This meant smuggling out their family members through the Soviet Zone into West Germany, usually over the Helmstedt–Marienborn border crossing. Charles once described disguising the wife of one top scientist as a female British Auxiliary Territorial Service officer – the women's branch of the army. 'We drove her through two Russian checkpoints from West Berlin to Helmstedt and into West Germany. She was a good actress and she spoke a little bit of English but fortunately she wasn't questioned and nobody spoke to her, so she was all right. And the Russians probably wouldn't have known anyway.'

British intelligence officers like him, moving regularly across zones, were just about tolerated by the Russians in these early days. But that soon changed and throughout 1946 the atmosphere became 'touchy and difficult', as Charles put it. This was where he first became conscious that something new and very dangerous was in the air in Berlin. 'People had to be pretty careful that it never broke out into any kind of violence,' he said. 'And I don't think it ever did. But this became a sort of mutual hostility. That's where I first became conscious of the fact that there was a Cold War, just a few weeks after the war ended, we were into the Cold War.' With the changing political realities in Europe, Charles had entered a terrain that was becoming as much John le Carré as James Bond.

But now it was time to go home. He handed in his Webley service revolver to the British Area Security Officer on Flottbeker Chaussee in Hamburg and was demobbed in August 1946. Having, as a twenty-two-year-old, been driving around Europe in that very spiffy red BMW roadster, Charles, back in London, was reduced to a second-hand Austin. Car status was the least of his worries. As it was for so many, finding a job after the war was hard and humiliating. He had a glowing reference from the director of Naval Intelligence, Vice-Admiral Edmund Rushbrooke ('He served in the German campaign and showed himself to be conscientious and hard-working, with initiative, energy, common sense and plenty of personal courage . . . [T]he information he obtained was of considerable value'), but even that wasn't opening doors. As someone who'd volunteered for the military, the law that guaranteed conscripts their jobs back did not apply to him. At the *Daily Sketch* they told him they already had some thirty to forty men coming back. And in spite of a good word from FIU friend and *Daily Mail* stalwart Ralph Izzard, the *Mail* also turned him down. With just one year's experience in journalism as a copy boy, he had to admit that he wasn't, in his words, 'a very attractive proposition'. He tried the Joint Intelligence Bureau and even went for a job in the City. No takers there, either. But then his former Naval Intelligence comrade, journalist Brian Connell, suggested that he try the BBC.

'They'll take anyone on,' he told him.

2.
COLD WAR WARRIOR

Thousands of young voices raised in praise of a dictator, political slogans shouted in chorus, rhythmic clapping, stamping feet and marching to arms. The people of Leipzig had seen it all before. Only the names had changed – a foreign dictator this time – and brownshirts had given way to blue.

CHARLES WHEELER, BBC GERMAN SERVICE,
LEIPZIG, 26 JUNE 1952

The British Broadcasting Corporation that eventually hired Charles in October 1946 was, as he put it, 'terribly orthodox and bureaucratic'. His ability to speak German like a native had opened the door to his job in Naval Intelligence and, with his passable French, proved vital for his unit making its way through France and Germany after D-Day. But at his interview with the BBC's overseas news editor, Arthur Barker, he was given a curious piece of advice: 'Never ever speak a foreign language.'

Exercising a kind of warped consistency with this idea, the BBC drafted Charles into its Latin American Service based at Aldenham in Hertfordshire and appointed him as a sub-editor 'in training'. Speaking barely a word of Spanish, and even less Portuguese, Charles's job was to write news summaries for translation and broadcast by a team of mainly native speakers. He was awarded a starting salary of £380 a year with annual increments of £30 – if he did well. The work was almost like a factory production line, though it gave the fledgling journalist a useful lesson. As he put it, 'What you had to do was to try and do a whole day's news in very short items – not more than about four lines a story. It was a marvellous exercise in compression, and I used to have great fun trying to get forty or fifty stories into a ten-minute bulletin and write them absolutely as tightly as I could.'

By May 1947, Charles had graduated to sub-editor proper, and then won a permanent, 'established' post with the BBC, migrating to what was known as the 'Talks Department' of the European Service by the following year and joining an army of émigrés from all corners of the continent. He kept his head down, plugging away at copy-tasting, writing news stories from the wires and occasionally press reviews. But 1948 would also offer some lively and intriguing developments in both his life and career.

That summer, Charles was offered the opportunity of joining the BBC's team covering the London Olympics and leapt at the chance to get away from the grind of the newsroom. The Games were being held for the first time since 1936, when they'd been staged under the triumphalist gaze of Reich Chancellor Adolf Hitler in Berlin. By contrast, the London that hosted the 1948 Olympics was struggling to return to normality after the war, with a population still living off food stamps and rations. In spite of – or probably because of – this, the national broadcaster went big on the event, hoisting the five-ringed Olympic flag above Broadcasting House next to the Union Jack and setting up a dedicated Olympic Service with an international broadcast centre at the Palace of Arts in Wembley.

Charles threw himself into the work with the Olympian energy and stamina for which he would become famous among colleagues, and his efforts won praise from the BBC bosses.

Charles had spent the first few years of his adult life in the military and so, despite the austerity of post-war London, he clearly relished the new freedom the capital had to offer. His monthly pay packet was enough to rent a small flat in Marylebone and buy a motorbike.

One of the first trips he made on it was back to Normandy. He'd kept in touch with siblings Solange and René, in whose house he'd stayed at the liberation of Granville in July 1944. 'Bicoulette', as Solange was known, and her brother were still in the family home where Charles had once lodged. Evidently, it was a passionate reunion. Several weeks later, a lovesick Charles received a letter from René written in French: 'I'm writing to you from the living room, where I know you have so many memories of Bicoulette, who speaks about you so much, so much. Rather too much for my liking in fact. But I also know what this all means and how much hidden suffering there is – and how this mutual feeling quickly took hold of both of you, the pull of violent emotion.'

René couldn't resist a bit of leg pulling and added, '*Mon cher* Charles . . . Solange thinks you forgot her very quickly because she has no news; that she doesn't even know if you received the little packets she sent you in which she put all of her heart; that she is disgusted with all men who are never sincere; and that she would have been better off listening to declarations of love from any other idiot than you.'

When Charles got back from his trip he found another letter waiting for him in his flat in Luxborough Street. It was from the Admiralty. His old outfit at Naval Intelligence wanted to know if he'd like to come back for a couple of months to 'undertake an interrogating job' in Germany. 'The job is undoubtedly interesting,' Royal Navy Commander Malcolm Saunders wrote, 'and I know with your experience of RNFIU [Royal Navy Forward Interrogation Unit] you will be well able to perform the work.' The BBC were reluctant to let him go at first but the Admiralty were determined to get their man. Charles was eventually given leave of absence, departing for Naval Intelligence HQ at Minden, 60 km west of Hanover, in October, and seeing out the rest of 1948 there.

Why did NID want him at that time? The summer of 1948 had seen a flare-up in the Cold War; the Soviet Union unilaterally declared that the four-power administration of Berlin was over and that the Western Allies no longer had any right to be there, blockading all roads, railways and canals into their sectors in an attempt to force them out. The immediate result was the Berlin Airlift, when the British and Americans began dropping food to relieve what was, in effect, a siege. At the same time, the Joint Intelligence Committee in London was running Operation Matchbox, a policy of encouraging high-level scientific and technical defectors from the East. Such defectors had to be assessed, both for their usefulness and to establish that they weren't enemy agents. This was where Charles's expertise was needed.

At the end of his stint, the Admiralty asked the BBC if they could keep him for another two months, as he was 'engaged on work of national importance' – the officers in charge also seemed to appreciate Charles's lively company over a post-supper whisky, and wanted him to stay because of his 'pleasant personality which has made him a distinct asset to the Naval Mess at Minden'. The BBC politely refused, saying that Charles was up for promotion, but had to be actually working at the BBC in order to get it. He returned to England. This was to be the last time he was actively employed by the intelligence services – but his next career move would reveal that the cord had not been completely cut.

Charles was itching to get out of the newsroom in London but he wasn't sure if the life of a foreign correspondent was for him. And then, near the end of 1950, someone wandered into the newsroom and asked, 'Does anyone here speak German?' Charles put his hand up. Although it wasn't mentioned at the time, an urgent replacement was needed for somebody in the BBC Berlin office due to unspecified 'alcohol-related problems'. Almost before he knew what had happened, Charles was being given a voice test for radio – 'Deepish baritone; rich blend; slight nasality. The voice level is apt to be weak, but apparently out of shyness' – and was once more on his way back to Germany.

Charles was soon to discover that the post of 'BBC liaison officer' (also known as BBC German Service representative) based in the BBC Berlin office at Lancaster House, the HQ of the British Military Government in Berlin, wasn't viewed by the military or the BBC as a purely journalistic one. As the job title implied, it was a quasi-news administrative and intelligence role, reflecting the BBC's close relationship with the British security services at the time – a Second World War connection that had continued into the Cold War. In early 1950s Berlin, the lines between news and propaganda could certainly become blurred.

Charles's new job was to be the first point of contact for the British military and intelligence services in Berlin and to receive visitors, often dissidents, to the office. He was to provide dispatches, political commentaries and 'talks' for the BBC's Eastern Zone radio programmes, often largely based on intelligence reports shared with him. But the exact balance to be struck was at times unclear, although his natural bent was clearly journalistic. Indeed, an internal BBC report on his progress in Berlin would observe that it might be 'occasionally necessary to remind him that his work is not that of a normal correspondent', as he was showing too much 'enthusiasm for news-getting'.

The Broadcasting White Paper of 1946 had set out the case for the independence of the BBC. The Licence and Agreement of November 1946 arguably rather undermined it by stating that the BBC's External Services should also accept information from government departments to 'enable the Corporation to plan and prepare its overseas programmes in the national interest, or, in other words, to deploy the national broadcaster against the new emerging Soviet 'foe'. Charles himself was quite clear-eyed about what he was doing. 'I knew that the stuff I was sending back was being used in the [BBC's Eastern Zone

Programme] propaganda broadcasts into Eastern Europe,' he told the *Independent* newspaper in 1997. 'That was the job in those days. That didn't mean it was lies . . . I suppose I was a Cold War warrior.'

Radio was seen as an important weapon by all sides in the Cold War, as it had been in the Second World War. Both MI6 and the West German Social Democratic Party (SPD) wanted the BBC to broadcast the names of possible informants in the Soviet Zone to their East German listeners to warn them of the danger. And the Information Research Department, the IRD, set up by the British Foreign Office in 1948 to counter Soviet propaganda in the satellite states – and now infamous for its covert 'black ops' in later years – was also counting on the cooperation of the BBC office in Berlin.

That very close relationship between the BBC and the intelligence services was nowhere more obvious than in the person of Major General Sir Ian Jacob. He had been the military assistant secretary to the War Cabinet since 1939. Jacob had also been at Yalta with Churchill and had been offered, but turned down, the job of head of MI6 right after the war. Now he was controller of the BBC's European Services, soon to become head of the BBC's Overseas Service, and later director general. He advocated a 'more vigorous reply' to Soviet propaganda from the BBC, and, when the cabinet approved proposals for the Information Research Department to support the government's new 'publicity policy', Jacob was clear that the Overseas Service of the BBC would play a principal role in providing 'advice'. What that meant in practice was that, while the government could not exert direct editorial control on news output, formal structures were put in place to allow the IRD an opportunity to influence programmes.

Charles's official attachment to Berlin was to be only for four months and so, by March 1951, he was already, reluctantly, preparing to leave. A week before his planned departure, the head of the BBC's German Service, Lindley Fraser, received a typewritten letter from General Geoffrey Bourne, Commandant of the British Sector, expressing concern that the Russians and the Americans were winning the propaganda war through superior technology and effective jamming. He was pushing hard for a powerful 100kw transmitter to be set up in the city to improve the signal and the reach of the BBC's programmes throughout Soviet-controlled East Germany. It seems that Charles had been doing some strategic lobbying of his own because General Bourne finished the letter (a copy of which was shared with Charles) by saying:

> I take this opportunity of asking you to tell my friend Sir Ian Jacob once again that we are making full use of the BBC liaison officer and that again I regret the rapidity with which individuals are changed around. Wheeler, who has done just over four months, tells me that he leaves next week and he estimates that he took three months to get into his stride. I quite see that you don't want BBC representatives to get completely into the Berlin groove and that they become less useful in the more general work of the European Service. Nevertheless, I firmly believe that anything less than one year is unprofitable.

Intervention from the top brass did the trick and Charles's four-month attachment became three years.

He found himself very much in demand. Luckily, what was expected of him working for the BBC in post-war Berlin also converged with his own interests as a journalist and his response to the times. But decades later, Charles would admit that not all of his colleagues were as relaxed about the job of the 'BBC Berlin liaison officer' and the relationship with the military and intelligence services: 'The domestic service had nothing to do with the propaganda side. My counterpart for domestic news in Berlin, Patrick Smith, was totally straight and disapproved of what I was doing. He thought I was just a propagandist. But I didn't see myself like that.'

This was mainly because Charles found very little difference between the East German regime and the Nazi regime: 'People behaved in the same way, the police acted in the same way, people shouted in the same way – it was incredibly similar.' Charles's scripted radio offerings for colleagues in the German Service back in London and for the 'Talks' Department (usually for the stable of well-known presenters to read) come across as onslaughts against East Germany's economic failures and political repression, tracking the gradual withdrawal of liberties under East Germany's brand of Marxist–Leninist state socialism that ordinary people were experiencing on a daily basis. Charles was outraged by this, and for him the job was less about delivering the anti-Soviet propaganda that the IRD desired than bearing witness to the assault on personal freedom that he saw taking place around him. As Patrick Major has observed in his essay 'Listening Behind the Curtain: BBC Broadcasting in the

Cold War', 'Charles Wheeler hardly concealed his sympathies for those who have right and courage on their side.'

Installed in the Berlin office, Charles was producing items for the 'Eastern Zone Programme', developed the year before his arrival in Berlin by the BBC's German Service. Specifically aimed at listeners in the Soviet Zone, it provided regular news, interviews and features, such as *Briefe ohne Unterschrift* ('Letters without Signature') and *Die Zwei Genossen* ('The Two Comrades'). *Die Zwei Genossen* was essentially a reworked satirical sketch show that the BBC had broadcast during the Nazi period. The two oafish Nazi officers lampooned in the original show were easily transposed into two Communist Party officials.

The hugely popular *Briefe ohne Unterschrift* was a regular nightly feature that ran until 1974. Letters from the listeners themselves telling of life in the GDR, its daily hardship and frustrations, read out by actors and commented on by the London-based presenter Austin Harrison, were the source material for the programme. Some of them were collected through a secret system of drop-off points around the city but many were delivered in person from East Berlin and other parts of the Eastern Zone. And so, the BBC office in West Berlin became a kind of meeting-house and sanctuary. People streamed in to talk, get advice, have a coffee. On some days, Charles would receive ten different visitors. While they were there, he encouraged them to write to the BBC and to tell their stories. It is possible that this correspondence allowed British intelligence services to trace and communicate with dissidents in the East.

The visits were not without risk. There is a framed photograph from those days hanging in Charles's old study in Sussex. Charles is leaning forward behind a solid-looking desk, looking quite intently at the man in front of him with a rather affectionate half smile. He looks very young, hair still ungreyed, unlike the man facing him, whose head shows streaks of white on a much stockier frame. There's a huge map of Berlin behind Charles in the picture. On the back of the frame, Charles has glued a typewritten explanation: 'With his back to the camera is one of my regular visitors from the interior of the Soviet Occupied Zone. The border between East and West Berlin was still open. But a visit to the BBC could have cost him ten years in the political prison at Bautzen.'

That threat didn't put them off. As Charles filed at the time, 'West Berlin remained a place of refuge for many a Soviet Zone German who cared to buy a railway ticket to his capital.' Among them was an elderly farmer who had travelled from Frankfurt an der Oder, on the border with Poland. This farmer, Charles told me, was an occasional contributor to *Briefe ohne Unterschrift*. He came into the BBC office one day and handed Charles a brown envelope. 'This is for you – a wedding present.' Inside the envelope was a small postcard-sized oil portrait on wood of an aristocratic-looking woman holding a dog. It looked pretty good even to Charles's untrained eye. The man said he'd got it from a Russian soldier in return for two sacks of potatoes to make vodka. 'I can't take it. I'm not getting married,' Charles protested. 'You will one day. Keep it. Besides, I've already been through two checkpoints to get here and if I'm searched on the way back home . . .' the farmer trailed off.

Another visitor was Robert Bialek, a high-ranking East German bureaucrat and former head of the Police Section of the Central Secretariat of the ruling SED, the Socialist Unity Party of Germany. He had become increasingly disillusioned with the regime and defected to the West towards the end of Charles's tenure. He began working for the BBC, giving talks on life in the GDR that his erstwhile colleagues in the East considered treasonable. A couple of years after Charles left Berlin, Bialek was lured to an address in the Wilmersdorf district, bundled into a large black Mercedes V170 by Stasi agents and driven to East Berlin via an unguarded crossing, never to be seen again. Questions were asked in parliament. But for Charles, the responsibility for the Stasi's capture of Bialek could be laid at the door of a British double agent running MI6 in Berlin. Someone he knew, in fact. George Blake.

Blake had replaced Charles as the Forward Interrogation Unit's commanding officer in Hamburg in 1946 and Charles spent a month showing him the ropes and introducing him to his contacts. He'd found Blake charming enough – though he couldn't say he actually liked him. He didn't particularly trust him, either. As Charles famously said of Blake, 'He smiled a lot, smiled rather too much – he smiled at breakfast.' Blake was secretive and hard to read. Charles suspected he was already a spook and remembered him fooling about with invisible ink, 'playing gramophone records down telephones . . . a sort of lifelong professional intelligence officer who obviously got an enormous kick out of playing around with these sorts of toys.' And then they'd lost touch until a strange encounter, seven years later in Berlin.

WITNESS TO THE TWENTIETH CENTURY

On a cold April day in 1953, Charles was standing outside Berlin's Gatow military airport waiting for a plane to touch down. On board was a small group of British diplomats, recently released after almost three years in a Korean People's Army prison following their capture at the start of the Korean War. They emerged from the cabin, smiling for the photos taken by members of the press corps huddled in around them. Charles walked up to one of them and said hello. The reaction, according to Charles, was surprising: 'He spun round, almost jumping in the air.' It was George Blake. Charles told him he now lived in Berlin, suggesting a drink later that evening. 'No. No time. Have to go,' he said, flustered, and hurried away.

Unknown to Charles or, at this point, to anyone in the West, during his time in prison in Korea, George Blake had gone over to the Russians and become a KGB agent. As a high-ranking MI6 officer, Blake would go on to betray dozens, maybe hundreds of British agents, at the cost of many lives, including, according to Charles, Robert Bialek's.

Replaying the scene in his mind, Charles concluded some years afterwards that Blake's unease at seeing him was because he assumed Charles was still involved in the intelligence game, perhaps MI6 itself, and thought he was in danger of being rumbled. Charles's interest in Blake was journalistic but, as he would later say, being a BBC reporter in Berlin at that time was, if nothing else, most definitely 'a Cold War kind of job'.

It's clear, looking through Charles's reports from Berlin through 1952 and early '53, that, however informal, his relationship with the British intelligence services had not ended. Charles described how the intelligence services, specifically the IRD men in Berlin, would pay him regular visits in the BBC office. Peter Seckelmann, his main contact and a friend, would turn up with bits of intelligence they had obtained from sources in the East and, if of interest, Charles might use them in the scripts he sent back to the German Service in London. As he told Michael Nelson, author of *War of the Black Heavens: the Battles of Western Broadcasting in the Cold War*, the IRD men would produce pages of cyclostyled information, which he was not allowed to read himself. They read it out to him, paraphrasing the contents while he took notes. 'It was all done on an old boys' basis,' said Charles. In return, he would give the IRD 'snippets' from his own sources.

But Charles seemed to make a distinction between the IRD men and MI6. To some, it might appear like equivocation, but he always maintained he never knowingly gave information to MI6, feeling perhaps that went too far beyond what his remit as a journalist should be, apart from one occasion when a young German engineer approached him to be put in touch with the service. Charles actively discouraged direct contact, thinking it was simply too dangerous for someone resident in East Berlin, and so relayed the information himself.

This close relationship with the intelligence services had inevitable consequences. The Communist regime in the Soviet Zone was fully aware of what the BBC was doing and made very little distinction between the Western radio stations and the governments of the West. In 1952, Charles was denied a visa by the Soviet authorities for that year's Leipzig Fair. While not exactly creating a major diplomatic incident, the story made it into the *Daily Telegraph*, which reported the Soviet consul as saying, 'Mr Wheeler's visa had been denied because he had been dishonest in his application' and 'falsely described himself as a journalist'. In fact, the consul stated, he was, 'an enemy agent'. Charles kept a cutting of the article, which no doubt had greatly amused him.

The scripts and news 'talks' that Charles was sending back to Bush House in London from spring 1952 described an increasingly dysfunctional East Germany, tightening its grip on everyday freedoms in the context of mounting mutual suspicion between the Soviets and their erstwhile allies in the West. He was drawn not just to events themselves but to the absurdities and Orwellian 'doublespeak' that were part of life in the East when viewed through the refracting lens of Communist edicts and bureaucracy.

'A few days ago a friend and I made an experiment,' began one of Charles's dispatches from June 1952. 'My friend sat in a state-owned restaurant on one side of the Potsdamer Platz, which means he was in the Soviet Sector of Berlin, while I was in the British Sector. Within ten minutes we were talking on the telephone. There is nothing very remarkable about that – except that to bridge the fifty metres between us, our voices had to travel 900 kilometres by radio to Frankfurt, by telephone line to Munich, and from there over Prague.' Charles explained why: the East German authorities had dismantled Berlin's automatic dialling system and split the city's telephone network, 'calmly announcing that it was the Western authorities who had done it as part of their policy of splitting Berlin'.

The following year, the East German government was

calling on the people of West Berlin to throw out their political leaders and Western troops; otherwise, the East German regime declared it would be forced to take further 'security measures'. In a report from this time, Charles bore down on what that term actually meant: 'It was intended as a justification in advance of action to be taken in the future . . . Let me make a point that is insufficiently realised outside Berlin and the Soviet Zone. These security measures are not aimed directly at West [Berlin]. They are aimed at the people of the Soviet Zone – the only people in Eastern Europe who enjoy the privilege of contact with the West.'

And then there was the story of Walter Gies, the carpenter sent to Buchenwald concentration camp in 1943 by a Nazi 'people's court' for listening to an 'enemy' radio station. At the end of the war, liberated from Buchenwald, Gies returned to his job and home in Saxony – by now Soviet occupied. But in early 1952, Gies found himself arrested once again. This time, as Charles reported, he was sent to Sachsenhausen, sentenced 'in the name of the people' by a Communist court to nineteen years hard labour – for listening to a Western radio station.

The aspect of this particular 'cold' war that engaged Charles more than any other was one that recurred throughout his life and cut across political lines: as he put it, the resistance of people to oppressive governments. At a highly choreographed SED youth rally in Leipzig on 26 June 1952, the parallels between the new Communist rulers and the old Nazi order he had witnessed first hand as a child were just too obvious to ignore: 'Thousands of young voices raised in praise of a dictator, political slogans shouted in chorus, rhythmic clapping, stamping feet and marching to arms. The people of Leipzig had seen it all before. Only the names had changed – a foreign dictator this time – and brownshirts had given way to blue.'

Charles was documenting the build-up of pressure on people in the Soviet Zone that would lead to rebellion. The atmosphere in 1952 was becoming increasingly tense. In a speech lasting more than six hours to the conference of the Socialist Unity Party (SED), Walter Ulbricht, the party's general secretary, presented the party faithful with measures more radical than anything seen since 1945. The conciliatory tone of previous years towards the Allies has been extinguished: 'Our national armed forces must be filled with hate against the American, British and the French imperialists.'

Extraordinarily, less than a decade after the Holocaust, anti-fascist fighters who had become prominent citizens in the new East German order were now becoming targets of unwelcome and paranoid attention by the authorities. They were seen as agents of the West and of the recently created state of Israel. The anti-Semitic Communist show trials in Czechoslovakia had set the scene, and, after forty-eight hours of questioning and a demand to make a collective declaration against Zionism and 'Joint' (the Western relief agency responsible for distributing food parcels in the East), Julius Meyer, Salo Loser and other Jewish leaders from Dresden, Halle and Erfurt defected to West Berlin. It was a serious blow to the international standing of the GDR, damaging the plans of the East German Communist Party to 'mount a defence of their anti-Jewish policies by Jews' as Charles put it in his script from 26 January 1953. The 4th General Conference of the

Association of the Persecuted by the Nazi Regime was cancelled and within weeks the organisation itself was disbanded.

The East German regime was patently failing to convince its population of the merits of its ideology, according to Charles. The country was 'haemorrhaging people', as he put it.

While still calling for German unity, the Soviet forces had effectively sealed the border with Western Germany, but Berlin itself remained reachable. And the BBC was reporting it all, helped with information from visitors to the office and intercepts from the IRD men.

Charles estimated that in January 1953, more than 25,000 people left Germany's Soviet Zone and came to West Berlin as refugees. He described an unfolding humanitarian disaster. On the 26th he reported, 'For the past week, refugees have been flooding into West Berlin at the rate of over a thousand a day.' This was a city badly damaged during the war, afflicted with soaring unemployment and barely coping with the numbers. 'It is becoming more and more difficult to find a bombed disused factory or a burnt-out office block with an intact roof in which a few hundred refugees can be sheltered,' Charles wrote. 'Lack of mattresses can be overcome by the provision of straw – though this, like almost everything else, must be imported from the West. But West Berlin is running out of floor space on which these people can lie.'

Charles was witnessing an evaporation of hope. And he found it hard. His reports were becoming infused with less of the prescribed political critique and more with his response to the suffering he was seeing. 'They are finding it daily more difficult to follow West German leaders' exhortation to hold out. There can be no more anxious, impatient and easily disillusioned observers of the progress of West European unity and defence than the people of the Soviet Zone,' he wrote on the predicament of those hundreds of thousands who had chosen not to leave East Berlin.

Stalin's death in March 1953 brought some concessions and change with the announcement in June by the Communist authorities of the New Course. This policy, aimed at the Soviet satellite states, was intended to correct some of the mistakes of the past with political and economic liberalisation, a return of some farms and businesses to private owners and lowering prices for certain food and public transport. A very personal dispatch from Charles on 13 June, two days after the announcement, begins, 'Until Thursday it was a rather depressing week. There had been an unusual number of letters and visitors from the Soviet Zone all asking the same rather desperate questions: "How much longer is it going to last? Is there nothing that you can tell us that will give us some hope of a change that will help us to hold out?"' Hardly a usual relationship between a journalist and his listeners. But Charles advised that those who could hold out should put off becoming refugees and hoped he was saying the right thing. When news came of the new concessions, he must have been relieved. As well as a better deal offered to farmers, small businesses and consumers, there was a relaxation of travel and, most surprisingly, an admission by the ruling Communist Party that they might have got some things wrong.

But three days later, the East German regime – and its Soviet masters – would receive a violent shock to their authority.

Sensing the regime's weakness, the people hit out. In his dramatic, on-the-ground coverage of these events, Charles demonstrated for the first time the skills of the formidable foreign correspondent to come – and his knack of being in the right place at exactly the right time and conveying what that feels like to an audience at home.

In the early afternoon of 16 June 1953, Charles was sitting at a pavement cafe on the Kurfürstendamm in West Berlin. Peter Seckelmann, from the Information Research Department at the British Embassy, pulled over in a car and called out to him. He asked Charles whether he'd been over to the Soviet sector of the city that day. Charles said he hadn't. 'I think you should,' Peter replied. 'I've heard there's trouble on the building sites there, and if I were you I'd go and take a look.'

That could only mean the Stalinallee, a broad avenue where identical blocks of flats were being constructed in Joseph Stalin's favourite wedding-cake style, the East German regime's flagship project. The workers there were considered the best in the GDR, at the vanguard of the 'march towards socialism', according to the Communist Party press. If they were the source of the trouble, thought Charles, something important must be happening.

Charles went straight there and marched through East Berlin alongside the protestors for the next three hours. It was the smiling faces of the strikers that he noticed first: '. . . their own delighted surprise that what they were doing was possible . . . Their morale was high and, as they marched, their numbers growing, through streets lined with cheering clapping people, it soared,' as he wrote in his dispatch from the scene.

The next day, 17 June, it rained. Charles was out again early on the streets of East Berlin but he wondered whether the rain would drive the strikers to shelter and dampen the enthusiasm of the day before. Far from it. He watched as some of the demonstrators climbed the Brandenburg Gate, lowered the red flag and scrambled down again. Meanwhile, others had filled the Potsdamer Platz. There were building workers, railway men, factory workers, shopkeepers, clerks, boys and girls from the Communist Youth movement 'happily disposing of the outward signs of Communist rule', from red flags and banners to the portraits of Stalin and the Litfaßsäule, advertising pillars plastered with Communist posters – everything was being set alight. When the strikers shouted at the People's Police in the former Gestapo building to join them, Charles saw the officers throw their uniforms out of the window and desert. That was the sign the strikers needed to carry off furniture and police files and set those buildings alight as well. Charles felt he was witnessing a revolution.

Though he didn't know it at that moment, the uprising had spread beyond Berlin. In Magdeburg-Neustadt, the strikers – young men and women from one of the Soviet industrial plants – broke down the doors of prisons to free those inside. One of the 300 political prisoners who escaped took a train to Berlin and managed to get to the BBC office to tell his story to Charles, who recorded it: 'We heard shouting in chorus, "We are coming to get you out!" One by one our cell doors were broken open. The guards, the People's Police, offered no resistance even though they were armed.' In fact, the erstwhile guards even helped the prisoners find their personal belongings before they got away.

It looked like the government must fall and that the revolt was succeeding. And then the Red Army took over. Witnessing it all in close-up in East Berlin, Charles was transformed from writer of anti-GDR diatribes to on-the-ground foreign correspondent. His report crackles with tenseness and immediacy. 'Violence began when the police attacked the strikers with truncheons. The strikers withdrew and used stones. Then the Soviet Army took over. Using trucks filled with troops in full battle order and armoured cars, they swept through the streets, scattering the strikers in all directions . . . Then came the tanks. And, here and there, the shooting started.'

At first, Charles said, the strikers thought they were firing blanks. They were wrong: the Red Army was actually using live rounds on workers. The first casualties were carried away. 'It was rapidly becoming a hopeless cause. One cannot fight a modern army with stones, sticks and bare hands.'

At 3p.m., the Russian Garrison declared martial law. By the next day, the authorities had imposed a ban on the assembly of more than three people and East Berlin had been sealed off. 'Every exit to West Berlin is guarded by tanks and troops and the streets surrounding the government office block have been turned into what is virtually a military camp.' It was, Charles reported, 'a divided city, now divided as never before'.

Even though the 'revolution' had been so swiftly crushed, Charles remained hopeful about what he'd witnessed. 'In spite of the casualties, I believe that the demonstration was well worthwhile. It was neither influenced, nor started, nor supported by the West. It was the people of East Berlin – and also the people in several big industrial towns in the Soviet

Zone – giving the most vivid demonstration that a Communist dictatorship has ever had of the true state of affairs in a country whose leaders are dependent on weapons of war for their own protection. The Socialist Unity Party has suffered a blow from which it can never recover. And the Communist leaders in Moscow have been given a lot to think about too.'

Indeed, in Moscow the events in East Berlin led to a Kremlin coup headed by Nikita Khrushchev, which saw the fall of Lavrentiy Beria, the first deputy premier since Stalin's death. Chief author of the New Course policy, Beria was suspected of favouring German reunification. The Soviet Union was checked, if not militarily, then in terms of confidence and prestige. Charles's immediate analysis of the repercussions of the uprising, given in a radio broadcast a week later, is sharp and far-sighted. But it's clear from his dispatches following the rising that he found it hard to accept that this would-be revolution had been completely defeated.

On 25 June, Charles wrote, 'Nothing can wipe out the East German people's newfound knowledge that they have a strength of which up to a few days ago they dared not dream. Slowly a picture is emerging that is deeply impressive – a picture that finally disposes of the Communist legend that the riots were started and led by agents from West Berlin.' Charles believed that because of this first truly spontaneous uprising by the workers against a Workers' Republic, the Soviets would never try to roll into West Berlin because it had been made clear that they lacked popular support even in Communist-ruled areas. 'It's not too much of an exaggeration to say that the people of Eastern Europe have made a true contribution to world peace.'

In his mind and in his broadcasts, Charles would return to the events of these two days again and again, writing 'news talks' for the European Service on the first and second anniversaries of the East German Rising. Looking back many years later, Charles would reflect that the people who had taken part in it, and in other upheavals and revolutions among Moscow's Warsaw Pact allies, had acted as a 'powerful deterrent to a Third World War. One day, perhaps Western historians will acknowledge that debt.' But the people of East Germany would have to wait another three and a half decades to achieve their goal of political freedom.

In the autumn of 1953, Charles was told that his three-year posting had come to an end. He was desperate to remain in Berlin and keep covering the story, and lobbied hard to stay there, petitioning a number of the bosses back in London, as his correspondence at the time shows. Charles was even prepared to leave the BBC and tried the Canadian Broadcasting Corporation for the job of Berlin correspondent. But that petition was also unsuccessful and he returned to London.

His time at the BBC Berlin office had left its mark, though, not just on Charles but also on the listeners themselves. A group enigmatically codenamed the East German Sixtus 2 wrote a letter to the BBC on his departure from this 'city surrounded by red'. It seemed that the open-door policy at the BBC had made a lasting impression: 'It is not through his vivid reporting alone that he has won so many friends among his listeners. He has also by his human qualities won a place in the hearts of those listeners who visited him in Berlin. He had time for every visitor and always had the necessary understanding and the right word for their cares and worries. It was this that his visitors valued and gave them the feeling that he was the right man in the right place.'

Charles had caught the reporting bug. In an attempt to avoid a return to the 'Talks' department at Bush House, where, as a sub-editor, there would be few opportunities to venture out of BBC premises, let alone to report or go in search of interesting stories to cover, Charles went for an interview with the head of home reporters. He was rejected, though – he told me because he was unable to take the interview seriously enough when asked to role-play a live commentary on the inauguration of the Royal Yacht *Britannia* in Clydeside. He yearned for something more engaging.

Salvation came in the form of Michael Peacock – later to become BBC's head of news. He gave Charles a path into television with the chance to be part of the newly relaunched flagship programme *Panorama*. First broadcast in November 1953 as a fortnightly show of forty-five minutes, the programme was then given a weekly one-hour slot. It has survived to this day and stands as the world's longest-running TV news programme. Charles was drafted on board as part of the programme's glittering young team of producers that included Ludovic Kennedy, Jack Ashley, Malcolm Muggeridge, Robin Day, Catherine Dove and Woodrow Wyatt – with presenter Richard Dimbleby fronting the show.

Broadcasting from Lime Grove in west London, this was an entirely new way of news-telling. Even in these earliest days of television news, *Panorama* was already stretching the medium

– more in-depth, more analytical, with pieces sometimes fifteen minutes long. It gave reporters and guests space to share their insights with the viewers on the issues of the day. The magazine format also meant there were plenty of opportunities for lighter items, where Charles could indulge his more mischievous side. He told us as children about the famous spaghetti-growing-on-trees prank produced by the team for April Fool's Day in 1957, and he was also proud of giving the musical comedy duo Flanders and Swann their first break on national TV. And then there was Brendan Behan.

Conventional wisdom has it that the first time the word 'fuck' was used on British television was by Kenneth Tynan in the 1960s. According to Charles, it happened ten years earlier when Behan, the controversial Irish playwright whose latest play, *The Quare Fellow*, just opening in London, was invited onto the programme. Charles once recounted to me what happened after a *Panorama* 'minder' was sent off to bring him up to the studio from the BBC reception. Behan was notorious for his enthusiastic enjoyment of the hard stuff. 'Don't let him drink,' Charles told the minder as he left.

Behan had arrived at the studio fairly sober, it seemed, but was shown into the hospitality room and, for some reason, left there. He was drinking scotch *and* gin when Charles found him. Word got out. The editor of *Panorama* came down. 'You can't let him go on,' he said. 'He'll keep swearing or something.'

'No, it's OK,' said Charles, 'he's fine'. And so, Behan went on and every second word was 'fuck', but as he pronounced it 'fock' and was drunk and slurring his words, Charles said that almost no one understood what he was on about. But for all that, Charles only escaped a severe reprimand for what happened because the managers accepted that he'd done his best to help by grabbing the scotch and gin from Behan's clutches and pouring it down the sink before the situation became impossible to retrieve.

Three years after his immersion in the political drama of East Germany, in October 1956, Charles found himself once again at the edge of a popular uprising challenging the Soviet empire. He'd been trying to get visas to go to Poland, where worker-led demands for reform had found a figurehead in the person of Wladyslaw Gomulka and forced a partial thaw from the resolutely Stalinist regime. And then things blew up in Hungary. Another spontaneous popular uprising had begun. Charles and the *Panorama* team changed their plans. The BBC presence was pretty sketchy there. Radio had sent a correspondent to Budapest, but within hours of his arrival the airport was closed and international telephone lines blocked. Television news didn't send anyone at all.

The *Panorama* team had a rare and prized possession: one of only two portable cameras owned by the BBC able to record synchronous sound on 35mm film. It was, as Charles would later recall, a bulky piece of gear – to fly with it, they had to book cargo space. But it was deemed 'priceless' and, before leaving London, Charles had to promise not to take it into Hungary in case it was damaged, or worse.

The *Panorama* team, with the Hungarian-born writer and humorist George Mikes as reporter and frontman, flew to Vienna and drove straight to the Hungarian border. There, they found half a dozen buses ferrying medical supplies – plasma, penicillin, bandages and dried milk – to the hundreds of wounded in Budapest and began filming men and women who were exhausted but clearly defiant. The Hungarian frontier police had removed the red star from their caps and were flying the flag of the revolution: the red, white and green tricolour, with a jagged hole in the centre where the Communist emblem the hammer and wheatsheaf had been. Some of them recognised George Mikes from his regular broadcasts from London and he easily persuaded them to let the team through, hitching a ride into Hungary on a pile of coal in an open lorry. Charles's promise about the priceless camera was already forgotten. He was holding onto the precious cargo for all he was worth but, at one point, the driver took a bend too fast and Charles, losing his balance, dropped the camera tripod overboard, completely smashing the head. The *Panorama* teams were apparently unfazed. 'We dumped the thing in a ditch,' and, as Charles put it admiringly, ace cameraman A.A. Englander, already celebrated for his arthouse work, 'hand-held his unwieldy camera for the whole of the trip.'

They spent just over three days in west Hungary and the drama of the moment was captured on camera in all its intensity and emotion. They filmed eyewitnesses to a massacre – the security police, the detested AVO, had machine-gunned a peaceful demonstration in Magyaróvár, killing around fifty unarmed men and women and wounding many more, including several children.

But for most of the people to whom Charles spoke, it seemed that the uprising was victorious. The fighting in Budapest had already died down and the Russian troops had apparently withdrawn. 'At Sopron University students had taken over the town after locking up local party officials,' he remembered. Standing on the steps of the new Revolutionary Council, a woman tells Charles (who is, unusually for a producer, seen on camera at this point), 'We hope that our country will be entirely free so that we can work, and we can have free connections, new scientific connections and that our students will be able to go to the West, see the Western institutions and we can be good friends with the Western people.'

The *Panorama* team flew back to London on Saturday 3 November – sound-camera intact, though missing a tripod, of course. And there were no repercussions over Charles going against orders in his deployment of it in Hungary – the editors knew perfectly well that if he had not, they would never have got the story. The film they'd shot was processed overnight. But events were moving faster than they could keep up with. The next day, four Russian divisions attacked Hungary with tanks, artillery and MiG fighter-bombers. 'We heard the news in the cutting room at Lime Grove. Most shattering of all was the BBC's re-broadcast of the last appeals to the West for help, before Free Hungarian Radio went dead for the next thirty-three years,' Charles recalled when he revisited Hungary five decades later to make the radio programme *After the Uprising*.

The *Panorama* film was already out of date, filled with Hungarians celebrating the liberation – Charles, Catherine Dove and the rest of the production team deliberately left it like that, knowing it would be all the more poignant. They expected their story – that countless Hungarians were being killed in the Soviet invasion of Hungary – to lead the programme. But that day there were two other big stories in the running order: America was voting in a presidential election and Britain and France were at war with Egypt over its newly elected leader President Nasser's forced nationalisation of the strategically vital Suez Canal.

Michael Peacock, the editor, wanted to lead with the Hungary film. Charles recalled how the head of department, Grace Wyndham Goldie, 'a kind of pre-incarnation of Margaret Thatcher', stepped in and told them, 'Our boys are dying in the Middle East. You will lead with Suez.' Charles and Catherine Dove argued hard for a change of tack. They tried to sway the decision their way by invoking the fourteen-day rule (also known as 'the fortnight gag') imposed on broadcasters by the government. This rule, originally adopted voluntarily by the BBC in 1944, banned comment for a fortnight on television or radio about anything being debated in parliament. It meant there could be no filmed report or even an interview on Suez, just an item with the BBC's defence correspondent and a map. The tactic did not work, however, and Suez, not Hungary, got top billing.

In fact, Charles and the *Panorama* team's report was cited in a fiery parliamentary debate on the role of the BBC some ten days later. The report had included an interview with the elected leader of West Hungary's revolutionary committee. Charles later said, 'He told us that by intervening at Suez and diverting world attention from Hungary, Britain had wrecked the revolution. This will put the Russians in a position where they can in fact act with impunity because the world's eyes will be on the Middle East and not on Hungary.' The Red Army would be back, he had warned them.

Many felt that British military action in Suez had distracted the world's attention from Russia's brutal suppression of the uprising and deprived London and Paris of the moral authority that might have deterred Russia. But, writing in the *London Review of Books* four decades after the uprising, Charles reflected that researchers and historians had concluded that Suez may have made it less difficult for Russia but the suppression of the revolution on 4 November was probably inevitable.

But more personal interests were beginning to occupy Charles's thoughts. Oxford-educated, talented and lively, his colleague Catherine Dove was the only woman on the *Panorama* production team. She'd battled alongside him to get the Hungary story high on the running order and she'd been a major player in the April Fool's spaghetti-tree spoof. One day she called in sick with a cold. Charles went to her flat with a sustaining portion of chicken soup. Within a few weeks they were engaged.

Charles and Catherine married at the end of May 1958 at the former Royal Bavarian Chapel, a small Catholic church around the corner from Piccadilly Circus. Charles's relationship with the BBC was about to change too. *Panorama* wanted him to take up the job of deputy editor of the programme, but ever since he'd covered the events of the East German Rising he'd set his heart on being a reporter. The position of deputy editor would have kept him in the role of a producer, on a fast track to management. A decision had to be made – and it was one that would dramatically change the course of his life.

He turned down *Panorama* and applied for the post of 'news correspondent in foreign countries'. And now he heard he had been successful and had been appointed as the BBC's South Asia correspondent, to be based in Delhi.

After the wedding, Catherine was to stay in London until she had completed a production assignment. Then she would join Charles to take up their new life together in the Indian capital. That, at least, was the plan.

3.

ONE CHEER FOR DEMOCRACY

Ceylon has been ruled by a Cabinet composed very largely of mediocrities, and led by an inexperienced eccentric, whose only strength lies in his possession of dictatorial powers . . . It's difficult to see how either Mr Dahanayake or the present government can last very long.

CHARLES WHEELER IN COLOMBO, *FROM OUR OWN CORRESPONDENT*, BBC RADIO, OCTOBER 1959

Charles was meant to leave for Delhi just two weeks after his marriage to Catherine. But on the eve of his scheduled departure, he was diverted to the British colony of Cyprus, which had erupted into violence between its Greek and Turkish communities. This was Charles's debut appearance as a television reporter. Opening with a shot of him at a typewriter, carefully coiffed, he cuts a glamorous figure as he speaks slowly to the camera: 'Last week showed how near Cyprus is to becoming another Palestine. There are the beginnings of inter-community warfare. Men who had been living alongside other men peaceably for years are killing with meat cleavers because the victim belonged to another community.'

Then, almost without a pause for breath, Charles was sent to Jordan to cover the upheavals taking place in the summer of 1958. King Hussein's cousin – Faisal II, King of Iraq – had been killed in a military coup on 14 July. There were grave concerns that Hussein was about to suffer the same fate, with Jordan falling under the sway of pro-Nasser radicals. The Jordanian army had only been 'Arabised' – that is, relieved of its senior British officers – two years earlier. Now, in order to bolster Hussein's rule, the British were back – and Charles with them, flying in from Cyprus with two battalions of British paratroopers. He explained to viewers the problem facing the king: 'His country is on the verge of bloody revolution . . . Every day that passes without the threatened explosion is a positive gain but it's a gain at a price. No one in Jordan denies that the explosion has been held off so far by the presence of a British military force [but] in the modern Arab world the importation of foreign troops is a cardinal sin.' It's an insight that would not lose its relevance over time.

From Amman, he finally set off for Delhi, four months later than planned. Charles settled himself into the house at 18b Rajpur Road in Delhi's Civil Lines district. This had been the cosmopolitan centre of the city, where the British worked and lived before Edwin Lutyens designed and built New Delhi. Charles's new home backed onto what residents called The Ridge, a forest corridor where India's ancient Aravalli Hills begin and, in those days, still home to honey badgers, hyenas and the occasional leopard. As the BBC's new South Asia correspondent, covering the whole Indian subcontinent on his own, Charles's patch stretched from the North West Frontier's Khyber Pass down to Colombo in Ceylon, and the Maldive Islands, nearly 4,000 km to the south.

WITNESS TO THE TWENTIETH CENTURY

Those early days were lonely. It was three months before Catherine joined Charles, finally arriving on the SS *Chusan* ocean liner at the end of October 1958 from Southampton. But she had something to tell him that would shake him to the core.

While Charles had been on the road almost constantly from the time of his marriage, Catherine had been in London, working on a series of three programmes called *Press Conference*, where four journalists interviewed a politician. One of the members of the panel was John Freeman, a former Labour MP and deputy editor of the *New Statesman*. He was sixteen years her senior, magnetic, attractive and intellectually impressive. Catherine now told Charles that she had fallen in love with Freeman and wanted a divorce.

He was devastated. And he felt publicly humiliated. Buried deep in a box of his cuttings is a piece from page two of the *Daily Herald*. There's a large picture of Catherine on their wedding day with white flowers in her short, dark hair. 'Freeman and the BBC man's wife: as soon as she's free, we will marry' is the headline. Decades later, we were chatting about heartbreak, marriage and relationships in the bathroom of my parents' home in Sussex. Charles was taking a long soak, as he always did after several hours of heavy gardening. And then he suddenly said something that startled me: 'When Catherine left, it was the only time in my life when I really felt like shooting myself.'

Charles had planned a belated honeymoon in Kerala on the Malabar Coast soon after Catherine's arrival. Despite her stated intention to leave him, they took the trip anyway. It must have been extremely difficult. Several decades later, on a family trip we made together to Kerala, Charles told me about 'an unpleasant afternoon' he spent drinking with some tea-planter members of Catherine's family in the Kerala hills, 'half-cut on gin and tonics', then sleeping it off on the veranda, legs draped over the long arms of the planter chairs. If there were any attempts to patch things up, they came to nothing, and Catherine returned to England.

Ruth and Cyrus Jhabvala, Charles's new neighbours, took him under their wing. 'Jhab', as he was known to friends, was Charles's landlord as well. A distinguished Parsee architect, he had built the house at 18b as well as the adjoining home that he shared with his Polish-German wife, the writer Ruth Prawer Jhabvala, whose novel *Heat and Dust* would win the Booker Prize in 1975, and their three young daughters. Jhab introduced Charles to his Delhi, taking him on one of his renowned tours of the old pre-British Mughal part of the city: Humayun's Tomb, the Qutub Minar, a poignant synthesis of Hindu and Muslim tradition, and, of course, Delhi's Red Fort. As they walked around the sandstone monuments, I imagine Jhab enthusiastically regaling him with stories of fallen empires, conquest and treachery.

Charles was alone, miserable after his short-lived marriage to Catherine. Yet he was determined not to let it derail him. As was to be expected, the expat community welcomed the BBC's new man in Delhi, and invitations to parties and luncheons at clubs like the Gymkhana were soon forthcoming. But the cocktail circuit was not what Charles was there for and, even if it gave him the chance to make important contacts in diplomatic circles, he resolved not to spend too much time in the capital or at the BBC Delhi office in Hanuman Road.

With a new brief and a vast subcontinent to be reported on, he would throw himself into the job.

The most high-profile and prestigious foreign postings for a BBC correspondent were still in Europe and the United States, but, just ten years after the end of the British Raj in India, many British people still felt a powerful attachment to the region. Charles wasn't just broadcasting to a British audience, though. His dispatches, mostly for radio, would be aired on the BBC's Overseas Service (created in the 1930s as the Empire Service and renamed the World Service in 1965) as well as the domestic channels. The defining stories of Charles's posting and their importance became clear within his first six months there. Neighbours India, China and Pakistan were caught in a Cold War nexus, with Russia and the United States vying for influence, threatening peace in the region. Meanwhile, the integrity of independent and secular India was being undermined by separatist movements on its eastern borders and Hindu–Muslim communalism in many of its states and cities. Holding it all together was the towering but increasingly tired figure of Prime Minister Jawaharlal Nehru. Having constructed the nation's political institutions in the aftermath of imperial rule, he was now grappling with the business of governing this massive and diverse country – democratically.

Interpreting events on the Indian subcontinent for both a British and world audience was never going to be a straightforward undertaking. It was little more than a decade after the bloody legacy of the Partition of India following independence from 200 years of British imperial rule. The fledgling democracies created in the image of Westminster were already struggling. Coups and crackdowns in Nepal, Pakistan (at the time, comprising both West Pakistan and East Pakistan, now Bangladesh), Burma and Ceylon, as they were then known, put the robustness of the 'gifts' of empire into question.

Charles was the only BBC reporter covering the patch, with no producer and little more than a typewriter and a tape recorder to do his job. The distances were huge and getting the stories on air was always going to be one of his biggest challenges when outside Delhi. Reports had to be filed by phone or, if the quality wasn't good enough, by telex for a radio presenter in London to read out.

The declaration of martial law in Pakistan in 1958 by President Iskander Mirza and General Ayub Khan, the Commander-in-Chief of the Pakistani Army, 'to avoid bloody revolution' was one of the first events Charles covered when he took up the new post. Pakistan, created on religious lines and divided from India by Partition, was already following a very different political course. Charles reported that the October coup was carried out with no violence and chilling efficiency: 'Two men took over an enormous country of two wings separated by a thousand miles. At a single stroke, they abolished the constitution, the government, parliament and all the political parties and there was not the slightest sign of opposition,' he reported. Pakistan, he pointed out, was on the verge of ruin and its people demoralised.

'There is a view,' continued Charles's BBC dispatch from Karachi, 'the country was too underdeveloped to handle democracy.' This was certainly the view of General Ayub Khan, who with sinister simplicity put it like this: 'The politician's only weapon is his mouth, and we closed it.'

President Mirza might have read the ominous signs from Ayub and the military, but at the time, he and the general, now appointed prime minister, were apparently on the same page. Charles interviewed them together soon after the coup in early October. The interview was picked up by both the Indian and the Pakistani press, presumably not a little irritated that a Brit had scored one of the first sit-downs with the new rulers. They still reprinted large chunks of it though. The Pakistani newspaper, *Dawn*, in a piece headlined 'No Forsaking of Democracy' quoted Mirza saying that despite the imposition of martial law, 'indirect elections' would soon be held with voting rights 'for those people who understand what they are doing'.

'We have got to go back to democracy,' Ayub insisted. 'We must make it work. But unfortunately, in the first flush of independence our fellows adopted a system the people did not understand.' Pakistan's new rulers laid out their stall: for financial reform, food production and a better standard of living. Charles registered a quite favourable first impression of this new dictator duo after their dramatic takeover: 'Both of them strike one as relaxed and confident [but also] modest in talking about their personal capabilities.'

And then, before the month was out, Ayub had deposed his president as well. Mirza skulked off to live the rest of his days in London, and his fellow Sandhurst graduate, the tweed-wearing general, brought in a penalty of up to fourteen years imprisonment for criticism of the regime. A week before Ayub moved himself into the Presidential Palace, Charles had used his dispatch to reflect with some prescience, 'Is there not a danger that the army, basking in the artificial warmth created by an uncritical muzzled press, will become convinced it's become indispensable to a nation's well-being?'

The Indian establishment watched the sharp turn Pakistan was taking away from democracy with some trepidation. Commentators in the Indian press were pointing out that many of the elements that had led to Pakistan's military takeover were present in India too – namely corruption, nepotism, inefficiency, red tape and waste. As Charles put it in one of his reports, 'Independent India has a record of sound democratic achievement that can't be equalled among the undeveloped countries of Asia, but it would be living in an illusion to think it couldn't happen here.' India's own armed forces would be kept firmly in check in the years that followed, arguably to the detriment of the nation's security when it came to the crunch. But while politicians nervously eyed events unfolding in Pakistan, their attention was being forced to another of the country's neighbours. China's harrying and repression in Tibet could no longer be ignored. Nehru, who for years had turned a blind eye to the situation, found his hand forced.

The young Dalai Lama's flight from Tibet came after weeks of especially intense fighting between Khampa tribesmen and the Chinese occupiers of the country, who claimed Tibet as part of the People's Republic of China. By March 1959, a popular uprising was being brutally suppressed by China, the fighting had reached the edge of the Tibetan capital, Lhasa, and the young, fresh-faced 'God King', Tibet's spiritual and political leader, received a summons to attend Chinese headquarters in the city. He never went. The Dalai Lama, a believer in non-violence, had been an outspoken proponent of Tibet's liberation and its independence from China since the invasion of 1949. His supporters understood the danger and declared he would not be allowed to fall into Chinese hands.

'The fate of the Dalai Lama is unknown,' filed Charles for the BBC News Bulletins desk on 28 March from Delhi. This had turned into a major international story. The Chinese launched a massive manhunt – but Charles said 'reliable information' suggested that he was heading south through Khampa rebel strongholds. For three weeks there had been no firm news, no public sightings. And then, on 2 April, the Reuters team in Delhi broke the story that the Dalai Lama had safely crossed into India and would be given asylum.

It soon became clear that he was heading for Assam – the town of Tezpur at the foothills of the Himalayas. Charles got himself to the BBC office at Marshall House in Hanuman Road to pick up the tape recorder before joining the other Delhi-based reporters at the airport. The Reuters team had hired a plane and were charging the other reporters the price of a seat to cover their costs to fly the bumpy 1,000 miles to Tezpur. For the next week, they all set up camp at the Tezpur Station Club, the favoured watering hole for numerous British tea-planters who had stayed on after Independence. Droves of international press soon outnumbered the Tibetan émigrés and supporters also holed up in the town.

'What I remember so vividly, waiting for the "God King" to arrive, was this sometimes savage competition between Fleet

Street's finest,' Charles would recollect much later. Weird and flamboyant stories started popping up, many of them, according to Charles, filed by the *Daily Mail*'s 'star' reporter, later turned novelist, Noel Barber, which he said subsequently proved to be 'make believe', such as the Dalai Lama suffering terrible injuries and multiple fractures along the route. Journalists were getting frantic calls and cables from the news desks in London asking why they had missed the stories their editors were reading in the *Mail*. Of course, this wasn't the first or last time Charles witnessed journalists better suited to fiction-writing playing fast and loose with the truth, but it always shocked him.

The Dalai Lama had walked for a week, 224 miles down from Tawang in Arunachal Pradesh where he had been resting. Charles got his first sight of Tibet's twenty-three-year-old leader as he arrived on 18 April to a fanfare of Tibetan horns and a chorus of barking dogs, raising his arms and greeting the press and his supporters with a broad smile. His spokesman announced, 'All that the Dalai Lama wishes to say at the moment is to express his sincere regrets at the tragedy which has overtaken Tibet and to fervently hope that these troubles would be over soon without any more bloodshed.'

Once the full official statement had been delivered that morning in Tezpur, and his Holiness had left for a breakfast of fried eggs and cereal, there was a mad rush by the journalists to find a place from where they could file – in those days, that meant getting hold of a long-distance telephone line. 'The competition was sharpest between the two picture agencies, UPI [United Press International] and the AP [Associated Press], both of whom had ace cameramen on the story,' Charles remembered.

The real prize was to get the first picture of the young Dalai Lama, who everyone had heard of but no one had seen. But getting the photographs down to the agency news desks in New York and London called on inventiveness and, in some cases, downright skulduggery. It was possible to send photographs through wirephoto technology, involving a portable copier and transmitter, but this required a stable long-distance telephone line. The photos of the Dalai Lama could only be wired from the nearest big city, Calcutta, a two-hour flight away. 'UPI had decided it was going to go its own way. It sent its vice president from Tokyo to Tezpur to make sure they got the story and no one else did. The way they were going to do it was to hire a bigger aircraft, choose their own route and above all not allow anyone else but their own men on the plane.'

UPI had even invested in on-board processing equipment so as not to waste any time in the air. On the AP plane was a full cargo of rival members of the press, including Charles. The AP man was rushing everybody along to get on the aircraft so it could leave. As they boarded, they could see UPI's plane had just taken off. 'The pilot was so excited that he actually started taking off before we'd got the door shut,' said Charles. 'There were no seats on the aircraft. We were sitting on the metal floor of the Dakota plane that normally carried tea chests, holding onto each other. Some brave guy managed to shut the door before we were ten feet off the ground. It was actually a rather hairy situation.'

When they finally reached Calcutta, they could see the UPI plane was already on the ground. UPI had sent their pictures and then, according to the other reporters covering the story, they 'stuffed everybody else' by blocking a further six lines that they didn't need. It was some time before Dennis Lee Royle, the AP photographer, managed to get his pictures of the young Dalai Lama away.

'I was in the bar in the Calcutta hotel, helping the AP photographer to drown his sorrows,' recalled Charles. 'He thought he was going to get fired because he'd been so thoroughly beaten by a chief competitor. Someone walked into the bar and called out his name . . . It was a cable from his office. It said something like, "UPI has bearded Lama circulating around world. Your Lama unbearded. Please clarify urgently which is correct Dalai Lama." And of course, he realised he was OK – he had the picture, he had the scoop.' What in fact had happened was the UPI man in charge of making sure the pictures got off first had grabbed a picture of a man from a pile of photographs and sent it down the line without checking. He was, it turned out, a bearded Indian security officer, not the smooth-faced young lama.

A few months later, in September, Charles, working with the cameraman for Visnews, Prem Prakash, got the first ever television interview with the Dalai Lama. He spoke in Tibetan, his interpreter close by. Charles was keen to know what he made of the Indian prime minister's juggling on Tibet – he had incurred Chinese wrath by granting the Dalai Lama asylum but was still reluctant to make an international stand on China's suppression of Tibet and its refusal to uphold the highly contested agreement signed in 1951 that tied Tibet to the Chinese 'motherland' but also guaranteed its regional autonomy.

'The Indian people, especially Mr Nehru, were very pleased to receive me in India. However they can help, I know the relationship between Indians and Tibetans has always been very important.' He added, 'Naturally I am very sad. The Chinese are killing and threatening with more and more strength. This is still happening, such as in Eastern Tibet. I have hope that the situation will become more peaceful and safe for us to return.'

A year later, Charles would be reporting on news of terrible atrocities from Tibet, commenting that 'all that is Tibetan is gradually being extinguished'. The story is of ethnic cleansing with mass deportations, 'merciless humiliation and sheer horror'. Khampa resistance fighters were being flayed alive and dissenting lamas flogged in the streets. Reflecting on the role of Britain and the United States, Charles would wonder, five decades later, if more could have been done to secure worldwide recognition of Tibet as an independent state back in the early 1950s. His conclusion, and that of his colleagues at the time, was that these two Western powers simply didn't want to get involved. 'They didn't want to upset the Chinese – any more than they do today.'

Not upsetting the Chinese had been of paramount importance to Nehru as well. Not just to avoid another world war or infectious instability on India's borders but because Nehru saw China, and especially its prime minister, Zhou Enlai, as a natural ally and a political soulmate. Nehru's vision of India was as a promulgator of a non-aligned, pragmatic international movement, and the signing in Peking back in 1954 of the 'Panchsheel', the Five Principles of Peaceful Coexistence between India and China, was integral to this. But giving the

Dalai Lama asylum had threatened the relationship, angering the Chinese leadership, who were now accusing India of inciting the Tibetan rebellion. Nehru himself finally gave vent to popular feeling about the anti-Indian Chinese propaganda that was coming at them from their erstwhile friends, charging the Chinese with using the language of the Cold War 'without regard for truth and propriety'.

Charles found one of the most entertaining and instructive of places to witness all this unfold was from the press gallery of the Lok Sabha, India's parliament. Watching debates here and in conversations with fellow journalists from papers like the *Times of India* and the *Hindustan Times*, Charles did some of his most effective news-gathering. He was evidently keen to give the listeners not just a narrative of events but a glimpse of how this post-colonial example of parliamentary democracy was faring. It soon became clear that the deteriorating relations with China had become a major focus of the house. Nehru's reluctance to engage on the issue in the chamber finally gave way in the face of MPs' persistence. 'Very gradually . . . the facts have been drawn from the reluctant Mr Nehru,' filed Charles in his report after one Prime Minister's Question Time in August, and 'enough has come out to show that India's relations with China are in fact much worse today than are her relations with Pakistan, who has long held the position of enemy No 1.'

Then, on 25 August, the Chinese attacked an Indian outpost at Longju on the China–India border. The worry was that attacks on nearby Himalayan states could follow, and so Charles went north, up the perilous road to Sikkim, which had only just opened to light traffic after a series of landslides. Filing a story from Sikkim presented him with his biggest hurdle yet. There was no radio station there, no telex machine available and no functioning long-distance phone line either. But, as he later wrote, 'The night clerk at a tiny, sleepy post office was equal to the challenge.' The clerk's solution may well have made Charles the last BBC foreign correspondent ever to send a dispatch by Morse code. Neither of them actually knew any Morse beyond 'SOS', but the clerk had a code book and so each letter of the entire report was tapped out using this and sent to the main post office in Calcutta, transcribed there and telexed to London.

It was read by the presenter in the studio a few hours after Nehru declared that an attack on Bhutan or Sikkim would be treated as an attack on India herself. Questions were now revolving around India's preparedness, and whether firm words could be translated into firm action. 'If the Indian government does have a policy for defence against China, then the secret has been remarkably well kept,' wrote Charles, deploying a heavy dose of what was becoming characteristic irony in the dispatch.

Nehru was coming under fierce personal attack for his evasiveness. Charles summed up the mood, reflecting that this was probably the most trying week for the PM since he came to power after Independence: 'Members of Parliament are getting increasingly restive at the prime minister's habit of keeping vital developments from the House. Parliament, it's being said, has become – like the deceived husband – the last to know.' Most damaging, and almost unheard of for a man who had been the embodiment of his party and of Independent India, was a loss of confidence from the public, as 'confusion gives way to suspicion that the man at the top is losing his grip'.

Nehru eventually told a shocked parliament that the Chinese had been occupying a large part of Ladakh in the northwest and according to Charles he published the texts of sixty increasingly angry notes and letters that had passed between Delhi and Peking since 1954. One of those was a letter from Mr Nehru's old friend Zhou Enlai, who said India's traditional frontier with China in the north-east, known as the McMahon Line, was illegal because it had been created by the British.

In this febrile atmosphere, with Nehru's leadership being called into question, an unexpected and unlikely reprieve presented itself. Pakistan's president Ayub Khan dropped in to meet Nehru – for the first time. This was an important moment for Charles's listeners as relations between India and Pakistan after Partition, in a new Cold War setting, commanded world attention. The photographers and reporters, Charles among them, took in how strikingly different the two men were in appearance and in style: Nehru in his elegant three-quarter-length white Achkan jacket, wearing the handspun cotton topi synonymous with the Swadeshi movement against British rule; General Ayub, tall and dapper in an impeccably tailored dark suit and tie as he descended the aircraft steps onto the runway at Delhi's Palam airport where the two men were meeting. The visit was judged a considerable success. Charles and the rest of the accredited press were ushered into a large room before the meeting for a short press conference. His report recorded, 'It was the first glimpse that India had had of a man who has been portrayed as a minor monster – a sort of oriental Mussolini with a Sandhurst veneer . . .' The Indian reporters hadn't really expected to like him, but they did, 'not so much for what he had to say but the way he said it, and for his friendly and confident approach.'

Charles reported how, with the help of a successful visit from General Ayub, Nehru had managed to take the heat out of the situation and dispel growing doubts around his leadership. He added, 'It's doubtful if a month ago the general would have made the same impact. His appearance was beautifully timed. He arrived just when the Indians, badly shaken at the loss of an old friend to the north, were ready to make another.'

A few weeks later in Ceylon (now Sri Lanka), a different kind of diplomatic incident blew up – but this time, Charles was the cause of it. Ceylon's prime minister , S.W.R.D. Bandaranaike, had been assassinated by a Buddhist monk at the end of September 1959. A state of emergency was put in place and strict censorship laws introduced by the new prime minister, Wijeyananda Dahanayake, aimed at silencing growing calls to keep the Buddhist clergy out of politics. Some press claimed Dahanayake's party had been put in power by the clergy and they were in fact the ones pulling the strings. Charles travelled to the capital Colombo to report on the aftermath and to interview the new PM. He'd been filing shorter news reports for ten days but his dispatch for the *From Our Own Correspondent* programme was a longer, more reflective and analytical offering. Technical difficulties stopped him from getting the recording to London, so he cabled his script for the presenter to read. It was coruscating about Dahanayake, his cabinet, the role of the Buddhist clergy and the censorship policies aimed at muzzling the Ceylonese press and stifling opposition voices: 'In some respects, Ceylon last week reminded me of Pakistan exactly a year ago, just before General Ayub Khan removed the politicians and established military rule. In Ceylon, the conditions for a takeover are there; what is missing is a man with the necessary following.'

But it was the next paragraph that stung the most: 'As it is, Ceylon has been ruled by a Cabinet composed very largely of mediocrities, and led by an inexperienced eccentric, whose only strength lies in his possession of dictatorial powers . . . It's difficult to see how either Mr Dahanayake or the present government can last very long.'

Unsurprisingly perhaps, the Ceylonese government and some parts of the press took great umbrage at this. The BBC was seen by many as a mouthpiece of the British government, and so the broadcast was regarded as a major slight. The *Times of Ceylon* newspaper led the charge, stating, 'The BBC has descended to undignified scorn and uncharitable abuse, which does great violence to its reputation for fair-mindedness in the presentation of news and comment. The BBC owes the people of Ceylon an unqualified apology.' Ceylon's *Sunday Observer* published several extracts of the offending dispatch under a seven-column streamer headline, but its coverage was less hysterical. In fact, it repeated Charles's view that press censorship had been introduced by the government under pressure from the Buddhist clergy.

Charles was not prepared for what happened next. The Ceylonese government banned BBC broadcasts on Ceylon Radio airwaves for five months and delivered a strongly worded protest to London through Britain's acting high commissioner in Colombo, with the message that, 'The broadcast contained unwarranted criticisms of the new government and was of a nature likely to impair friendly relations between the two Commonwealth countries.' Members of the Ceylonese Parliament were incensed, with one female MP condemning the 'grossly improper, impertinent and impudent comment made by the BBC'.

Charles sent a series of telexes back to London. He assured the editors that his piece was written after rigorous censorship had been in force for several days; the premier had refused the opposition request for a recall of parliament; and press and opposition had been printing cartoons and mocking pieces about his vanity. He insisted, 'My piece was a distillation of ten days of intensive reporting.'

The BBC issued a formal apology to Ceylon's high commissioner in London but that wasn't enough to stop the controversy developing into what had become a major diplomatic row. Before long, it had reached the top of the British government itself. A personal message of regret from Harold Macmillan, the prime minister, was conveyed to the Ceylonese government, informing them, 'I know that you will fully understand that Her Majesty's Government has no responsibility whatsoever for the contents of dispatches from BBC correspondents . . . I greatly regret that anything should have been said to add to the burden which you took up in such distressing circumstances especially since we have such warm feelings of goodwill towards you and your country.'

Macmillan's somewhat lofty response was widely reproduced in the Ceylonese press and did enough to take the heat out of the political situation, although the matter rumbled on at a local level for quite a while. When Charles wanted to return to Colombo the following week, the *Ceylon Observer* was so outraged that it printed a front-page story reminding readers of his previous transgressions, adding that, 'In spite of this, "wheel-again Wheeler" as you might like to call him, has applied for permission to cover the opening of parliament.'

Some of the British press picked up the story. Charles's father sent him a cutting from the *Daily Telegraph*, whose columnist came to Charles's defence but also took the opportunity to indulge in some bashing of the public broadcaster: 'The BBC has already apologised twice. For all I know they may go on apologising indefinitely. The one person who is unlikely to receive an apology is Mr Wheeler, whose reputation as a commentator is thus cheerfully thrown to the wolves . . . The BBC plainly does not expect, desire or deserve to be served by people of independent mind and judgement.'

In fact, the BBC backed their man up. Charles was half expecting to receive his marching orders over the offending broadcast. He wrote to Tony Wigan, Head of BBC News, when things had calmed down slightly, wanting to make it clear that his dispatch had not been an outpouring of untempered opinion: 'I am sorry to have caused this incident . . . I should like to say that my remarks were not an expression of any personal frustration at censorship or anything else. They were meant as a considered attempt by a reporter with no axe to grind, to sum up as news, a development that had not yet been fully reported or properly interpreted because local critics of the government – both press and parliamentary – were silenced by censorship and because other foreign correspondents had left

Colombo before the government took the action it did. It was also an attempt to redress the balance; I felt that in my several meetings with the prime minister I had been misled and that I had in turn misled the listener,' he wrote. More contritely, Charles ends the letter, 'I take your point about appearing in the guise of a protagonist and will be more careful in future.'

Charles later recalled that the BBC was 'very intelligent about it', taking the view that ultimately it was the editor's responsibility to stop the piece being broadcast. That was also reflected in the annual review of his work by BBC management, a regular exercise for all BBC staff, which noted with unusual insight, 'He didn't allow himself to be thrown off balance when an error of judgement in his reporting of Ceylon – which should have been eliminated in London – produced a sharp international reaction, but continued to send calm and balanced reports in circumstances which must have been difficult.'

Within a few months, Prime Minister Dahanayake had resigned. Charles felt vindicated, though wisely kept it to himself. But later, after many years had passed, he told an interviewer, 'Everybody thought he was an idiot. I was right as it turned out.' After Hugh Carleton Greene became director general of the BBC, Charles asked him what his personal view was of the episode. Greene replied, 'Charles, the thing to do as a foreign correspondent is to always sail as close to the wind as you can, and just make sure you get it right.'

There was barely time to brood over the rumpus in Ceylon before the border conflicts with China flared up again. The capture of an Indian patrol squad by Chinese forces and a violent clash at the Kongka Pass in Ladakh led to the deaths of ten Indian police officers. Afterwards, Charles detected a change in the Indian prime minister. He noted that 'his recent speeches were much more in tune with the country's feelings' and 'Mr Nehru has made small but distinct concessions to public opinion. His first reaction to the Ladakh attack was in effect anger at his own countrymen for their anger with the Chinese. His remarks went down badly – almost as badly, I think, as the Chinese attack itself . . . And equally interesting – there's been a change in his own mood. He now seems so relaxed, much less on the defensive about his own policies.'

A few weeks later, Charles was granted a rare television interview with Nehru's daughter Indira Gandhi, who had no formal role in her father's cabinet, but since the start of 1959 had been president of the Congress Party. Watching the black and white footage so many years later, I'm struck by her stillness. She and Charles are sitting outside by the side of a small pond. Gandhi answers concisely, her head slightly to one side, an enigmatic smile occasionally passing across her face like a shadow. Charles asks her what she thinks Indian people feel about the recent border issues with China.

'Angry, indignant and excited,' she replies, and waits for the next question.

'What about the criticism from within your own party on the handling of the China crisis?' queries Charles.

'They obviously think we should move our armies in at once and they are indignant because they also feel, I think, that we didn't protect our borders well enough . . . They are not aware of the terrain of the area,' comes the assured answer.

Charles recorded, and many modern historians have since concluded, that it was largely Nehru's handling of the relationship with China that undermined his authority in India as prime minister. But as Indira Gandhi said to Charles, 'I don't see what other kind of policy we could have adopted which would have prevented the situation. If China attacks us if we are friendly, would it not have attacked us if we had been hostile?'

For India, friends abroad felt more important than ever. The country's leadership might have had ambivalent feelings towards America but, as 1959 drew to a close, President Eisenhower received a euphoric reception when he arrived for an official visit to the country. Crowds lined the streets of Delhi, waving banners of support. 'Welcome Ike – Prince of Peace' read one. With each speech the US president delivered, admiration for him soared. 'Perhaps India provided the ideal background for the expansive Eisenhower personality – those Hindu wedding bands; those monster garlands of jasmine . . .' Charles observed in one report.

India's national press were reporting enthusiastically that the American president had been converted to the non-alignment approach of India, a position that avoided taking sides with the major powers, namely China, Russia or the US. Charles described Ike-mania gripping the nation: 'By the fifth and last day mutual goodwill had grown to such proportions that one of India's most sober commentators seemed to be speaking for millions when he talked of a "breakthrough" to a new and powerful relationship between the world's two biggest democracies.'

But during his last speech of the visit, Eisenhower felt he

had to put his hosts right that there was no new American–Indian partnership in the making, telling them that America was not a 'convert' to the Indian way in international relations, and that the world was divided into two groups of nations: 'those that believed in truth and individual liberty, and those that did not,' as Charles paraphrased it. The debate that ensued between the two leaders engaged and electrified the audience, including Charles, who reported, 'It was the one great moment of the visit – here were two statesmen in public debate; firm friends, laying bare the incompatible philosophies that divide them and doing so with deep conviction and entirely without animosity. It destroyed some illusions but nothing else, and it restored reality.' By contrast, Eisenhower's trip to Pakistan, which Charles went on to cover as well, was a much more 'brisk and businesslike' affair, conducted in a forty-hour flurry.

India and Pakistan had become the setting for another act of the Cold War drama, with the world's big Communist powers and the United States touting aid, influence and military might, while General Ayub, avowedly anti-Communist, and Nehru, the exponent of the global non-aligned movement, were simultaneously courting these great powers and keeping them at bay. But in India itself, the hallmark of Nehru's relationship with the Communist Party of India was mistrust.

The southern Indian state of Kerala had become the world's first freely elected Communist government in 1957. That dealt a humiliating blow to the ruling Congress Party, which was now in power across the country in every state except Kerala. The contrast between the Congress leaders' attitude to the Kerala state government and, as Charles put it, 'a much more militant communism abroad' was stark. He followed the Kerala story closely, from the month he spent there during his ill-fated honeymoon in 1958 to the 1960 elections two years later. 'If only they weren't Communists,' one of those tea-planter acquaintances of his former in-laws from the Kerala High Ranges had told Charles ruefully. 'We have to admit it, for sheer ability, intelligence and personal honesty there isn't a group of politicians to match the Communists in this state. They're young and keen; they work long hours; they're approachable and they're worth talking to because they know what they are talking about.' When Charles travelled down to take a look for himself, he encountered a brand of communism very different from what he had seen before. 'There is nothing of the police state about Kerala. People say what they like, and they don't go in fear of arrest. The proposed legislation is carbon copies of Congress-sponsored measures in neighbouring states,' he noted.

But two years after the election that brought the Communists to power, Charles was reporting from Kerala's capital Trivandrum that, 'The Indian National Congress, occupying the seat of power everywhere in India but for Kerala, is supporting a movement to overthrow by unconstitutional means an elected government.' It had all seemed to be going in the right direction, he observed in one dispatch. But important interests were challenged, and protestors took to the streets. The land reforms upset the high-caste Hindus. The Education Bill threatened the Catholic Church, which resolved 'to fight with a fervour reserved in more normal times for the Devil himself'. They all united behind the banner of the local Congress Party, who insisted that Delhi intervene to keep the peace. By the end of the following month, the Congress-led government had imposed 'President's Rule'. 'The government of Kerala is the only Communist government in the world that came to power in a free election. It can now be added that it was also the first Communist government ever to have been overthrown by mass direct action,' filed Charles.

On his very first visit to Kerala, Charles had wondered whether Communism there would be 'tied to an inflexible dogma dispensed from abroad, or will it take on an indigenous course suited to the Indian environment and tradition?' The answer to that question was easier to give with hindsight. By the time he returned to Kerala more than four decades later to attend a riotous family wedding in the state, the Communists had been elected and voted out several times over, alternating at regular intervals with Congress to run the state legislature – testament to the independent-minded Keralan voters, as well as the 'indigenous' course this brand of communism had indeed taken.

International VIP visits to Charles's patch were coming thick and fast, ensuring a regular stream of dispatches. While 1959 had seen the visit from Eisenhower, in 1960 it was the turn of the Russians. In February, Soviet president Voroshilov asked if he might visit Kerala but was politely told by Delhi that the state was not on his itinerary. The Indian government clearly didn't want him stirring up trouble with their homegrown Communists. The irony, as Charles pointed out, was that while Voroshilov was feted in the next-door state of Tamil Nadu as 'the head of a great and friendly state dedicated to peace and international goodwill', Congress leaders and a couple of senior cabinet ministers from Delhi were expostulating to a crowd in Kerala that 'there could be no co-existence between democracy and Communist dictatorship'.

The Russian Premier Nikita Khrushchev followed in March, but, unlike President Eisenhower's trip, it was not a great success. 'Both sides expected too much,' reported Charles. Khrushchev did not get the welcome he expected and was visibly grumpy about it. He then made things worse by choosing the Indian parliament as the platform to attack the multi-party system and devoting all of his five speeches to criticising the nature of Western aid. 'Even one's Communist acquaintances were embarrassed,' Charles noted in a radio dispatch from the visit, pointing out that 'Indian Members of Parliament are proud of their Westminster tradition . . .'

The Chinese Premier Zhou Enlai's diplomatic mission in April for six days of talks with Nehru brought about a far more significant encounter for Charles. The international press corps had flown in to cover the talks between the two premiers, and the Canadian High Commission gave a lunch party to welcome their national broadcasters and the media. As the BBC's man in Delhi, Charles was invited too. One of the other guests was Dip Singh, the Canadian High Commission's social secretary. She was ten years younger than Charles, self-composed, strikingly beautiful, well read and clearly highly intelligent. Dip found Charles pleasingly modest, even shy. And for such a handsome man, he had a singular lack of vanity, unlike many of the men she had encountered up to now. Charles was not so timid as to hold back from inviting her to lunch the next day.

He soon found out they had more in common than they

might have guessed. Dip, like him, had also lost a beloved older brother. Bakshi, she told Charles, had died of tuberculosis in a sanatorium in the hill station of Kasauli at the age of twenty-one in 1949. It was because of him that the family had left their home in Sargodha, in what would become Pakistan, to reach the TB treatment centre. As it turned out, they went just before India's Partition and the worst of the violence that tore apart the Punjab. Dip believed her brother had in some ways saved their lives, as her father, a prominent Sikh landowner, may not have left in time to escape the ensuing bloodbath, which claimed around one million lives and displaced twenty million. Dip was fourteen when the family left their home for the last time. Charles, of course, also knew something of what it felt like to have a childhood disrupted by conflict.

They had also both been married before. Dip kept the details sketchy. She'd had an arranged marriage at seventeen, which she left after five years, simply walking out of the home with barely more than the clothes on her back and a small piece of hand luggage. She had been living an independent life since then, even travelling to London in 1957 with a group of friends that included two Indian tennis players, Narendra Nath and Ramanathan Krishnan, who were playing at Wimbledon that year. She sat on Centre Court and, at the end of the tournament, danced all night at the Lawn Tennis Association Ball at Grosvenor House. Now she was living in a small, self-contained 'Basati' flat upstairs in her parents' house in Delhi's Golf Links neighbourhood. Charles was enchanted. But he had to tear himself away to file on the story that had already come to dominate his time in Delhi.

The talks between Nehru and Zhou Enlai hadn't gone well, bogged down in claims and counterclaims about the borders and the dates they were established. Discussions revolved around the disputes in the north and east, Ladakh and Tibet, the Aksai Chin and the disputed McMahon Line. From the Chinese, there was a grudging agreement not to advance any further, and from the Indians, not to repulse Chinese advances. Later commentators have reflected that Zhou's offer to give up Chinese claims to the east if Nehru had agreed to relent on the Aksai Chin might have avoided future conflict. But public opinion left Nehru little room for manoeuvre. The atmosphere in the press conference afterwards was, according to Charles's account for the BBC, very strained. The only Indian journalist who dared to challenge the statement from Zhou Enlai that the Sino–India friendship would live on 'for tens of thousands of years' was mocked by the Chinese premier himself, who, according to Charles, then took the opportunity to make jokes about Western imperialism at the expense of the Western reporters in the room – 'sallies that provoked gales of sycophantic laughter among a surprising number of Indian journalists'. As far as the substance of their dispute was concerned, Zhou Enlai left Delhi 'unmoved, undented, unbowed, uninstructed and unconverted', as one of the Indian commentators had put it. In Charles's view, the heat, for the time being at least, had gone out of the dispute. But 'Indians are resigning themselves to the inevitable Cold War with China,' he concluded.

In September 1960, Nehru travelled for his second meeting with Pakistan's President Ayub Khan and the signing of the Indus Waters Treaty. It took him – and Charles – to Pakistan's major cities. Everywhere he went, Karachi, Rawalpindi and Lahore, Nehru was received by hugely enthusiastic crowds. The question of how to divide the water around the Indus River Basin and the six tributaries that crossed India and Pakistan's borders had meant twelve years of quarrelling between the two countries. In a rare moment of diplomatic harmony, an agreement was signed in Karachi. This was a city where Charles greatly enjoyed himself. He became a regular at Farook's, whose tandoori chicken was far better than anything Delhi had to offer, he wrote to Dip. He also described to her how he was taken on a family trip to the beach by Gordon Slater, a local-based British diplomat, to go swimming with turtles, an experience that he treasured for the rest of his life.

The Indus River signing had gone so well that a further meeting was arranged between Nehru and Ayub Khan at the hill station of Murree, the Pakistan government's summer retreat, and a favourite haunt to entertain and parlay with foreign dignitaries. Legions of hopeful press and diplomats followed. The night before the 'Summit Conference', Charles wrote another letter to Dip, complaining of a 'madly rattling air conditioner' in the room. He couldn't sleep. Insomnia and restlessness were always a problem for Charles; his irrepressible energy wouldn't be stilled. He wrote that he'd been taking some soundings from officials at the UK High Commission who told him 'no one expects much to come out of the talks'.

Unfortunately, they were right. The Indus Waters Treaty, brokered by the World Bank, had resolved some long-standing issues and created a mechanism to sort out any future squabbles. But on the most problematic issue of the disputed state of

Kashmir, which was what Ayub wanted to discuss, Nehru refused to engage. Charles gathered accounts of the meeting from both the Indian and Pakistani sides, all agreeing that Mr Nehru hardly spoke. 'He admired the view, and he asked the names of the flowers in the garden . . . He even invited President Ayub to come to Delhi.' But Nehru was unwilling to budge on Kashmir, convinced, like most Indians, that any move from the status quo would only bring back communal riots that India had seen during Partition in 1947. The talks were over far sooner than expected and Charles prepared to head back to Delhi.

'HOPING MAKE SATURDAY AFTERNOON PLANE EXLAHORE CROSS FINGERS' he cabled Dip from Murree on Wednesday, 21 September. She kept the message for nearly six decades, tucked in the same small, grey Air India travel bag in which she'd carried her most personal belongings when she moved out of her first husband's house. On the back, she has noted down in pencil when she calculates he should land: 5.45 p.m. on Saturday at New Delhi's Safdarjung airport, about half an hour's drive from Charles's house in Rajpur Road. She has also jotted down the name of a book she wants to get hold of from Bahrisons, their preferred bookshop in New Delhi's Khan Market: E. M. Forster's *Two Cheers for Democracy*.

Charles was counting the hours before the weekend, when they would be able to spend another Sunday together – a late Sunday lunch at 18b had already become their tradition. Charles's cook David, a Christian from Kerala, made a regular Sunday roast dinner just the way he thought his English boss would like it. Charles and Dip would rather have eaten a lamb curry or stuffed parathas but the lifeless peas and carrots with chewy goat dressed as lamb were always lovingly prepared. They complimented David effusively, ensuring the tradition continued unthreatened. When David finally said goodnight, they would retire to the sofa and listen to Mozart's Clarinet Concerto, their favourite piece of music. Matters were slowly coming to a head between them. Shortly before Charles met her, Dip had appeared in a Canadian Broadcasting Corporation documentary on India called *Revolution by Consent*. She'd been volunteered by the High Commission as the producers were looking for a guide and translator for the project. So elegant and poised was her performance, interpreting and managing interviews with villagers and officials, that she had ended up on screen nearly as much as the presenter himself. When the producer of the programme sent a letter from Canada suggesting she might like to come and try her luck at a broadcasting career, Charles was alarmed. It was time to make his own intentions a little clearer – though Dip could have had no doubt about his feelings towards her. The letters he wrote to her in those early courting days before they married, which she kept safely all her life, are full of impatient passion and tenderness. But 1960 had been especially busy for Charles, with intense scuttling around the continent, ensuring that Dip and Charles's hearts definitely had time to grow fonder, as the business of news-gathering kept them apart more often than not.

For almost a month, Charles criss-crossed the subcontinent to support preparations for the Royal Tour at the end of January 1961. This was to be the first visit of a reigning British monarch since George V came for the Delhi Durbar fifty years earlier and, of course, since independence from British rule. The BBC would go big on this major broadcasting event and sent their head of outside broadcasts, Charles Max-Muller, to join Charles recce-ing locations and events ahead of the Queen's arrival. The BBC duo went first to Calcutta, where Charles noted in a curtain-raiser broadcast that the Victoria Memorial – 'a curious blend of St Paul's, the Taj Mahal and the Old Bailey' – had been turned into a museum devoted to Victorian India, with an Indian curator who was 'an ardent Victorian still. Every stone, he tells me the other day, speaks of Her Majesty's greatness.'

In Jaipur – where the tour would start and where the Maharaja and Maharani's ancestors had traditionally entertained British royalty – the plan was to re-enact the moment in 1876 when the Queen's great-grandfather, Edward VII, then Prince of Wales, entered the City Palace on a 'bejewelled elephant'. The Queen was to be provided with her own mount to ride in state to a reception followed by a two-day tiger hunt.

In Peshawar, Charles and Max-Muller discussed the logistics of radio coverage with Rashid Ahmed, the director general of Pakistan Radio. They found him likeable and 'businesslike'. Less appealing to Charles were some of the British officials. He especially took against the 'unimpressive and clerky' UK deputy high commissioner, who 'didn't have the courtesy to ask us for a drink'.

While royal and presidential visits were a clear news priority for the news desk in London, like all foreign correspondents, Charles also had a certain freedom to deviate from the news-planning diary. Among the leaders of state governments, kingdoms and nations that he'd met so far on this posting, the Wali of Swat made a particular impression. Charles pitched a profile on him for BBC Radio: the Wali, otherwise known as Miangul Jahanzeb, was the de facto monarch of his district in North-West Frontier Province. He was also its religious leader, Commander-in-Chief and political head in a region of blood feuds and tribal justice. On an earlier visit, Charles had reported that it 'works quickly and smoothly, without the benefit of lawyers (who are not allowed to practice in this corner of the Commonwealth), or of the public hangman, who is considered unnecessary'. The Wali was a good-looking man of fifty who wore Western dress and spoke 'faultless English'. His father had united the warring tribes some forty years earlier. Charles suggested that in Swat, the 'rifle is to the frontier tribesman what the umbrella is to the City of London Englishmen in midsummer – a precaution but also an ornament.'

'Frankly,' the Wali told Charles, 'I'm a dictator and the system works very well.' Education was free, there were hospitals and mobile dispensaries and an 'advisory council' that met four times a year. The people were well housed and they grew enough food for their own use. Charles also judged Swat's hotel to be 'one of the best on the Indian subcontinent'. The Wali had built it himself. He explained that it lost money, but he had been putting up all the visitors at his own modest brick bungalow and found it difficult to look after them 'properly'. Not usually an advocate of dictatorship as a form of rule, it seems Charles was quite taken with the Wali's small dominion.

Now visiting the district, he wished for one more thing. He wrote to Dip, 'It's in places like this, that I miss you most of all.

How I wish there were no such things as visas and that I could bring you here . . .'

Charles and Dip had been planning a surreptitious weekend away together on his return to Delhi when London called to tell Charles to head for the airport. Not for the first time a romantic getaway had to be cancelled in deference to the gathering of news. There had been a coup in Nepal. Charles had travelled to Kathmandu the year before to report on the opening of the country's first parliament. He had walked into a magnificent chamber, taking in the 'suitably cosmopolitan', light-green contemporary sofas for the new MPs, and had seen the silver throne studded with rubies belonging to King Mahendra, who in 1950 had returned from exile to lead the overthrow of the ruling Rana clan and bring democracy to Nepal. Charles had been surprised to spot on the wall, among the life-sized portraits of the Rana prime ministers, a small portrait of Hitler. No one could tell him what it was doing there.

Maybe it was a bad omen because now Nepal's experiment with democracy was over. The new MPs had barely had a chance to settle back into their smart new sofas before parliament was wound up. King Mahendra threw the whole government into jail, including his softly spoken prime minister, BP Koirala. From his hotel in Kathmandu, at midnight, Charles wrote to Dip:

My own darling,
I wish I could talk to you about all this, it is quite fascinating . . . I have spent another day talking to all

sorts of normally well-informed people only to find no one who even pretends to know what it's all about. Up to last night it had seemed comparatively simple – the King had dismissed and arrested the government, allegedly on grounds of inefficiency and corruption . . . He has now arrested every politician of any consequence in the country – including the Speaker of Parliament – and even those politicians who were yesterday hailing his move as a Godsend . . . Perhaps the most depressing thing about the whole affair is the utter apathy of the mass of the people – the King is an incarnation of Vishnu so he must be right, and the politicians must have been charlatans.

There was great interest in the story; Charles managed to contact the Nepal Congress Party, who gave him a statement from their general secretary, who was in hiding. 'It was strong stuff, so I filed it,' he said. He had been trying to get the Indian correspondents covering the story to use it, 'but they declined – they have to live here . . . The [Nepali] papers have swung into line, printing editorials praising the King's wisdom and judgment.'

Charles was baffled by the actions of the King who had staged a successful revolution nine years ago. 'Everything is so uncertain that I can't possibly decide when to leave. Why the coup? I am no further than when I arrived and I don't like to leave until I am fairly certain in my own mind what the whole thing is about,' he agonised in his letter to Dip, his journalistic instincts and desire to get back to her battling each other. Handwritten on the back of the letter, he has added,

'Now it's Sunday – and I miss you more than ever – we should never be parted on Sundays.'

Perhaps the answer to Charles's questions lay partly in the growing popularity of Prime Minister Koirala, whom the monarch had arrested at a public meeting, supported by 200 men of the Royal Guard. Back in Delhi, Charles made Koirala the subject of his offering for the BBC's *From Our Own Correspondent*'s Christmas Eve broadcast. The 'young and energetic' BP Koirala had been in prison before, jailed by the British as a member of the Quit India Movement. Now he was behind bars again. He was, according to Charles, a 'social democrat with drive' who, with his encouragement of the peasantry to stand up for their rights on land reform, his twenty-one-day walking tours to explain his policies to the people personally, may have been going 'too fast, too soon'. Despite suffering from throat cancer, Koirala would spend the next seven years in jail, and then the rest of his life mainly in exile.

The British Queen's first visit to India took place from January to March 1961. Charles lauded both her stamina and her unstuffy demeanour during the seven-week trek around the continent. 'The effect of the Queen's personality was considerable, and the credit is entirely hers, for the tour was long and demanding,' he stated in his broadcast of 4 March. He told his listeners that despite the stiff and 'blessedly misleading' regal photographs, 'the Queen the public saw was responsive, the reverse of pompous and even shy – not at all the popular conception of a British monarch; and quite unlike the usual touring foreign dignitary with his laboured repertoire of indigenous gestures and his posings in native hats.'

But the positive account did not extend to Her Majesty's advisors. Charles suggested they had mishandled the more political aspects of the tour. He reported how feathers were ruffled in India when it was learnt that she would be making a speech in Pakistan, while the United Kingdom representative in Delhi was 'neither consulted nor forewarned'. In Nepal, where much of the government remained in jail, her speech was royally bungled, according to Charles's dispatch. An expression of sympathy for the King's controversial action in closing down parliament was included and then deleted, but not until after the original text of the speech had already been distributed to the Nepalese press and radio. The issue didn't just reverberate in Nepal but in India too, where, according to Charles, 'All too many people are saying that the Queen's advisors are not only showing themselves to be inconsistent, backing parliamentary democracy here and autocratic regimes next door, but are quite needlessly displaying a bad bet on the wrong horse.'

The killing of a tiger by the Duke of Edinburgh during the hunt laid on in the Indian city of Jaipur a month earlier had already provoked some negative headlines in Britain. 'Does Philip need another rug at the Palace?' asked the *Daily Mirror*. In keeping with family tradition (the Queen's grandfather George V had shot thirty-nine tigers in Nepal in 1911), another tiger and rhino hunt was planned for the Royal Party in Nepal. But this time the Duke – who had just taken up the presidency of the World Wildlife Fund – pretended, Charles later said, to have an injured index finger, a 'whitlow', to avoid having to pull the trigger. That honour was bestowed on the foreign secretary, Alec Douglas-Home, the 14th Earl of Home, also accompanying the royal couple.

Perched on top of an elephant in a howdah basket, observing from the sidelines with the other accredited press, Charles provided what may have been the first and last radio commentary of a royal tiger hunt for the BBC. It sounds like a wholly unedifying spectacle, even for those days. The tigers were already cornered and corralled, ringed by dozens of elephants and beaters flapping white sheets, before the party was summoned. Lord Home was invited to take a shot. Charles, not a fan, nevertheless conveyed a sense of being caught up in the excitement. In the recording, he goes for it like a football commentator at a Wembley final, starting with a hushed urgency: 'Everybody is in position now, the Earl of Home with his rifle at the ready, the Queen watching, her camera ready. And about six . . . seven . . . eight beater elephants are moving in front of elephant grass about seven feet high . . . not very fast . . . A hundred yards away is a patch of clear grass. Anything may come out at any minute . . . Some grass movement there . . .'

A long silence. Then, suddenly, the sound of gunshots, elephants trumpeting, the mahouts shouting and calling, and Charles going into overdrive:

'And we can hear it . . . now it comes! Tiger straight off towards the other elephants! I don't think he's got him, he's still in the ring . . . [more gunfire] . . . I think the foreign secretary missed but I may be wrong.' He wasn't. Two hours later, the tiger had made eight appearances and the foreign secretary had missed another three times. It was left to Rear-Admiral Christopher Bonham-Carter to deliver the *coup de grâce*.

But it was all wearing a bit thin for Charles. Seven weeks of traipsing around the continent with legions of visiting press and royal correspondents from Fleet Street, hours of watching the Royal Party aiming at wildlife, waiting for directions from the Palace flunkies, was enough to drive the most patient of hacks to drink. Charles would often tell the story, perhaps with a hint of remorse, how after a few too many at a bar in Peshawar one night, he muttered, 'I wish that bloody woman would go home.' His unguarded comment was overheard, and word got out. Shortly afterwards, when his name was put on a list of journalists for a visit to the Queen's Picture Gallery in London, Charles said the Palace phoned the BBC and told them if Wheeler comes to the Palace, we will call out the Guard. 'I was persona non grata for the next five years.'

Soon after the Royal Tour, Charles was summoned back to England for discussions at Broadcasting House on his next move. He had a month of home leave, so based himself with his parents at their house in the Surrey village of Dormansland.

London was keen to send Charles back to Berlin for his next posting, but at this stage they were not committing themselves to keeping two correspondents in Germany, one there and another in Bonn, West Germany's capital. At his meeting in London, Charles told the foreign editor Donald Edwards that he would be happy to stay in India for another year, which the BBC agreed to. He also expressed a hope that the mandate of the Berlin job could extend to Eastern Europe, including maybe Moscow, and said he was willing to learn Russian. On this, Charles would not get his way.

Charles and Dip were now planning a future together, but the wedding would have to wait until the following spring, when Charles's divorce finally went through. The month in England felt long and Charles was piqued by jealousy hearing about Dip's busy life on the Delhi social scene, where she seemed to be as popular on the dance floor as she was on the tennis court. Perhaps thinking of when things went wrong at the very start of his first marriage, he was getting distinctly edgy about the attentions of one particular Maharaja's son. 'You seem to be getting on very well with the Indian nobility – think I should get back,' he wrote.

Charles told Dip he was feeling a bit empty, 'dull and depressed for no very good reason'. He went up to London to record a dispatch on Ceylon, where a State of Emergency has been declared by the new leader Mrs Bandaranaike, widow of the assassinated PM. He spent the rest of the afternoon in search of a recording of Mozart's German Dances and the fawn-coloured raincoat that Dip had asked him to bring back for her. In the gramophone department at Harrods, he locked himself into the small listening room with an armful of records. Liking nothing very much (except Dip's German Dances), he went back to the rack and found Mozart's Clarinet Concerto 'which reminded me of us at 18b . . . So I played it through twice – until an assistant interrupted me to say it was 5.30 and the shop was closing – which ended my daydream about us,' he wrote to Dip. Travelling back to Delhi via Moscow, he would arrive before the letter did.

*

Dip once said that the only fights she ever had with Charles over politics were about Kashmir. She came at it from a perspective influenced by her experience of Partition, and she saw it as 'my country right or wrong'. Dip was instinctively antagonistic towards any Pakistani claim on the region, given that the very creation of Pakistan by Partition had meant the loss of her own childhood home. She was also intensely loyal to any position taken by Nehru, whom she had met while still a schoolgirl and who for her symbolised the new, secular India.

Charles, reporting on Pakistan as well as India, had a more dispassionate view of the dispute. He had been struck by the intensity of Pakistan's feeling about the region and had noted that 'there is absolutely no disposition in Pakistan to compromise on Kashmir'. In the summer of 1961, it was Kashmir that led Charles to report, 'It is being said in Delhi, and it's unlikely anyone in Rawalpindi would disagree, that relations between India and Pakistan have sunk to their lowest level in many years. Yet only ten months ago, it was almost as widely believed that the two countries were about to put more than a decade of quarrelling between them and start living as reasonably friendly neighbours.'

President Ayub had just returned from a visit to see the newly installed US President Kennedy in Washington. After failing to get Nehru to engage on Kashmir at their last meeting, Ayub had been waging a campaign through his state-controlled press that severely provoked the Indian prime minister. Nehru accused Ayub of indulging in theatrics and of pursuing a policy of hatred against India. It was, said Charles, 'the sharpest attack Mr Nehru had ever made on a head of state'. In fact, as he went on, 'both President Ayub and Mr Nehru are prisoners of the highly emotional attitudes towards Kashmir, which both have a share in generating.' Charles bleakly concluded in his report that 'the outlook for continued peace on the Indian subcontinent must be poor'.

India's relations seemed to be souring further afield as well. The day before Nehru's departure for Washington that November, Charles reported on the US administration's charge that Indian policy was biased in favour of Russia, casting a blight on the visit. India–US relations had been blossoming with the election of John F. Kennedy. He had pleased Indians when, as a candidate, he announced that non-alignment was right for India, and as president he had upped US aid to the country. But on 13 August, when the first sections of a wall in Berlin to divide East from West were built by the East German authorities, India was slow to condemn Russia. More damagingly, in the UN debate on nuclear testing by the two superpowers, India's abrasive defence minister Krishna Menon pronounced that he saw no difference between the conduct of Mr Khrushchev and Mr Kennedy. There was acute reaction not just from the US but from within India itself, as Charles observed: 'Mr Menon has been attacked as shamelessly pro-Communist, and Mr Nehru has been criticised as responsible for a foreign policy which leading India commentators have called immoral, unprincipled and opportunist.'

While the international audience was gripped by India's part in the unfolding geopolitical drama, the country's internal strains and the pressure for separate linguistic states since Independence produced a story that was closer to home for

Charles and Dip. Charles was about to marry into a family of Sikhs: monotheistic, and distinct from Hindus and Muslims in their commitment to the equality of men and women and rejection of the caste system. On the surface, Dip's family had struck Charles as quite secular. Her father, Harbans Singh, was teetotal but all her siblings liked their evening whiskies. For all that, Beji, their mother, had schooled them in the Sikh creed, the Ardas, and daily prayers, and their religion was woven discreetly and naturally into their lives.

Yet, Sikh separatism never held much sway in Dip's household. This was evident in the family's ambivalent feelings towards Tara Singh, the seventy-six-year-old leader of the Sikh community. His campaign for a separate Sikh state in the Punjab, where Sikhs were in the majority, culminated in August 1961 in a 'fast unto death' aimed at pressuring Nehru to concede to his demands. The family's view may have been partly expressed in Charles's dispatch a few days into Singh's forty-seven-day fast. He reflected on Tara Singh's use of Mahatma Gandhi's 'fast unto death' tactic that 'while the weapon had survived, the motive hadn't . . . It's striking that all the great fasts since Gandhi's time have been devoted to creating new divisions.' Dip's older siblings had marched with the Quit India Movement. They may have admired Tara Singh's courage, but the founding principle of a secular India was an article of faith. However, Charles added, 'One cannot cope with a proud and aggressive people like the Sikhs by simply saying no, and by clapping their leaders in jail.'

It had taken Dip a while to introduce Charles to the family, unsure of how they might react to this shy but at times forthright Englishman. She needn't have worried. Her father bonded with him over their shared love of roses. Her siblings and their children took to him immediately. When he got to know Charles better, one nephew would tease her, 'He's more Indian than you are.' Subhag, Dip's eldest niece, remembers Charles as being 'not at all formal, not correct and proper the way Englishmen were in those days'. Over the years, those nieces and nephews – their partners, and their children too – would look to Charles for guidance and find a home from home with Charles and Dip whether it was in Berlin, Washington, Brussels or West Sussex.

'Goa – Our Delhi correspondent, Charles Wheeler, who is there, has sent us this report of the Indian blitzkrieg against the Portuguese Colony, and what may follow.' This was how the London-based presenter introduced Charles's report for BBC radio news. But it was hardly a 'blitzkrieg' and, according to Charles's report from the time, 'If it was a war, it was a remarkably non-violent one.'

Tension around the Portuguese colony of Goa on India's south-western coast had been building over many years. Charles summed up popular sentiment: 'To a country like India, this is very largely a question of self-respect. Indians have always felt very strongly about Goa. Here, as they see it, are the Portuguese still in Goa after fourteen years of independence, still running a regime that is illiberal and often brutal, and apparently determined to stay on forever.' The trigger for action soon presented itself. When the Portuguese fired on Indian fishing boats and a passenger steamer in November 1961, the

Indian government began preparations for Operation Vijay: the annexation of Goa.

Charles's original plan was to get ahead of the action by flying directly into the colony in early December. This was thwarted by the Portuguese Foreign Office, who sent a diplomatic cable in cypher to their London embassy informing them that 'PIDE [the Salazar regime's secret police] says that Wheeler's visa should be refused'. It duly was. Not to be put off, he hitched a ride with the Indian Army. When he arrived, he discovered that the army had sealed off the main land route into Goa and the accredited press were ordered to wait for official press communiqués from the Defence Ministry.

Charles told me that he wasn't going to let them keep him out either and, with a handful of other journalists, broke away from the main group and snaked down a backroad left unguarded by the military police.

Once through to the main town, Charles was surprised to find he had overtaken the Indian troops and tanks by a good few hours. When the tanks did eventually roll in, he reported with his soldierly eye that it had been a 'well-conducted' operation: 'good planning, superb logistics, speed of movement, perfect discipline'. There was 'no undue use of force', there were scarcely any casualties on either side, and no civilians were hurt. 'The Indian Army had reason to be pleased with itself,' he concluded, and noted that the local population 'undoubtedly preferred integration with India to Portuguese rule', which 'was never enlightened and in many ways repressive'. With Portuguese defences outnumbered by around ten to one, surrender came in less than two days.

1962 saw the governments and the popularity of their leaders tested in both India and Pakistan. In Pakistan, there was a highly cautious exercise in democracy, where the military regime allowed 80,000 men out of a population of 9 million to elect a national parliament. By contrast, India's parliamentary elections involved around 120 million voters who returned Nehru's Congress Party comfortably to power, with a slightly higher share of the vote than the first elections after Independence. And yet, as Charles reported, there was slightly less room for complacency in the results from the state assemblies holding elections. Eleven out of thirteen states were won, but Congress majorities were slashed in many of them. This would in fact be Nehru's last term as prime minister. His health was visibly weakening, and the succession debate was becoming more anxious. As Charles put it some months before: 'Mr Nehru is amassing a crushing inheritance for his unknown heir-to-be.'

A few days after the Indian elections, on 29 March, Charles and Dip were married by the Delhi Registrar of Marriages after a blessing and the Sikh Ardas at Sis Ganj Gurudwara in Old Delhi, where Dip's own mother Beji regularly worshipped. Charles's parents made the trip from England and, largely to please them, they went in search of a vicar for a Christian blessing as well. The Church of England turned them down on learning that Dip had no intention of converting. They had more luck with the Methodists – appropriately, for, while Charles senior was a firm atheist, Winifred's beliefs were deeply rooted in Welsh Methodism. The family gathered for a party at Dip's parents' home at Golf Links to celebrate the marriage, the champagne a present from her employers at the Canadian High Commission. A short honeymoon followed – with Winifred and Charles senior in tow – in Corbett National Park, a six-hour drive from Delhi but just a stone's throw away by Indian standards.

Charles's time in India was coming to an end, with his personal life completely turned around from the turmoil he'd experienced after his arrival almost four years earlier. His professional life was also going in the right direction. He had been given the job he wanted, back once again to Germany, now as a correspondent. The bosses in London concluded that he had 'grown in stature as a foreign correspondent' in the subcontinent, even though frequent technical problems meant he had often not been seen or heard live in news bulletins. As such, his upcoming transfer to Berlin would 'give him opportunities to show his capacity as a live contributor . . . from a post which is more continuously under the public eye.'

As Charles and Dip prepared to leave Delhi for Berlin, dozens were dying in a heatwave. 'This has been a week to long for home,' he wrote in his last dispatch before they left. The city was an inferno, in a 'shroud of airborne dust, which caked two million throats, and seared two million pairs of eyeballs'. That was Wednesday – by the end of the week though, luggage packed, he was wishing he could stay.

The country was feeling increasingly tense, and, like any dedicated hack, Charles was always reluctant to leave the story until he knew its ending. Sure enough, just four months after Charles's departure, China would attack India across the disputed boundaries in a month-long war that left India further humiliated. Three years after that, the worsening relations with its other neighbour would also lead to aggression by Pakistan.

In his broadcast 'On Leaving India' in June 1962, Charles said: 'India is a country in which events always seem to be moving to a climax. But in practice, they seldom do. As a reporter, one follows a lead or gets interested in a trend, or looks into a promising situation, to find that the thing has no substance whatever, or that the climax has been indefinitely postponed . . . Rather like the reader of a long and absorbing book, who reached the last page to find the author died before he finished the book, I feel a little cheated.'

A few days later, Charles and Dip left the heat and dust of Delhi in summer, bound for a Berlin in the grip of the Cold War.

4.
BERLIN REVISITED: IN THE SHADOW OF THE WALL

The average West Berliner is not the optimist he was. Talk to him, and he'll remind you of Peter Fechter and the bystanders, the helpless watching the helpless, and he'll say: 'They've written us off in the West.'

Charles Wheeler, 'Morale Sags in West Berlin', BBC Radio, August 1962

Berlin had changed. A city once so familiar to Charles had been disfigured by the Wall. This sinister creation had already become synonymous with the paranoid regime that ruled East Germany and was itself now leading many of its citizens to risk their lives trying to escape to the West. One of the early stories Charles phoned into the news desk in London was his report of the killing of eighteen-year-old Peter Fechter, shot by East German guards as he attempted to get over the Wall. He was just a few hundred yards from Checkpoint Charlie, the crossing point manned by the US Army and used by foreigners and Allied troops to enter East Berlin. The young bricklayer was hit in the back and stomach. He got through two barbed wire fences before he fell at the foot of the Wall itself, lying unaided for nearly an hour, in full view of onlookers, bleeding to death and crying for help.

At its outset, coils of barbed wire, then breeze blocks and cement, were what made up the Wall. It had been hastily erected overnight on 13 August 1961 to stop the exodus of around a thousand people a day from the Soviet Occupation Zone – by the end of the morning, all routes into West Berlin had been closed. Walter Ulbricht, the East German leader, called it an 'anti-fascist protection barrier'. Over the next year, the escapes became more ingenious and the Wall more solid, guarded and reinforced. By July 1962, when Charles had his first sight of this monstrosity, the death strip, the cameras, watchtowers and contraptions designed to keep their citizens penned in were all in place.

In the twelve months since, nearly thirty refugees from the East had been killed trying to escape into West Berlin. Shootings at the Wall were not in themselves big news. 'Hearing the sound of gunshot from our office, which was just around the corner from Checkpoint Charlie, was unfortunately getting to be quite familiar,' Jack Altman, who headed the Reuters office in East Berlin at that time, told me. But, as Charles explained to his BBC listeners, the death of Peter Fechter was different: 'The case of Fechter has had a very special impact on West Berliners, for he died in full view and within earshot of members of the United States Army.'

Correspondents effectively had a line to the police or to the news agencies, so, when there was an attempted escape, they would get a tip-off and rush to see what was happening. Within minutes of hearing that there had been an incident at the Wall, Charles had driven the fifteen minutes from his office to Checkpoint Charlie. When he arrived, he joined a small crowd of camera operators and reporters pressed up against the western side of the Wall. Some had pushed their cameras up because it was too high to see over. However, they could all hear the pitiful screaming of the wounded teenager on the other side. 'It took him about forty minutes to die. It was awful, you could hear him crying right till the moment he died. It was a horrible day. I think some of us felt that the American military police who manned Checkpoint Charlie could have, should have, walked out of their hut, twenty yards down the Wall, on the East German side, and picked him up and brought him back, in which case he could have been taken away by ambulance and perhaps survived,' Charles recalled. He didn't believe the East German police would have had the courage to interfere with the Americans if they'd done it.

'Escapee shot and left to die' was the headline in *Die Welt* the day after the killing. And from the *Berliner Morgenpost*: 'Yesterday at 2:12 pm: Murder at the Wall'. The paper, part of the virulently anti-communist Axel Springer's publishing group, whose offices overlooked Checkpoint Charlie, quoted Fechter's cries: 'Please help me, please help me!' adding: 'Ulbricht's concentration camp henchmen burden their consciences with another murder.'

In the few days that followed Fechter's death, the anger and bitterness spilled over, and the escape attempts continued: one eighteen-year-old girl dodged machine-gun fire and made it across, as did an East German soldier in uniform, laying down his weapons once he got to the other side. But a teenage railway guard was shot by his own colleagues as he ran across the tracks. He made it to the West but died of his wounds.

West Berliners, Charles estimated 700 of them, gathered at the Wall to protest about Fechter's death. On 18 August, a Russian military bus carrying reliefs for the sentries at the Russian War Memorial in the British Sector was stoned, the windscreen broken. But, as Charles observed, the targets of the demonstrators extended beyond the Russians – to the People's Police, the West Berlin police and, 'of all people', the American troops. Many in the city were upset not just by the Wall itself, but by the fact that the Allies had not pulled it down or at least taken more of a stand when it was first erected the previous year. That feeling was exacerbated by the killing of Peter Fechter. 'There was a lot of resentment from the West Berliners that the Allies, or the Americans in this case, simply stood by and watched this happen,' said Charles. But then, Berlin was on a knife-edge and Allied military commanders controlling the city were all too aware that if fire was exchanged and opposing soldiers killed during an attempted rescue, it might be the spark to set off a major conflict with the Russians.

Charles was especially struck by the demonstrators themselves. 'What was unusual about those sometimes quite average demonstrations was the numbers of respectable, stolidly German citizens who took part – the number of elderly men and women, even, who wanted to get at the Wall, apparently intending to tear it down, and completely oblivious of the consequences, personal or otherwise,' he wrote in a radio dispatch from that week.

One morning, a few days after Peter Fechter's death, Charles received a mysterious tip-off. 'I got a telephone call in my flat in West Berlin. No name given, simply a voice saying, "Peter Fechter's funeral, 11 o'clock, such-and-such a church", which was in East Berlin. So I went over and watched the funeral – no camera crew, nothing.' One other journalist was with him, the *Daily Mail*'s Berlin correspondent, George Vine, who'd received the same anonymous phone call.

The priest gave what Charles remembered as being a brave speech, referring to the monstrosity of Fechter's death, though it was carefully worded as the secret police in East Berlin were always watching. Charles didn't speak to anyone but, on his way out of the cemetery, his car was forced over to the side of the road by an ordinary-looking Trabant. According to Charles, six or seven East German plain-clothes policemen emerged from it – members of the feared and reviled Stasi, the secret police. Charles and George Vine, who he was giving a lift back to West Berlin, were arrested and taken to the Alexanderplatz police station.

Charles and George assumed that the Stasi were looking for names and addresses of any contacts they might have in East Berlin and were hoping to frighten the two men into giving them up. Before being led to separate interrogation rooms, George blustered his way into being allowed to go to the toilet, where he quickly swallowed the contents of his contacts book, page by page. Charles was calm, confident that he'd done nothing wrong. While the regime was brutal towards its own citizens, it knew better than to spark an international incident by being too heavy handed with a couple of Western journalists. 'There was nothing they could do, we hadn't broken any rules, we were in East Berlin as opposed to East Germany proper. We didn't need visas, we had British passports; we were entitled to be there as journalists.'

But Charles's confidence wasn't solely due to his following the rules and carrying a British passport. He was, of course, no stranger to the interrogator's art. From his own wartime role almost twenty years earlier, he knew exactly how to employ the tricks of the trade. Also, he was simply someone who refused to back down in the face of bullying from the authorities.

Some years later, recalling the incident in an interview with BBC Radio London, Charles explained that in that kind of situation, the best approach is not to make too much fuss or be abusive. Is that the way you handled it? asked Roger Clarke, the presenter. 'Very much the opposite,' Charles replied. Far from being intimidated, he and Vine – both fluent German speakers – clearly relished the opportunity to lay into their East German hosts, giving them a verbal blasting on the iniquities of the Wall.

'We really went for those two interrogators,' Charles said. 'And we went on and on, and I kept getting up and walking around the room and the interrogator kept on shouting at me to sit down. And it was a strange thing – I wasn't being brave. I could hear George through the partition screaming at his guy, calling him a Nazi and so on, and between us we managed to intimidate them. Eventually, they just let us go, but it was a chance to tell a secret policeman that the regime he was serving was an international disgrace.'

Tension continued to build throughout 1962. West Berliners were living not just with a wall in the middle of their city but one that completely encircled them. Any hopes for a reunified Germany in the near future were fading. They were coming to doubt the commitment of the Allies, and even suspected they might withdraw in order to avoid a major conflict, leaving them to be overrun by the Red Army. In another sign of Moscow's commitment to a permanent Communist state in East Germany, with East Berlin as the capital (which would freeze in place the idea of a divided Germany), the Russians withdrew their commandant, replacing him with an East German. This dealt a symbolic blow to the Four Power Agreement, signed at the end of the Second World War by the victors in Berlin. On 24 August, France, America and Britain sent strongly worded 'notes' to the Soviet Union in protest at the 'cold-blooded killings along the Berlin Wall . . . causing growing horror in the civilised world'. But the Allied protests and reassurances left the locals unimpressed. They might have raised a cheer a year ago but, Charles reported, 'The average West Berliner is not the optimist he was. Talk to him, and he'll remind you of Peter Fechter and the bystanders, the helpless watching the helpless, and he'll say: "They've written us off in the West".' That sense of abandonment stalked the city. It was a theme Charles returned to repeatedly in his reports.

Willy Brandt, the Social Democrat mayor of West Berlin, who would later become chancellor of West Germany, gave Charles a TV interview at the end of that traumatic August. He made clear that West Berliners needed more than vague platitudes about their security: 'The important thing now is that it should be made absolutely clear that West Berlin will not become a so-called free city with Soviet co-determination, but that West Berlin will be a Western city under clear Western responsibility,' he urged. While the idea of a 'free city', with the Allies relinquishing their occupation of West Berlin, was one that had been advanced by Krushchev and rejected by the Allies, it was still perceived as a real threat.

Almost immediately after Charles's interview with Brandt, a new crisis threatened the Allies' ability to control events and give the West Berliners the reassurances they were looking for. 'The shadow of an all-out nuclear war darkens the globe,' began a dispatch from Douglas Stuart, the BBC's Washington correspondent, in late October 1962. The international stage was set for war when, in reaction to the failed US 'Bay of Pigs' invasion of Cuba the previous year, the Russians deployed nuclear missiles on the island, ninety miles off the coast of Florida. Global destruction seemed a real possibility, and for several days Berlin felt like it was one of the most dangerous places of all to be. Troop convoys – Russian and American – were moving in and out of the city, the pressure ratcheting up, urgent messages being flashed between Washington and Moscow. For Berliners the fear was that, if Kennedy hit the missile bases in Cuba, West Berlin would be the site for Russian retaliation. Charles recalled his profound sense of insecurity many years later during what became known as the Cuban Missile Crisis: 'I was thousands of miles from Cuba, but in West Berlin, which the Russians could have taken in a day, I felt terribly exposed.'

Dip was seven months pregnant with me, their first child. She was beset by anxiety. Not just by the prospect of childbirth, for which she was – by her own admission – very unprepared. The current international events filled her with dread. 'Like so many others, I really wondered if I should be bringing children into the world,' she confided to me once. One night, with the crisis in full flow, the tanks were out in force in the British

Sector, patrolling the streets of our residential Charlottenburg neighbourhood. The sound outside the house was pushing Dip to her limits: 'They were blaring out messages from loudspeakers on the tanks, "Red Alert! Red Alert!".'

After a while, Charles rang the British military commander to complain, asking him, 'Is this really necessary? My wife is seven months pregnant and might have a miscarriage. She's getting very anxious.' The military commander apologised. He knew Charles, of course. But a conversation between two polite British men wasn't going to stop the loudspeakers and the intense fear of disaster. Kennedy's military chiefs had urged him to invade Cuba but, fortunately, the president chose to organise a blockade to the sea approaches to the island instead, and the Soviet Union backed down a short time afterwards. The use of the bargaining chip of de-escalating the threat of military invasion, as well as a secret agreement that the US would withdraw its own warheads from Turkey, led Khrushchev to announce on 28 October that the Soviet Union would remove its nuclear missiles from Cuba. The Cold War carried on – but a nuclear war had been averted.

The pregnancy also came to a successful conclusion. On 8 January 1963, Charles registered my birth at the Wilmersdorf Standesamt – the local registry office. His parents, Winifred and Charles senior, made the trip to Berlin from England for the christening, which also saw a group of new friends in Berlin appointed as godparents. Jack Altman, Reuters' East Berlin man, was happy to take on the job. The grandson of Ashkenazi Jews who had escaped to London from Russia following the pogroms of the early twentieth century, Jack was a bright, well-read and ebullient twenty-four-year-old Cambridge graduate in modern languages. His office was the go-to place for other Western journalists to check the wires or use the phone to file when they were on the East side of the Wall, which is how he and Charles first met. Despite their very different backgrounds, and the age gap between them, they were both natural disruptors and equally alert to pomposity in politicians and officials. They became good friends, though Jack would be a lifelong friend to Dip as well, admiring her sharp intellect and recognising in her a fellow devourer of literature. Being Jewish, Jack declined to make the godfatherly vows required by the Church of England ceremony and asked Winifred to stand in for him instead. Marjorie Mallalieu, the head of the Anglo-German women's group, the *Frauengruppe*, had become my mother's best friend in the city and was her obvious choice for godmother. She and her husband Paul, combining his calling as a published poet with being head of the British Security Services Overseas in Berlin, may well also have been quite valuable contacts to Charles (not least as doyennes of the Berlin cocktail party circuit who even facilitated an interview with W.H. Auden) – but first and foremost, they were dear friends.

Apart from the constant atmosphere of paranoia, Berlin in the early 1960s provided a series of more low-key irritants to a correspondent's daily life. When Charles first arrived, he was accorded a quasi-diplomatic status by the Allies. While that might sound like it brought useful privileges, it also meant that he wasn't allowed to apply for a visa to travel anywhere beyond the city because any application by an Allied official would imply a recognition of the East German regime as a separate state. The result was that to get out of Berlin by car he had to drive down the permitted autobahn corridor to Helmstedt in West Germany, 190km away, and often in the wrong direction to where he wanted to go.

In the spring of 1963, though, the Allies withdrew this status from news correspondents and so Charles, like any private citizen, could apply for a travel permit from the East German authorities. 'Often I have gazed at a map and envied the pre-war Berlin correspondent who could get into his car and drive due north to the lakes or, better still, to the Baltic coast,' he said in one offering for *From Our Own Correspondent*. He decided to celebrate his newfound freedom with a family road-trip to the Baltic and a day-cruise on the Warnemünde ferry. Dip jumped at the chance when Charles suggested it – life in Berlin was, after all, often intense and claustrophobic. While the city offered plenty of opportunities for socialising, the circle was narrower than what Dip had known in Delhi and certainly much more alcohol fuelled. Since the end of her first marriage, Dip had carved out a certain independence from her family. In some ways, her departure from India and the move to Berlin was an expression of that independence. Like Charles, Dip was a talented linguist. She spoke Punjabi, Urdu and Hindi and, determined not to rely too much on Charles to communicate, she attended German lessons and soon picked up the basics. But those early days had their difficult moments. This was a city like no other, and while the Berlin posting did not take Charles very far away,

Dip was often in the house alone with a baby who, by all accounts, suffered from bad colic and was hard to get to sleep. And so a trip to the East German coast was a very welcome prospect. Making up the party along with Charles and Dip was Subhag, Dip's twenty-year-old niece on a visit from Bombay, and, of course, my six-month-old self.

Charles drove off, visas in hand, passing through the barbed-wire border crossing just twenty minutes from our front door and, until now, an insuperable barrier, and entered what Charles called East Germany proper. The roads were empty, and we travelled through countryside charmingly devoid of modern life and filled with a sense of an earlier time to the busy East German port of Rostock. As we approached, Charles pointed out a sign declaring that this was the 'Gateway to the World'. 'The bad joke of all time' for the people of Rostock, he reflected, because the gate was shut to them, as was the *Warnemünde*, the brand-new ferry just brought into service between Rostock and Gedser on Denmark's southern tip. Its predecessor had taken East German citizens on short cruises close to the Danish mainland, but there had been 'too many ugly scenes, with passengers leaping over the rail and swimming for it, and plain-clothes People's Policemen splashing after them in pursuit,' Charles recorded later in a dispatch for radio about our little excursion. And so this ferry, the latest 'pride and joy of the East German regime', was made strictly off-limits for East Germans, even for day trips.

A small crowd was watching, waving from the dockside as we boarded the ship. They in turn were being watched by the naval guards, spaced along the quay, armed with sub-machine guns. Dip had persuaded Subhag to trade in her salwar kameez for a snazzy sailor top and camel pedal-pushers to match her own. They posed for Charles to take some photos on the deck in the June sunshine, unable to help but notice that they were virtually alone. The *Warnemünde* could accommodate 100 cars, five railway wagons and 1,500 passengers, and boasted a dining room for 400, a smoking room and dance floor, a creche, bars and shops – not to mention a huge team of stewards, pursers and nursemaids. But in addition to our little crew there were just five other passengers. What – or who – was it all for?

When he shared his impressions of his unusual trip to the seaside with BBC listeners the following week, Charles resisted the temptation to draw out any easy symbolism of what this said about the regime, drily concluding that, 'The People's own motorship is for foreigners only, and the People's chance of ever seeing Denmark, just visible across the water, is rather smaller than the prospect of a visit to Peking.'

It seemed like most of the city turned out to greet President Kennedy when he travelled to West Berlin later that month, on 26 June. The visit lasted only eight hours, but Kennedy gave the crowd just what they needed: a clear message of solidarity and a personal vow that the US and her allies would not desert them. There was also a very bracing dose of anti-communist rhetoric to the extent that, as Charles would report, Kennedy himself wondered if he had gone too far. But on that day, it provided the required medicine. As Charles later recalled, 'He made the kind of speech that West Berliners wanted to hear.

It was tough, it was a Cold War speech, and that was the mood in West Berlin at that time, and it went down very well.'

The inaction of the Allies in 1961 after the Wall was built had in Charles's view left the morale of the West Berliners badly dented. But that was restored with Kennedy's words in the Rudolph Wilde Platz: 'All free men, wherever they may live, are citizens of Berlin . . . and therefore, as a free man, I take pride in the words: *Ich bin ein Berliner*.'

To the annoyance of Kennedy's press people, the later reporting of the speech, as opposed to its immediate reception in West Berlin, slightly tainted its reputation. One of the key protagonists in how it was reported was none other than the Reuters correspondent in East Berlin and my recently appointed godfather, Jack Altman. Charles witnessed Kennedy's speech first hand from among the huge crowd on the square. Jack was on the other side of the Wall, sitting in East Berlin with a group of locals and watching on television. Exactly forty years later they were still disagreeing about the so-called gaffe around Kennedy's phrase. We were gathered on Christmas Eve 2003 at my home in Brussels. Charles and Jack were tucking into soup and cheese and maybe a glass or two of wine. '*Ich bin ein Berliner*' was intended to mean 'I am a Berliner' but was, apparently, met with laughter because the locals understood it as something far less grand. But, maintained Charles, it wasn't a gaffe at all.

'I was in there,' he said, 'I saw the crowd's reaction. No one thought he'd said anything wrong.'

'Ah,' said Jack. 'Well, I was with some old Berliners on the other side of the Wall, and they immediately laughed and said to me, "Kennedy just said he was a doughnut!"'

In some parts of Germany, 'Berliner' was the nickname given to a particular type of doughnut – a jam-filled one without a hole, to be precise.

'There were old Berliners in the crowd where I was too,' said Charles dismissively. 'In fact, it was you, Jack, who came up with the story in the first place!'

Jack, it seems, had filed a piece for Reuters thirty minutes after Kennedy's speech, mentioning what his East German friends had told him. Charles said that the BBC's Alistair Cooke then repeated the claim a few days later on his hugely popular radio programme, *Letter from America*, and got into immense trouble over it, with denials and counter-accusations being made.

Willy Brandt's memoirs throw some light on the episode. He was hosting the visit as mayor of Berlin. 'The crowd roared its approval when he declared that he was a Berliner – he had rehearsed the German sentence during a breather in my office,' he wrote. But for all that, the story of Kennedy's Berliner 'gaffe' has taken on a life of its own: Jack said that even on a recent visit to Berlin he'd seen an advert on TV showing Kennedy and a doughnut with the slogan, 'Communications can go wrong.'

An altogether less high-profile visit to Berlin was made the following month by the man who had lost the election to John F. Kennedy three years previously. For six weeks during the summer of 1963, Richard Nixon was on a private trip to Europe, supposedly taking time out from politics after a series of political defeats, most recently for the California governorship. This was his first sight of the Berlin Wall and Charles's first sight of him.

In the hallway of my grandparents' house, a framed press

cutting used to hang that Charles had sent them from West Berlin. It was from a local paper covering Nixon's visit to the East. The headline read, '*Die schärfste Polizeikontrolle der Welt*' – the sharpest police force in the world. There's a photo of Nixon surrounded by a group of what the paper presumes to be SED party apparatchiks and members of that hyper-efficient secret police force. In fact, most prominent in the group are none other than Charles Wheeler and Jack Altman, part of the press contingent assigned to cover the visit.

As Nixon recorded in his memoirs, he was getting frustrated at how his foray into the East was going. He blamed 'the oppressive number of Communist police who unsubtly accompanied us [which] meant we had hardly any chance to talk to the people. That night I decided to go back . . .' According to Charles, the American ambassador to Berlin, a friend of his, was the one who suggested to Nixon's people that he return later that day for a more discreet tour. Charles, he said, would be the ideal guide, given his knowledge of the city and the language. Charles agreed and met Nixon at his hotel.

Many years later, Charles told me that, as they drove around East Berlin, Nixon kept asking the driver to stop so he could meet 'the people'. 'Hello, I am Richard Nixon,' he'd say, introducing himself and handing out his business card. The visit passed off extremely well, as Nixon saw it. His memoirs record his general impression of his trip to Europe: 'From our welcome abroad, no one would have guessed that I had lost two elections in the past three years and that my prospects for a political comeback seemed extremely remote. Everywhere we went, we were received as if I were still vice president.'

WITNESS TO THE TWENTIETH CENTURY

This upbeat view doesn't quite tally with Charles's own account. 'Most of the people he stopped in East Berlin didn't actually know who he was,' he remembered, 'but he seemed completely oblivious to how they were responding to him.' By the end of the day, Charles was finding it all too much to take. On his return home to the house in Kirschenallee that night, he told Dip, 'That man is quite mad – and to think he might have become president.'

They called it the *'Wunder auf Lengede'* – the Miracle of Lengede. On 24 October 1963 a torrent of mud and water from a broken reservoir flooded an iron ore mine in Lengede near Hanover, trapping fifty miners deep underground. Over the next two weeks, the dramatic events at the mine had the world transfixed. It was a story of survival and solidarity, a sequence of intrepid and intricate rescues that attracted 400 newspaper journalists and some ninety radio and TV reporters from around the world – including Charles, Jack Altman and his Reuters colleague Freddie Forsyth, who would later go on to write the bestselling novel *The Day of the Jackal*. The story barely left the BBC home news bulletins for thirteen days and in television and broadcasting history, Lengede has a special status as arguably the first truly international rolling TV and radio news event. Charles got to the mine some thirty hours after seven men had been pulled out to safety. Hope was fading for the other forty-three still missing. And then, nearly 300 feet below ground and well below the water level, three miners were discovered, still alive. Charles phoned in his dispatch from Hanover, 'A narrow steel tube was pushed down from the surface through the ceiling of the gallery . . . In complete silence, the rescuers waited for a sign of life. For fifteen minutes nothing happened, then tapping on the tube. A tremendous cheer from the rescue teams, the bystanders, friends and then a light, paper and pencil and a microphone were let down to the men below.' He describes the operation as the three miners are hoisted up one at a time, 260 feet to the surface and to safety: 'The final stage was accomplished with a barely credible smoothness. It took two and a half hours from the moment the escape cylinder, empty, was lowered on a test run through the shaft, to the shout we heard . . . when the last man was safely above ground. Two and a half hours of tension that left one weak at the knees.'

Barely twenty-four hours had passed when there was another incredible discovery – eleven more miners, now ten days without light or food, crowded together in a cavern several feet above the flood water. The next evening, on 4 November, Charles updated Richard Dimbleby, *Panorama*'s presenter, on the rescue attempts. In television terms, this was a technically challenging moment, but hugely exciting: live television pictures, a reporter right at the heart of the action, coming in direct to *Panorama* from Germany. 'They've been terribly pessimistic up to now and they are still being rather pessimistic. But the drillers and the men themselves are more optimistic than the men in charge,' says Charles. It is nail-biting stuff. When pressed on air to assess their chances, Charles gives them a fifty-fifty chance of getting out safely.

It was during this time, according to Charles and Jack's subsequent accounts, that one of the reporters started to get creative with the actualité. The scene is still, after nearly five decades, clear in Jack Altman's mind. He told me: 'By that time we were all working in the same caravan that was being used as an office. A colleague flagged up the idea that the remaining eleven miners may have turned to cannibalism to keep themselves alive and was going to ring it through as a story. It was pure hackery, of course, and there was not a shred of truth in it. Charles was outraged. He leapt across the room and grabbed the phone from his hand to stop him from filing. It was a great moment. There was no way he was going to allow that story to be filed.'

All eleven men were finally rescued on 7 November, two weeks after the mine was flooded. A worldwide audience – gripped by the news for a fortnight – could, like the miners and their families, at last let out its collective breath. It had been a success for Charles, too. He had produced radio and television reports throughout the event, day and night, with what appeared to be a boundless stamina and enthusiasm. Until then, many of the stories he had been reporting on from Germany were only for radio and the Overseas Service. Now, he'd been catapulted onto the domestic bulletins and live television for several days in a row. In covering the events at Lengede, his on-the-ground, tell-it-like-it-is reporting combined with a new and evolving broadcasting technology that allowed for live TV coverage outside the studio, from the scene. It was a significant moment in broadcast news history. 'The biggest challenge (and opportunity) for Charles Wheeler during the year was Lengede,' his annual report from the foreign editor noted. 'He rose to the occasion . . . splendidly.'

*

SHIRIN WHEELER

On 22 November, when West Berliners heard the news that John F. Kennedy had been shot in Dallas, there was an immediate, spontaneous reaction. Thousands left what they were doing and headed to Rudolph Wilde Platz, the square where they had heard Kennedy's impassioned words only five months earlier.

Charles heard the news on the radio. His memory of that night was always very vivid. After about an hour, he also walked out to Rudolph Wilde Platz. At midnight, in cold rain, he watched as a man scaled a nearby lamppost. 'He climbed up on the top with a handwritten sign on which he'd written "John F. Kennedy Platz" – that's where the idea came from of renaming the Rudolph Wilde Platz.' As news spread, it seemed that life in the city came to a sudden halt. At the Berlin Opera House, they stopped the performance. The Vienna Ice Revue followed. 'The skaters didn't want to skate . . . People left restaurants. Berlin really closed down that night,' Charles would recall.

Walking through Berlin in those hours after Kennedy's death, Charles found a city in shock. He described to listeners 'a torchlight procession by students [that] sucked people out of their houses as it passed through the town. And in the square, the crowd seemed nearly as dense as that vast cheering mass who had come to the same place five months ago, and heard him say, unforgettably for them, "I am a Berliner". This time it was dark, and they were silent and miserable.'

His dispatch the next morning was one of many from around the world, but it was clear that, for the Berliners he spoke to, this was personal. 'West Berlin is a lifeless city today,' he reported. 'There's a feeling in the air of the kind that follows a major catastrophe – and one that's occurred at home and not several thousands of miles away. People here will tell you quite simply that they had a respect and admiration for this man that they never felt for a leader of their own.' A young woman, a secretary, told Charles that hearing of Kennedy's death was the worst news she had ever heard: 'The people here in this city were especially shocked because they regard Kennedy as their man . . . they felt his sympathy and they knew he was the only man in the West who would help them and protect them in their struggle for freedom.'

Ultimately, Charles felt that Kennedy was an enormously romantic figure, unlike any other Western statesman who had been to West Berlin over the years since the War. During his visit, Charles had seen how the Berliners were not only fascinated by him but enormously buoyed up by the reassurances he gave them – which in effect they took to mean that the Allies would stand by them no matter what, even being prepared to go to war to prevent them being swallowed up by the East Germans or by the Russians.

Ex-Nazis in high places were not a rarity in the West German capital of Bonn, Charles once observed. Reading through his dispatches during his three-year posting, I am struck by his regularly expressed view that most ordinary Germans seemed to want to keep their wartime Nazi past well and truly buried, or at least at a distance. It's surprising because most Germans I've known and worked with, roughly of my own generation, seem to possess a remarkable historical literacy and honesty about their country's past. So I began to wonder when the change came.

SHIRIN WHEELER

One possible starting point might be in Frankfurt in April 1964. Charles sat each day in the press gallery of the courtroom, specially constructed for the occasion, watching the trial of some twenty-one Gestapo and SS men employed at Auschwitz. Men who 'actually operated the extermination machine, rather than directing it from a desk'. Historians and commentators like Steve Crawshaw in his book *Easier Fatherland* have pinpointed these proceedings, known as the second Auschwitz trial, as a critical starting point in Germany's acknowledgement of its recent past. Listening to Charles's dispatches from the trial, the profound national reckoning that is to come does still feel some way off.

He described the twenty-one defendants as 'a fair cross-section of German males. Some are sleek and obviously prosperous with gold watch chains and expensive haircuts; others are so unremarkable as to defy description.' Herr Mulka, the former camp adjutant, a Hamburg businessman, was 'well-connected, like several of the accused'. Mulka, Charles reported, claimed he was only concerned with the paperwork, didn't ever go into the camp, never knew anyone who died and never heard any complaints from the inmates at Auschwitz. And yet, witnesses at the trial identified him as one of those at the top of the unloading ramp when the goods trains stopped at the camp and arrivals were selected for the gas chambers.

The evidence given is horrifying, especially from witnesses testifying against two particular sadists, Wilhelm Boger and Oswald Kaduk. They were the ones who grabbed the media attention. Charles was bemused at the apparent lack of interest of the West German press in the others: 'Of the nineteen other defendants one hardly ever reads a word . . . so that once again it is easy to disassociate oneself, to say, "What on earth have the actions of men like this to do with me? Or my country? Surely not the first in history to produce an occasional monster?"'

In his dispatch from the courtroom midway through the trial, Charles reflected that this process could not be about society exacting retribution: 'How can a life sentence be considered retribution for murder committed in the millions?' he asked. It had, he argued, a different kind of purpose. 'To the prosecution, the trial is an attempt to hold up a mirror to the German people, an attempt to make Germans look at and think about, not the psychopaths among the accused, but at the others, at the normal ones – at the doctors, and the dentists, the prosperous pharmacist, the Hamburg merchant, the people who always conformed, before Auschwitz, at Auschwitz, after Auschwitz.'

But in this respect, the chief prosecutor himself, Fritz Bauer, took the view that the trial had not been a success. Six defendants (including Rapportführer Kaduk and political department henchman Boger) were sentenced to life imprisonment, five were released and the others sentenced to prison terms of three to fourteen years. When the trial ended the following year, Bauer pronounced that the media had perpetrated a 'wishful fantasy that there were only a few people with responsibility . . . and the rest were merely terrorised, violated hangers-on . . . compelled to do things that were completely contrary to their true nature'.

One of those defendants – acquitted in the end – was a Hanover dentist who Charles had reported on some months earlier when the charges and defendants were first announced. He was charged with murder, last seen 'sorting out Jews as they came tumbling out of cattle trucks' and working in the camp's *Zahnstation*, the dental station of Auschwitz-Birkenau. And yet Charles observed that, compared to the others, his story had generated barely half a line in the newspapers: 'What intrigues me about this happily practising Hanover dentist is that he apparently intrigues nobody else . . . The truth is that the German reader isn't interested. Current murders – "adolescent strangles prostitute" – are news; mass murder, eighteen years ago, is politics.'

In the eyes of many Germans today, Charles maintained, the family dentist from Hanover was a persecuted man. And the prime reason for this, in his view, was that: 'Most Germans have been working so hard forgetting, that they never had time to grasp the enormity of the crimes that were committed.' In this, he added, 'The man in the street has been set a pretty shoddy example by his leaders.'

The person he had in mind was none other than the right-hand man of the German chancellor himself. For Charles, and other commentators at the time, Doctor Hans Josef Maria Globke, under-secretary of state and head of the German federal chancellery, was a symbol of what had to change. Doctor Globke was the ministerial counsellor in the Nazi Ministry of the Interior under the late Herr Frick, hanged at Nuremberg in 1956, and had been 'the textbook civil servant who committed everything to paper, invariably in his own meticulous handwriting'.

Charles had covered another major Nazi trial in Hanover six months earlier, that of SS Captain Günter Fuchs, during which he had also been struck by the ease with which the defendant had been so comfortably reintegrated into normal life and the severity of the charge against him – commanding the Lodz ghetto round-ups, complicity in the murder of 70,000 Jews and the direct murder of forty-six men, women and children. Summoned as a defence witness was Doctor Globke.

Charles – sitting in the Hanover courtroom's press gallery – heard Globke's statement to the court that the mass murder of Jews was a well-kept secret known only to very few. 'I didn't learn of the killings till after the war,' he claimed, to sceptical laughter from the public benches.

Globke didn't just come out of nowhere. As Charles pointed out, 'Under Hitler he was a senior civil servant, an expert in "race questions" and author of the official commentary on the Nuremberg Race Laws, the legal foundation for the persecution and the subsequent mass murder of the Jews.' Dripping with irony, Charles's position was clear: Globke was 'highly commended by the late Herr Frick for quite outstanding work on the Jewish question, and is highly valued today by Federal Chancellor Adenauer, who's refused repeated appeals from Germans of all shades of opinion to replace his closest collaborator with somebody whose background is less controversial.'

Already in September 1964, Charles was reporting on talks to allow West Berliners to see their families across the Wall in the East during the coming Christmas holiday period.

As those discussions continued, he also covered the amnesty granted to political prisoners by the East German leader Walter Ulbricht. Eight hundred of them were to be allowed to return to West Berlin. This was significant because Ulbricht seemed to be realising that 'He can't govern forever in a state of war with the people; that he can't, as Bert Brecht once said, dismiss the people and elect himself another.' There was a dawning recognition in West Germany too that the old policies were not working: 'Insofar as Bonn has pursued any policy towards East Germany, it has amounted to little more than waiting for a collapse that would prompt the Russians to surrender their satellite to free elections and reunification. But with time, this illusion has faded. For Moscow, East Germany is obviously a growing asset.'

The tiniest seeds of what would become known as the Ostpolitik of the 1970s were being sown. A search began for common areas of interest with East German leaders; as Charles reported, 'Bonn is looking for a new policy. It hasn't found one, but there are pointers, there are voices, some quite persuasive, advocating change.' A new generation of German politicians – among them, of course, Willy Brandt – and the press, were wrestling with questions that, as Charles put it, 'Twelve months ago would have been howled down, stifled in a surge of patriotic anti-communism.'

But despite these tectonic political shifts under way in Germany, as far as the BBC bosses in London were concerned things were slowing down in terms of day-to-day news. Both Charles and his editors were getting twitchy.

'I agree with his view that Berlin does not at present generate enough news to keep him stretched. I intend to use him freely outside Berlin and shall in any case not waste his abilities,' reads an internal note from the BBC's foreign news editor John Crawley.

And so, at the start of August 1964, Charles was sent back to

Cyprus to support the BBC reporting team there. Six years earlier, he had spent nearly a month on the island covering the flare-up of violence between the Turkish and Greek communities. But the situation now was even graver: attacks by government forces on Turkish Cypriot fighter strongholds and villages in the north; airstrikes by Turkey on Greek patrol boats and then on Greek Cypriot villages. On 8 August, 'economic measures' were imposed by the Greek Cypriot forces on the area around the village of Kokkina. Two days later, a UN Security Council call for a ceasefire was eventually agreed on by both sides.

Reporting these events was highly sensitive. Correspondents were regularly taken to task by the Cypriot authorities, who were nervous and defensive and had the BBC firmly in their sights. Two BBC journalists had been deported by the Greek Cypriot government: Peter Flynn in April of that year and in August, Jack Williams, based in Nicosia, was accused of 'groundless reporting'. Given the level of governmental suspicion and his own track record in such matters, it was almost inevitable that Charles would find himself coming into conflict with the authorities.

While talks were starting up in Geneva for a draft settlement in Cyprus, Charles was reporting on claims by Turkish Cypriot villagers that the government's blockade was deliberately pushing them towards starvation. He and other foreign correspondents had visited the villages in the north, where he said they had seen depleted grain stores and food shortages. It was a charge vehemently denied by the Greek Cypriot authorities, who put the shortages down to other factors and alleged that the Turkish Cypriots were hiding their food and deliberately misleading reporters and UN officials. But on 13 August, the press accompanied General Thimayya, the highly respected Indian commander of the recently arrived UN Peacekeeping Force, to Kokkina to inspect the situation. The general's widely reported comments to journalists at the scene supported the Turkish claims, earning him a strong rebuke from the Greek Cypriots, and so he agreed to hold a press conference in Nicosia the next day to 'mollify' them.

Charles's report on that press conference, where the general did indeed row back a bit on his earlier remarks, was filed for the radio bulletins in versions broadcast on both the domestic and Overseas Service. It concluded: 'General Thimayya's remarks about the blockade obviously did not satisfy many of the correspondents, whose own investigations have produced a consensus of opinion that the Turkish community's complaints are, broadly speaking, genuine.'

It tells one something about the position of the BBC and also of the sensitivities of this particular conflict that all hell broke loose. Once again, Charles had found himself at the centre of a storm. Within hours, the Greek Cypriot government made it very clear that the BBC's correspondent Charles Wheeler was no longer welcome in Cyprus. The BBC radio bulletins reported that Charles had been declared 'a prohibited immigrant' because the Cyprus government objected to a news item in the BBC's Overseas Service. The official statement from the Nicosia Ministry of Information went further, charging Charles with 'malicious' and 'irresponsible news coverage and communications'. He returned to Berlin to weather the storm.

A flurry of letters followed. There was a protest to the Cypriot Director of Public Information from Donald Edwards, the

BBC's editor of news and current affairs, who remonstrated: 'We are gravely concerned and a good deal puzzled as to the nature of the charges made and of the action taken.' He insisted the Cypriot government's case had been reflected in Charles's dispatch and 'We cannot accept the justice of the charges that this was either "malicious" or "irresponsible".'

It turned out that Charles was the victim of a gaffe by one of the overnight sub-editors in London. A cut-down version of his original dispatch had been rewritten and broadcast for the Overseas Service bulletins and, as Donald Edwards admitted to the Cypriot authorities, 'It could be argued that the shortened form . . . failed to preserve fully the balance of the original.'

Charles was very affronted – by his expulsion by the Greek Cypriot authorities but also by what he felt could have been a more robust defence of his reporting from his own managers. 'I am in no position to take professional disabilities of this kind lightly,' he wrote in a letter to BBC management. 'I was disappointed, I hope not unreasonably, by the absence of any expression of confidence in its [the BBC's] correspondent – private if it could not be public – by the BBC.'

It seems like the incident and Charles's own spirited defence of his methods caused no lasting rift between him and the BBC management, except perhaps a confirmation – as if they really needed it – that the management route was not one that interested Charles. As Donald Edwards noted in Charles's end-of-year review, 'He clearly prefers to be a correspondent abroad more than anything . . . Organising or management does not appeal.' And so it was settled.

*

By spring 1965, Charles was preparing for the posting that would excite and provoke his imagination like no other assignment up to now. He had arrived in Berlin at a time when the world was gripped by the possibility of another global conflict, with the divided city as its most potent symbol. Unlike in India, where communications had hampered his reporting so that he was often sending down written scripts for others to read, in Germany his broadcasts had been heard by listeners around the world. Through reports on events like Peter Fechter's death, the Lengede mining disaster and the Auschwitz trials, Charles was honing an economical writing style that could be by turn elegant and impassioned, and, when necessary, sharply ironic. These would be the distinguishing elements that would colour his journalism over the course of his long career. Charles had repeated his offer to John Crawley, the BBC's foreign news editor, that he would be ready to take a 'crash course' in Russian if there would be a chance of sending him to Moscow. But London had a different plan for him – one that would establish him as the BBC's leading foreign correspondent and be the making of him professionally. He was to go to the United States initially as the 'Washington number two'.

Dip and Charles packed up their trunks – and me and my four-month-old sister, Marina – and travelled to the port of Bremerhaven. Here, we boarded a cruise liner, the *Bremen* – named after the city of Charles's birth – and sailed across the Atlantic to New York. As Charles's photos from the deck show, the seas were rough on the voyage, but he was soon to find himself completely in his element.

5.
PROTEST AND UPRISING IN 1960s AMERICA

They talk about police brutality in these terms: 'They push us around. They arrest us for nothing. They call us n*****s . . . We've had this for years – for as long as we can remember.' And the point simply came when somebody decided he wouldn't take it any more.

CHARLES WHEELER, BBC TELEVISION NEWS, WATTS – LOS ANGELES, AUGUST 1965

Charles and the family arrived in an America convulsing with violence and in the grip of momentous change. He would later say of the time that the country seemed ripe for revolution. It was a volatile period but also laced with an optimism, a society on the cusp of change, even if it didn't seem to take much to spark trouble. Having witnessed the rise of the Nazis at first hand as a child, the brutal nature of America's racial conflict spoke deeply to Charles. There was something distinctly recognisable about the uniformed white men, the heavily armed state troopers and the demagogic public officials of the South, mainlining prejudice and bigotry and feeding on an ideology of racial supremacy. 'The supremacy of one race and the consequent debasement of another has always been a recipe for murder,' he would later observe.

SHIRIN WHEELER

In the humid month of August 1965, taking up his new job in the BBC's Washington bureau as North America correspondent, Charles covered the signing of President Lyndon Johnson's new Voting Rights Act, filed TV and radio reports from Watts in Los Angeles on the eruption of violence there and interviewed Dr Martin Luther King on the issue of Black representation in the city of Washington itself. Charles found in the civil rights movement, and in particular in its leader Dr King and his supporters, a singular grace and dignity. This was something to tell the world about, and radio and television news was a chance to get voices on air that few had heard before in the UK – the clearly stated arguments of a new generation of Black leaders and the first-hand accounts of ordinary men and women in Black communities.

Despite a terrifying white backlash, Dr King had already taken on the segregationist system of the South and found an unlikely ally in the White House. Texan-born President Lyndon Johnson had signed the Civil Rights Act into law the previous year. In March 1965, just before we arrived in America, the landmark march from Selma to Montgomery took place. The movement had now turned its sights on the issue of voting rights and, as yet undeflected by his own flawed handling of Vietnam, Johnson allowed himself to be pressed by King to take up the cause of voter obstruction.

Through such barriers to voter registration as literacy tests, poll taxes, intimidation and violence, Black people in the South had in effect been denied their rights under the constitution by white politicians and officials. The new law gave the federal authorities powers to clear these obstacles. In President

Johnson's words: 'This Act flows from a clear and simple wrong. Its only purpose is to right that wrong... Millions of Americans are denied the right to vote because of their colour. The right to vote is the basic right without which all others are meaningless. It gives people, people as individuals, control over their own destinies.' President Johnson himself called it one of the most monumental laws in the entire history of American freedom and he urged Black communities to go out and register, adding, 'The time for waiting is gone.'

The passing of the Voting Rights Bill on 6 August 1965 was one of the first stories Charles filed for BBC TV News from the US. It is perfectly possible that British TV viewers of the mid-1960s might have thought the nitty-gritty details of an argument about voting rights in a region of America 3,000 miles away a little arcane, but Charles correctly saw in this an issue of profound importance about the state of America and its place in the world and he was determined to cover it.

Within a few days of the Act passing into law, Charles travelled to Madison County in Mississippi, where, till then, only 2 per cent of an adult Black population of more than 10,000 had been able to register their vote. Charles focused the story on one seventy-six-year-old man, a First World War veteran and cotton picker, who had managed to sign up to the federal register for the first time, having always been turned away in the past. 'He said that he'd got scared. But today, he had no reason to be scared. Being illiterate was no longer a barrier, neither was the colour of his skin. He couldn't write, so the federal man filled out the form for him. "You don't need to sign your name," the official said, "just make a mark here." "I don't think I can." "I'll make it – just put your hand on top of mine."'

This was history being made, a moment as poignant and portentous as the election of a president or a victory on a battlefield, expressed through the tenderly reported dialogue between an election official in Mississippi and an elderly Black man as he finally, after a lifetime of refusal, exercised his rights. By the time that particular office in Madison had closed, nearly 300 people from the Black community had been registered to vote. Twenty-four hours before that, across the whole county, the total had been just 218. Over the next five years, following the passage of the Act, the US Justice Department estimated that almost as many Black people registered to vote in Alabama, Mississippi, Georgia, Louisiana, North Carolina and South Carolina as in the entire century before 1965.

The veteran civil rights campaigner Julian Bond, a member of the famous Student Nonviolent Coordinating Committee, whom Charles came to know and greatly respect, once observed that reporters have a tendency to look for the spectacular rather than the significant. But one of Charles's keenest instincts was to seek out and recognise the significance of a historic moment in those people most often kept out on the margins – as on this day in Madison County, at the very beginning of his American journey. The Voting Rights Act was celebrated as a major victory. But for many Black Americans, change was coming far too slowly. On the very day that hundreds of people in the Black community of Madison County were registering to vote for the first time in their lives, rioting broke out in the Los Angeles neighbourhood of Watts. Charles left Mississippi, heading west on the first available flight. By the time he got there the worst of the rioting was over, but, to a reporter who had seen the charred remains of Caen and Hamburg and Berlin two decades earlier, it looked like, as he put it, a 'city emerging from war'.

His first report was for radio and has the slightly breathless quality of a war correspondent after a battle, aware that fighting could break out again at any moment. Speaking from a telephone box on Central Avenue, he described what he could see in quick-fire phrases: 'burnt buildings, looted shops . . . lot of police milling about, National Guardsmen . . . with fixed bayonets, sub-machine guns. But it's calm, . . . [people] are friendly . . . and we've been asking them what the causes of the riots were.' Thirty-four people had been killed, more than 1,000 injured and 4,000 arrested. Of course, most of the victims were Black, as were the rioters and looters. But as Charles remarked later, 'To the people who did this, this was not a riot but a revolt.' The residents of Watts were happy to tell this middle-aged white Englishman of how they'd put up with years of racist abuse and outright violence from the authorities.

Charles delivered the message of the neighbourhood of Watts to camera verbatim, in terms that would not be used on TV news today. But for a journalist who was known for his exacting linguistic precision, he would have been well aware of the powerful punch it would pack: 'They talk about police brutality in these terms: "They push us around. They arrest us for nothing. They call us n*****s. They say we stink. We've had this for years. For as long as we can remember." And the point simply came when somebody decided he wouldn't take it any more.'

In his piece to camera, Charles is standing by the side of the street, a striped awning and a shopfront that seems to have been spared by the rioters behind him. There is a sense of real urgency in his voice. The tone is immediate, clipped and yet empathetic. We aren't in any doubt whose side Charles is on – for him, being objective doesn't necessarily mean being detached.

Years later, for a special radio programme to mark Charles's eightieth birthday, the BBC's Jeremy Paxman, a friend and colleague, put it to him that it must have been hard to be 'dispassionate' in that situation. But Charles quite simply didn't believe in trying to be dispassionate and, as he told Jeremy, he had come to believe while covering the race riots in Watts that 'the violence was justified because it made white America listen. I used to go around saying this at Washington dinner parties and people were absolutely horrified at the idea that a journalist was saying burning down buildings was a justified form of protest. But I believe it was. They were really the victims. They were burning down their own ghetto.'

Martin Bell, a fellow BBC foreign correspondent, told me why he thinks that report from Los Angeles was so impactful at the time and why, for many years, lecturing to audiences on the business of news, he has cited the report from Watts as an example of journalism to aspire to. 'He didn't just talk about mindless violence and destruction. He explained why they'd done it. He got inside the minds of the rioters themselves. If ever there was a sharp intake of editorial breath in the newsroom it would have been after that report.'

And it wasn't just Charles' coverage of Watts which worried

some senior editors at the time. 'On some topics he has to make an effort to remain objective', said one annual report. 'He does need to guard against a recent tendency to moralise when the first requirement is factual reporting,' said another.

The next day, a curfew remained in place. Troops set up pickets outside the buildings that were left intact. The words 'Blood Brothers' had been painted on windows to indicate Black-owned businesses, and because of that some were spared from the flames, but many weren't. Charles filed another radio piece in which he spoke to people waiting in line for food outside the Student Nonviolent Coordinating Committee offices, asking them to explain the cause of the riots. One theme resonates.

It was in Watts that Charles first heard the two words that, as he put it, were soon to echo across America: 'police brutality'. Watts was also the first place to draw attention to the problems of its Black communities through large-scale violence – the first, too, of several riots that he would cover around the country as African-American communities in city after city boiled over with rage at the continuing experience of poverty, poor housing and neglect. In his reports, then and afterwards, Charles challenged the narrative of many of the US networks and their accounts of a 'senseless' violence. It was clear to him the underlying cause was that Black people were being treated as an underclass, as second-class citizens, and now they were demanding equality. And in Charles's mind, the spark for Watts and subsequent 'uprisings' was the indiscriminate use of weapons by the police.

Watts also seemed to challenge the creed of non-violence and the leadership of its apostle and father of the 'movement',

Martin Luther King. Two weeks after Watts, Charles met Dr King for the first time, in Washington, D.C. King told him that his faith in non-violence had not been shaken by the riots. In fact, said King, 'It depends on the leadership and the emphasis of the march. I am convinced that if we'd had non-violent marches and demonstrations in Los Angeles, we wouldn't have had the riots.' But King had been in for a surprise. When he went to Watts, he found that he wasn't in tune with Black inner-city residents, who told him in no uncertain terms that his philosophy of non-violence was simply not up to the challenge of what they were facing on the streets.

The reports from that first August in the US – the 1965 Voting Act, the registrations of voters in the South, the riots in Watts – lurched from euphoric legislative and political wins to the frustration and fury of communities faced with police brutality and entrenched, enduring racism. In so many ways, those stories held for Charles the essence of the civil rights and race story that would dominate his broadcasts from America for several years to come and his own preoccupations for the rest of his life. Even when the American establishment's own focus apparently turned elsewhere, Charles stayed faithful to this story.

The Washington that our family moved to in 1965 was not quite the one that images of the Capitol and the White House projected across the globe. Their gleaming white columns and domes might have suggested a modern, democratic form of classical order and power but it was built on an anomaly. Due to its status as the nation's capital, Washington, D.C. had no elected mayor or elected local body to represent its citizens: it was a federal district, not part of any state and run directly by a special committee answering to the federal government. It so happened that more than 70 per cent of those citizens were African-Americans. In a report at the time on the Washington that 'the tourist doesn't see', Charles observed that the 'ghettoes' in the capital were not as shocking as the slums of Los Angeles but that the conditions 'for revolt' were still there.

Charles had discussed the issue of Washington, D.C.'s lack of local democracy with Dr King in that first interview. King saw it essentially as a question of Black representation and local self-government at the heart of America's democracy and demanded what he termed 'home rule' – in other words, an elected mayor for the capital – telling Charles that the Black population had effectively been disenfranchised. President Johnson was forced to take up the cause, stepping in and creating a new post of mayor commissioner. The aptly named Walter E. Washington, the great-grandson of an enslaved American, was nominated to the post in 1967. Following the signing into law of the Home Rule Act of 1973, he became the city's first elected 'home-rule' mayor two years later.

Meanwhile, we had settled in to life on Veazey Street, in a well-heeled, tree-lined, solidly white neighbourhood near the city's National Cathedral. My Indian mother Dip was a notable exception here, as this was a city where there was virtually no racial mixing. The racial separation was so entrenched that I only found out later that the city my sister and I grew up in had an African-American population that far exceeded any other ethnic group.

Charles always seemed to be coming and going, especially in the early days when either the more predictable timetable of the civil rights campaign, on the trail of Dr King, or the painful eruptions of violence around the country would send him out of the door even before London could call. My mother often had to navigate her way alone through the racial politics of the time on the domestic front in Washington, guided by her instincts and the fact that she was herself an outsider, as a non-American woman of colour, albeit in a position of privilege.

She received an early lesson in the complexities of our new life in America from within her own home. Each week, a woman called Gloria came to help clean the house. One day, Dip invited her to bring her sandwiches outside on the front lawn to have their lunch together. Gloria, a young African-American woman in her twenties, was taken aback and replied that she would rather not. The thing was, she said, she was worried that people might see them and think she'd stepped out of line. Dip knew not to insist and suggested instead that they stay inside and eat on the porch where the fly screens concealed them from public view. Over the next few months, though, she persuaded Gloria to enrol for a course in secretarial skills so she could work in an office and develop a career rather than clean other people's houses for a living. Dip's own education had been disrupted by the Partition of India and the loss of her father's wealth and property. She was passionate about women's education and would herself sign up for a course in Russian at the American University.

Charles and Dip were comfortable in Washington despite its

evident divisions – intellectually and socially engaged, holding parties that became known for their spirited conversation and diverse guest lists, as well as for Dip's speciality, prawn and egg curry. But one invitation they would never extend was to the new British ambassador. John Freeman arrived in Washington not long after we did, accompanied by his wife, Catherine Dove – Charles's former wife. The BBC bosses were apparently concerned that this awkward situation might compromise the corporation's position in Washington or, worse still, feed the gossip columns if Charles had to attend official engagements at the embassy.

Charles's BBC colleague in Washington, Gerald Priestland, in his recollection of the time, wondered, 'Was Washington big enough for the three of them – four, including Dip? London worried more than I did; but in the end the stiff upper lip prevailed and there were no displays of horsewhips, gauntlets or pistols at dawn in Rock Creek Park.' In fact, Charles told me later that Catherine had said on several occasions that they should 'get the families together'. He – and no doubt my mother – was having none of it.

For the first half of his posting, Charles shared the Washington beat with Priestland, who was officially the senior correspondent, roughly dividing radio and television between them in three-monthly stints. The TV part involved more travelling around the country; three months of radio allowed for something approaching a stable family life. At least that was the theory. In practice, Charles just wanted to be where the story was. Gerry, as Priestland was known, was on his second posting to the States after a spell in London. Charles had arrived in America as the replacement for Leonard Parkin, who would go on to have an illustrious career with ITN News as a star presenter, but who had been described by Priestland as his 'assistant' or second in command. It should have come as no surprise to anyone who knew him that Charles was not going to play second fiddle to Gerry Priestland.

Priestland was to find himself on a steep learning curve. Charles was 'a challenge from the start', he later wrote, while noting that, while Charles was a newcomer to the United States, the Washington bureau 'now had two number ones'. They were very different people. Gerry was a Charterhouse and Oxford man and the BBC's youngest foreign correspondent when he took up his first posting in Delhi in 1954. Charles had ended his formal education at seventeen, his only academic qualification the School Certificate. And while Gerry was still a schoolboy, Charles, though only four years older, was serving as a naval intelligence officer in the war, facing danger behind enemy lines and interrogating Nazi commanders.

Priestland was all too aware of how their different experiences of life played out in their professional roles as journalists. In his autobiography, he recalled the occasion when he'd let a BBC camera crew, newly over from London, go in to film a riot in Miami without him. They came under attack from the crowd and one of them was hurt. Charles told him that he had been irresponsible: 'A good officer stayed with his men and did not allow them to go swanning off into no man's land. He was probably right.'

The Washington bureau also received a shot in the arm from Charles's relentless work rate. With him, the pace was never going to be anything but frenetic. Gerry described Charles as having 'nerves of steel, the taut discipline of the soldier and apparently no use for sleep'. Charles's stamina was renowned, even perhaps slightly dreaded by producers and crews. David Coxon Taylor, Charles's US-based producer in the 1990s, remembers that even later in life his drive was barely affected. Some thirty years younger than his colleague and mentor, David told me he would mentally and physically prepare himself for Charles's arrival in Washington. 'It was rather like preparing for a marathon. I knew we wouldn't be sleeping much, barely stopping to eat. So, a few days before he arrived in town, I needed to make sure I was fit, ready for the challenge.'

It was mainly the bigger stories of 1960s America that gripped Charles as he increasingly developed into a sharp political analyst of that country – but he was still an on-the-day news reporter and, as such, had to cover whatever items his editors in London wanted. Distractions from important issues like Watts and the civil rights movement were not welcome but had to be dealt with. While as a father, Charles indulged his children and his own mischievous streak, he didn't have much time for the frivolous when it came to filing a news piece.

According to Adam Raphael, the *Guardian*'s Washington correspondent at the time, 'Charles was basically a serious man. I don't think I am. I came across this newfangled hobby called the frisbee and I wrote a typically over-the-top piece about the new craze sweeping America. And then Charles received a very irritating call from the news desk in London saying, "Why are we not covering this?"' Caroline Ellis, the BBC's office assistant and producer in Washington in the

1960s, told me that Charles put down the phone to London and began yelling, 'Bloody hell, bloody BBC. Damn the bloody news desk, damn bloody Adam Raphael and damn his bloody frisbees!' But Charles usually fought the battles he could win. And this wasn't one of them. The frisbee story was duly covered and broadcast to the nation. (As for Charles's colleague, Caroline Ellis was later introduced to Adam Raphael by Charles and Dip and went on to marry him. Marina and I were bridesmaids at the wedding, held at the District of Columbia Court of General Sessions in 1971, in dresses sent over from Bombay by our aunt Anup Masi for the occasion.)

Charles was similarly unenthused by the prospect of coming face-to-face with Beatlemania, but duly went to cover a Fab Four press conference held at the Astor Tower hotel in Chicago in August 1966. Though, unlike the popularity of frisbees, this did at least have some merit in news terms with the potential to set off the powder keg of US politics at the time, as it was the first time the group had been in the States since John Lennon's notorious off-the-cuff comment that the Beatles were more famous than Christ. This had proved to be incendiary, with the flames originally fanned by a disc jockey in Birmingham, Alabama. The Beatles' popularity had taken a big knock across the whole country and the atmosphere at the press conference was bad-tempered. Charles reported how some Baptist ministers had threatened their congregations with expulsion if they attended the Fab Four's concerts but that the protest lost momentum when the Ku Klux Klan got in on the act and started setting bonfires all over the country, burning the blasphemous Beatles' records and merchandise. 'Nobody wants to be associated with the Klan, so many of the former Beatle supporters have gone back into the Beatle camp,' Charles told his viewers. The story received a full quota of Charles Wheeler gravitas and, with a tilt at the Klan, managed to pick out elements that tied it to the wider problems of contemporary America. But watching it back, I still detect signs that he was filing it slightly under sufferance.

In our age, where news is conveyed around the world at the touch of an iPad or smartphone screen, the way stories were filed from the US during Charles's time might strike people as rather antiquated – a case of fingers crossed, almost. True, the satellite two-way had come into being and Charles had been one of the first to use it, for live interviews from Washington with the London TV newsroom. But as far as getting the filmed reports back, all undeveloped films were put in purple BBC 'onion bags' and shipped overnight to London. As Rona Christie, Charles's Washington producer, told me, 'We would go to the airport hoping to find a "pigeon" – someone in the check-in queue we knew, who could carry the film for us. That would save time at the other end at customs in London, so it could be taken to the lab, processed and get on air.' For Charles back in Washington, however, it meant that he was rarely able to see anything being edited, and he hardly ever saw any of his own finished reports, which might appear on British television anything up to two days after being filmed.

On a hot and humid day in the summer of 1966, Charles was back on the frontline. Watching his report, you can spot his unmistakable thick, slightly greying hair at the left edge of the frame. His head is close to Martin Luther King's, his face intent, listening but glancing watchfully around – perhaps for a flying brick, a bottle, or maybe to check the camera crew are OK, ready with the shot, well placed to put a question to the civil rights leader. Around them are braying, frenzied crowds, many with Confederate flags. Some are brandishing posters of the Alabama governor and self-avowed segregationist George Wallace. They are shouting obscenities at the marchers and threatening the reporters too, who surround King.

These pictures weren't filmed in the Deep South, however, but around Gage Park, a solidly white district in the south-west of Chicago. This was the starting point for King's Northern Campaign, 'penetrating white neighbourhoods and suburbs in America's northern cities, putting housing on the nation's radar – in particular to challenge the city's segregated housing practices and underinvestment in poorer neighbourhoods,' as Charles reported.

Charles was part of the press corps travelling with Martin Luther King. In Chicago, they joined King and some 600 people from the city's Black ghetto, along with dozens of TV crews and reporters. But in full view of the cameras, they soon came under attack. More than a thousand whites lined the streets, pushing into the marchers, screaming murderous and obscene curses.

There were loud bangs and smoke. Young white men were throwing powerful firecrackers called cherry bombs (which would be banned in the US at the end of that year). Dr King was knocked down and, crouching next to the young Jesse Jackson, Charles took cover. 'I've been hit so many times, I'm immune to it,' King remarked. But he was not expecting such vitriol – 'I've been in many demonstrations all across the South. But I can say that I have never seen, even in Mississippi and Alabama, mobs as hostile and as hate-filled as I am seeing in Chicago.'

That day, standing near King, Charles heard something that haunted him. People on the pavements were shouting, 'King go back to Africa' in thick East European accents. He didn't refer to this in his reports, but he would later reflect that these were people who had probably been taken in as displaced people, or 'DPs', by America at the end of the war, and had 'taken on this white racist feeling about the Black revolution'.

The *Los Angeles Times* reporter at the scene called it 'an afternoon of almost uncontrolled terrorism'. Also part of the gaggle of journalists travelling with King was Charles's old Berlin friend Jack Altman, who had decamped to Chicago and was now working for *Time* magazine and the *Chicago Sun-Times*. Jack remembers one moment in the park as he tried to file his story from a phone booth: 'Charlie and I had got separated and suddenly I found myself surrounded by these white guys, rocking and pushing at the box. It was terrifying. I shouted for Charles. He'd fought in a war – he knew how to deal with this sort of thing. But he'd been swallowed up by the crowd. Then, thank goodness, they suddenly for some reason lost interest.'

Charles felt that King was brave, but Chicago was too much – even for him. It wasn't long afterwards that King famously said, 'I don't mind saying I'm tired of marching. Marching for something that should have been mine at birth. I'm tired of living every day under the threat of death . . . I want to live as long as anyone . . . sometimes I begin to doubt if I'm going to make it through. I must confess I am tired.'

But King and his team had deployed their non-violent tactics to great effect to (in a word often used by him) 'dramatise' the struggle. From the early days, campaigning to change the segregation laws and in the marches from Selma to Montgomery, every march and action announced by King attracted dozens of TV cameras and reporters. They made the news virtually every night. Television was playing its part in the momentum for change with documentaries tackling the subject of race relations and nightly news programmes from CBS and NBC expanding to reflect a growing interest, pricking at the conscience of white America. And then the cities erupted.

Across sixty days in June and July 1967, there were riots in thirty-eight American cities alone. First Tampa, then in Cincinnati, Atlanta, Newark and Detroit, leaving seventy-nine people dead and thousands injured, homeless, with property destroyed and neighbourhoods decimated. Violence and heavy-handedness by the authorities inevitably directed at the Black community seemed to be a recurring theme triggering rage and frustration.

Charles found himself criss-crossing the country to cover the unrest. Sound recordist Eric Thirer, only twenty-four years old at the time, remembers: 'We did an endless trail when it heated up around the country. Night after night. We'd finish one riot, get onto a plane and go onto the next.'

Detroit was the bloodiest. Forty-three people died and over a thousand were wounded. The vast majority were Black. 'No one who saw it will ever forget', Charles would later recall. And he certainly didn't. Detroit was the fourth or fifth riot he had covered since he arrived in the United States, and he found it the most frightening yet. Everywhere, in every direction he looked, there were fires. Looters going for every shop they could see. But, he said, there was no mob violence, no attacks on individual whites. It was the police and state troopers that worried Charles: 'The danger to life and limb came from the forces of law and order,' he reported. The police had tooled themselves up to the eyeballs. They had even brought their own weapons – long guns, hunting rifles – as well as heavy machine-guns mounted on tanks and, Charles said, 'They blazed away at everything that moved.' Charles wasn't a war reporter and never wanted to be one, but in America in the 1960s he found himself reporting on what was going on in the cities as if from the middle of a war.

A nationwide commission later found that the police did use unreasonable and disproportionate violence against the rioters. The head of the force told Charles later that it took the authorities years to track down the stash of arms that the Detroit police had amassed to do battle with their own citizens.

If the streets were terrifying, the scenes in Detroit's hospitals that night were truly appalling. The sheer numbers of people being brought in on stretchers hauled out of the back of police trucks, overflowing into corridors, put Charles in mind of military casualty clearing stations. He felt that what he saw there spoke a great deal about American society itself and the persistent and dehumanising racism experienced by its Black citizens from every quarter. In his report, we see half a dozen Black men handcuffed to beds and stretchers. One young man is propped up on his elbows looking around in dazed slow motion, others are barely moving. Off camera, but recounted later, Charles asked a young white doctor why even the injured and those apparently close to death were manacled to stretchers. 'These people are animals,' replied the doctor in a chilling, matter-of-fact tone.

The timing of the '67 riots seemed to astonish white America, to whom it had appeared that civil rights were being won at an impressive pace. But the previous year, Charles had suggested, 'The crisis in American cities is rapidly becoming an issue to rival Vietnam.' Little seemed to have happened to change that idea. Many predicted that a white backlash after the violence would be manifested in the results of the US local elections at the end of that year. But in fact, 'racism lost', as Charles put it. The elections saw the defeat of candidates who, like Louise Hicks in Boston, had run racist campaigns. And in Cleveland, Carl Stokes – a forty-year-old lawyer and civil rights worker – became the first Black mayor to be elected in a major American city.

But for the 70 per cent of Black people in America living in the country's northern cities, nothing much about their everyday lives was changing. 'Poverty is as permanent a condition as the colour of their skin,' noted Charles in a report that he filed later that year from Chicago.

After the riots in Los Angeles and Detroit, many predicted that Chicago would be next. The city had one of the largest Black populations of any American city and the problems with housing, poverty and relations with the police were manifold. But as Charles reported in his story broadcast at the start of

August 1967, decisive action by the Black community itself, and in particular its own newspaper, the *Daily Defender*, may well have helped to avert an eruption. The 'Keep a Cool Summer' campaign saw a massive volunteer effort across the city as well as outreach to the ghetto, where Charles visited to speak to members of the gangs who had signed up to a truce. Sitting on the stoop of a house in a Chicago neighbourhood, a group of boys and girls – members of the Blackstone Rangers, a kind of umbrella group for the gangs – tell him that, while they are not about to defect to the non-violent approach of Martin Luther King, they are committed to keeping the peace.

When unrest finally did come to Chicago the following year, Charles would be there to witness it. But the people out of control were the police themselves. As a government-appointed inquiry put it, it was in effect a 'police riot'.

The mood was simmering – 'a powder keg', Charles called it. King and his followers had set their sights on poverty, economic injustice and housing. At the same time, King became more vocal against the war in Vietnam, calling for an end to the war and to the 'forc[ing] of young Black men and young white men to fight and kill in brutal solidarity'. In 1967, nearly half a million American soldiers were fighting this American war. Of the 246,000 men drafted under the infamous 'Project 100,000' that lowered the qualification standards of the draft, 41 per cent were Black, although Black Americans only represented 11 per cent of the population. With the future head of the Black Panther Party Stokely Carmichael applauding from the front pew, King had told a congregation at Ebenezer Baptist Church: 'There is something strangely inconsistent about a nation and press that will praise you when you say be non-violent toward Jim Clark [the sheriff of Selma] but will curse and damn you when you say be non-violent toward little brown Vietnamese children.'

America was pouring millions of dollars into Vietnam, which King argued should be going to fight the War on Poverty. This drove a wedge between King and his old ally in the White House. King broke with President Johnson over Vietnam. Anti-war demonstrations were breaking out on student campuses around the country against the draft. Johnson was facing criticism from all sides. Dr King accused him of undermining the War on Poverty by pursuing a war on foreign soil. And he went further still, calling for a 'radical redistribution of economic power' and for America to 'bridge the gulf between the haves and the have nots'. He argued that desegregation and voting rights had not cost America a penny but now it was time to spend billions of dollars to ensure jobs and an economic future.

This shift in focus split support in his own constituency. Many were worried about more violence, the likes of which had already been witnessed the previous summer. Others in the camp, like Stokely Carmichael, were not convinced by King's brand of multiracial civil rights ecumenism. White liberal Washington, it seemed, was also alienated by the new rhetoric – pushing traditional allies too far, threatening privilege and power.

But Martin Luther King still had friends on the Hill determined to make the powerful listen. Among them was Senator Robert Kennedy, who went down to Mississippi and, confronted by the poverty there, declared that 'we are not doing what we should in this country'. Kennedy suggested that King bring the poor to Washington to force white America to look at what was going on. But before he could get there, on 4 April 1968, Dr King was assassinated at the Lorraine Motel, supposedly a safe haven for Black travellers and a favourite among musicians recording in Memphis. He died almost instantly, standing on the balcony outside his room. The reaction was swift. Riots broke out in more than a hundred American cities in an outpouring of grief and anger.

Charles learnt of Martin Luther King's assassination as he sat on board a plane with around a hundred other correspondents ready to take off for a conference organised by President Johnson in Hawaii. They piled out of the plane. Johnson cancelled his programme and declared a day of mourning. The president spent most of the night on the phone to mayors around the country, begging them to use the least possible violence in restoring order.

'As I record this report it's just after midnight, about 6 a.m. in England. The president is in the White House situation room, usually the nerve centre in foreign crises like Cuba and the Arab–Israeli War. Outside, infantry are stationed in the White House gardens, there are tanks in New Hampshire Avenue and a machine-gun nest on Capitol Hill. Washington is now quietening down. But the fires are still burning,' Charles relayed to the listeners.

The BBC in London sent reporter Martin Bell out to help Charles cover the story from Chicago, where he reported scenes of arson and violence: 5,000 troops and 8,000 National Guardsmen camped out in the city's Jackson Park and eleven lives lost. The capital saw three days of violence, two nights of curfew, millions of dollars of property damaged and, as in Chicago, thousands made homeless. Charles found a ray of optimism in the behaviour of the occupying forces of law and order in Washington. With the memory of the Detroit carnage no doubt seared in his mind, he observed the troops had pulled out when it looked like a confrontation with rioters or looters was imminent and, 'No soldier fired anything more lethal than a tear gas canister . . . Human life is valued above property . . . Washington has shown that you can put down a riot without using machine-guns.'

But the head of Washington's Black Power Committee, Chuck Stone, also a fellow journalist (later founder and president of the National Association of Black Journalists), had a less optimistic message. In the aftermath of the rioting that spread across America after King's assassination, he told Charles, 'Unless the conditions, which are the festering ground for the riots are removed, unless the slum housing, the unemployment, the discrimination – the whole pattern of grievances that force the Black man to live in a second-class citizenship, unless that pattern is overhauled completely, there will be more eruptions, more insurrections and rebellions, not just in the next few months but in the years to come.' Prescient words.

Chuck Stone would become a regular visitor for Dip's famous curry suppers at our house in Veazey Street. I remember him always signing his name in the guest book in brown ink, using his own pen. Perhaps because of Dip's experience of the independence movement in India, whose moral leader Mahatma Gandhi was an inspiration for Martin Luther King's creed of non-violence, Chuck was as intrigued by and interested in Dip's life and ideas as much as by Charles's.

Determined to keep faith with King's intentions and his commitment to non-violence, the movement, under King's successor, Ralph Abernathy, went ahead with the Poor People's Campaign, which King had planned just before his death. Two months earlier, he had wept at the sight of small and hungry girls and boys with no shoes in the town of Marks in the Mississippi Delta – a typical delta town, in theory racially integrated but in reality far from that. This small community, in Quitman County – America's poorest county in its poorest state – was a fitting place to start the campaign for economic justice, setting off with a mule train of fifteen covered wagons in mid-May.

At the start of the month, the recruitment drive for marchers to join the caravan to Washington was on. Charles joined some of the young activists who had taken on the mantle of King's mission in Marks. But many people in the town were reluctant to join the protest in case they lost what little they had in terms of work and housing. Others weren't convinced they could make a difference. In one of his first reports shot in colour, Charles took the viewer past the town's bright white clapboard houses with their impossibly green lawns, up to the railway track that separated what they called the 'coloured section' from the white part of the town. Electricity crossed the track 'but people rarely do,' observed Charles. The pictures show tin-roofed wooden shacks in various stages of neglect, stray planks hanging off here and there, standing in pools of rainwater. The town didn't earn enough income to tackle its slums but was too small to qualify for federal poverty schemes. There were no council houses, no plans to rehouse the poor. No future unless it could attract industry. These are the people, Charles tells us in the film, that Martin Luther King wanted to bring to Washington 'to demand their share of the national cake'.

In Marks, Charles met Mrs Margaret Franklin. Standing on her porch in a sky-blue dress and a green head scarf, she was a dignified and serious woman. She listened intently to a bearded young man in glasses and a natty grey suit. 'Bring the kids,' he entreated. She had five young children at home and five chickens too, she told him, but what could she do in Washington? She'd rather they came to her and explained why she received no public assistance. Old beans, black-eyed peas, bread and occasionally some meat were the family's staple fare. The recruiters urged her: 'People like you are what it's all about.' She eventually promised to think about it.

Charles returned to Marks thirty years later in 1996, accompanied by James Figgs, the same man who had guided Martin Luther King around the town. There was no sign of Mrs Franklin or her children, though the shacks were still there, standing in pools of stagnant water. 'Is anybody living here now?' Charles asked Figgs, incredulously. 'Someone has always lived here,' was the answer.

Perhaps in 1968, residents like Margaret Franklin were right to wonder what difference it would make if they went to Washington. But many did go just the same; people who had never left their towns before. They joined the civil rights protestors to form the caravan of carts, boarded trains in Virginia and walked the last few miles along the Potomac

River to arrive in the neoclassical heart of the city. By the time they arrived, though, presidential candidate Robert Kennedy had also been shot.

Kennedy, familiarly known as Bobby, was endowed with a naturally infectious charm. Buoyed up by the growing anti-war movement, he had entered the race for the presidency in spring 1968. The previous autumn, Charles had been invited, with a few other foreign correspondents, to Hickory Hill – the senator's home in Virginia. When he arrived, he found Bobby in the pool. Charles went over and immediately asked if he planned to run against Johnson. Every time he pushed the point, Kennedy laughed and dived under the water.

Charles accompanied the charismatic middle Kennedy brother on his famous Nebraska campaign train in April 1968. Watching him speak to the crowds about preserving their small towns and family farms and ending the war in Vietnam, Charles firmly believed that had Robert Kennedy escaped the assassin's bullet, he would have won the nomination in Chicago and gone on to win the 1968 election. In fact, moments before he was shot in a hotel in Los Angeles, Kennedy had heard the news that he'd taken the California primary. Charles would say later that the death of Robert Kennedy was one of the things that had moved him most deeply as a journalist, along with the East German Rising and Hungary in 1956. 'I found him extraordinarily compelling. I was impressed by his shyness as much as anything, and I liked him as a person,' he said, in a rare endorsement of a political leader.

In Washington, Charles watched as the Poor People's marchers hammered the first stake into the ground to set up

'Resurrection City', a camp of canvas and plywood in Lafayette Square. The Reverend Jesse Jackson was elected as 'mayor' of this encampment. As a young activist, he had stood beside Dr King at Gage Park, demanding decent housing, kneeling on the ground next to Charles as marchers and reporters tried to avoid the rocks raining down. Now Jackson was presiding over a makeshift city in the mud that, alongside some 3,000 civil rights protestors, included poor whites from Appalachia and Mexican-Americans from California. Perhaps this inspired his later 'Rainbow Coalition' rallying cry. Some years later, Charles would report on several bids by Jackson to run for the White House. He was electrified by his speeches, feeling that he might become the country's first Black president. It was not to be, of course. Not this time, not that man.

But the Poor People's Campaign and 'Mayor' Jackson's Resurrection City outraged Washington's largely white establishment. Press and politicians alike bemoaned the possibility of disease and 'unauthorised camping'. Joseph Califano was President Johnson's chief assistant for domestic affairs at the time. He described the reaction of white Washington to Charles: 'It was sloppy, messy. It was very offensive to Americans who looked at the Capitol grounds, the Washington Monument, the Jefferson Memorial, the Lincoln Memorial as great and beautiful places. We had legislation in the house, the [Fair] Housing Bill . . . We almost lost the Bill because of the Poor People's March. I'm not just talking about the reaction among conservatives; it was across the board: liberals, moderates, conservatives were all offended by that march.'

Resurrection City and the Poor People's Campaign lasted

only a few months, its makeshift tents eventually torn down by police as the protestors began to abandon the site and the mud took over. Nearly thirty years would go by before Black Americans held another demonstration in the nation's capital.

*

Charles returned to Watts, the scene of the riots he had covered as a newly arrived Washington correspondent, a couple of times over the years to see how things had evolved: once in 1969 and again more than two decades later when police violence again sparked riots that saw Watts and other neighbourhoods in Los Angeles once more engulfed in flames. On both occasions, he found people encountering many of the same obstacles – from social neglect and poverty to institutional racism. The massive investment needed at state level to bring about any meaningful transformation had never happened.

Although by then living in Britain, Charles was in Virginia covering a death penalty story for *Newsnight* when the call came from London. Following the acquittal in April 1992 by a predominantly white jury of the LAPD officers accused of brutally beating an unarmed Black man, Rodney King, Watts had erupted. On the bumpy flight to LA, Charles and producer David Coxon Taylor talked about the story, bouncing around ideas, testing angles and script lines. What really lay behind the riots? What part did police brutality play? How had things changed since '65?

David and Charles arrived while Watts was still in flames and walked for six hours straight down Michigan Avenue from South Central to Koreatown. 'We just captured interviews and sequences as we went and edited the film right through the night for the following day's *Newsnight*. Charles was at his best on that story,' recalls David.

Charles tried to retrace his steps from more than twenty-five years earlier and find a Black-owned community and business centre that had been built in the wake of the 1965 riots. At the time, Ted Watkins, founder of the Watts Labor Community Action Committee, told Charles that the answer was to provide jobs and social services – with homelessness being the acute issue to address and a reason for the unrest. When Charles and the crew got there in April 1992, they found Teryl Watkins, the daughter of its founder, exhausted, standing by the burnt ruins of the centre, her father's life's work. Despite her remonstrations – 'We are Black like you! We've been here for years!' – armed rioters had driven straight at the gates of the centre, smashing them, burning down offices and many of the shops inside the complex, shooting as they went.

And yet with great eloquence, Teryl Watkins told Charles: 'We are not resentful. This is a clash of the classes. I truly do not feel that the condition that exists here in LA right now is a racial condition, it is definitely a class condition. It is the economic underclass taking a little bit of what everyone else has in America – of what is shown to them, drilled every day into them on the tube [TV], of what most people have and these people do not. They represent a whole community of people who don't have a connection with the rest of affluent America.' Watkins explains that 75 per cent of people in her neighbourhood were on welfare, many homeless, many unemployed for twenty-five years.

After the first riots in Watts in 1965, Martin Luther King had come to a similar conclusion: that racial justice in America could never be achieved without tackling the condition of poverty and poor housing. Charles noted that King was mounting a challenge to the American capitalist system, calling for such things as the redistribution of wealth. As Charles reflected later, 'In making King a national hero, America has glossed over his radicalism, conveniently forgetting that in the last two years of his life he was preaching socialism.'

I think when it comes to the struggle for Black justice and equality, Charles would have appreciated US President Barack Obama's words that 'progress sometimes goes in zigzags and sometimes backwards'. In January 2021, less than seven months after the killing of George Floyd on 25 May by Minneapolis police officers, Raphael Warnock was elected to the US senate – Georgia's first senator of colour and pastor of the Ebenezer Baptist Church, where Martin Luther King once preached.

But as 1968 wore on, with its assassinations, the continuing war in Vietnam and the erosion of Johnson's vision of the Great Society, some might have wondered whether progress was in fact in full retreat. As Charles would reflect, by that year, 'America's brief infatuation with civil rights seemed like history.'

6.

CONSPIRACY AND COVER-UPS: THE UNDOING OF AMERICAN PRESIDENTS

I thought, this man is really not telling the truth and he's the President of the United States. And I think my feelings about Vietnam were governed by this too.

CHARLES WHEELER ON LYNDON B. JOHNSON,
GREAT LIVES, BBC RADIO 4, 7 MAY 2004

Growing up in 1960s America, the Vietnam War was everywhere. TV was strictly rationed by Charles and Dip to half an hour a day with, exceptionally, a favourite film on occasion. But one day my father brought in the small TV set from the spare room and put it on one of the dining-room chairs so we could watch the CBS evening news as we sat down to supper at the table. There was a special report from Vietnam that he didn't want to miss. The strangeness of what appeared on the screen was not lost on my five-year-old self. It was in colour, like my absolute favourite film, *The Wizard of Oz*. But this was real, and the forest the men were walking through was a jungle. A war was being played out before our eyes while we sat at home eating spaghetti and meatballs. Across the nation, more and more people were tuning in as new technology allowed the networks to beam this faraway war into their living rooms. The pictures were changing minds and attitudes. All too aware that our father was often away making his own TV appearances, we were grateful that 'Fa', as my sister and I called him, didn't have to work over there, in a land filled with soldiers and death.

By 1968, the Vietnam War had come to dominate the news and the political agenda. As Charles reported to listeners and viewers back in the UK, it was a year that brought assassination, protest and division to America in its politics and on its streets, undermining even the position of the presidency in the minds of many.

At the end of January, as Tet, the Vietnamese lunar new year, began, Viet Cong and North Vietnamese forces mounted surprise attacks on cities across South Vietnam and attempted to invade the US embassy compound in Saigon, just a few streets away from where many of the American reporters and TV crews were staying. Though they'd been aware that the North Vietnamese had been planning an offensive, the Americans were nonetheless caught on the hop. Panic was in the air. The reporting of the Tet Offensive, especially in the US television networks' no-holds-barred nightly bulletins, challenged the tenuous narrative that Johnson and his circle had been spinning: that the US was winning the war. Viewers witnessed the summary execution by Saigon's police chief of a Viet Cong suspect on 1 February, the horrific moment captured by an NBC cameraman. Reports from the US news networks were now not just showing the mounting number of body bags (more than 400 Americans killed in the week that followed

Tet) but pictures of fighting in the heart of Saigon, raising the spectre of possible American defeat.

The widening divide between what viewers in America and around the world could see on their TV screens was happening in Vietnam and the US administration's official version of events led high-profile American journalists like the avuncular CBS TV newscaster Walter Cronkite to go there and see for himself. Cronkite was a household name. He was trusted, affable, authoritative, with a cast-iron reputation for objectivity and a unique place in American homes and hearts. Normally based in the CBS studio as an anchor, when his report from Vietnam aired on 27 February it was watched by millions. 'To say we are closer to victory today is to believe the optimists who have been wrong in the past... We are mired in stalemate,' he pronounced from the newsroom after the broadcast, concluding, 'The only rational way out will be to negotiate, not as victims but as an honourable people who lived up to their pledge to defend democracy and to do the best they could.' Cronkite's broadcast may well have played a key role in conditioning American public opinion against the war, or at least Johnson's handling of it. Polling data showed President Johnson's approval rating dropped to 26 per cent after the report aired. He'd certainly predicted as much, famously reported as saying, 'If we've lost Cronkite, we've lost Middle America.'

Pressure was building on Johnson from all sides and yet the administration still insisted there was light at the end of the tunnel, and that, in fact, Tet constituted a Communist defeat. As Charles had reported on the first Monday of February 1968, Johnson had sent two of his principal cabinet officers, Secretary of State Dean Rusk and Defence Secretary Robert McNamara, to be questioned by members of the White House press corps and drum home that message, in the face of mounting evidence to the contrary. Charles delivered his assessment from outside the White House: 'If anything can help to carry President Johnson and the country through the present crisis of confidence it's honesty . . . the country is in the mood to listen but not to be bamboozled.'

While the president himself was the driving force behind the escalation of the war, he was, in Charles's view, especially in the early years of the presidency, also swamped and pushed by the Kennedy hand-me-downs – the 'Harvards', as Johnson called them. They were much more poised and polished than the Texan LBJ, who felt intimidated and at an intellectual disadvantage.

'They were enormously persuasive people. McNamara in particular always seemed to be two or three steps ahead of Johnson. And as soon as Johnson gave way to the pressure, the chiefs of staff at the Pentagon, as much as the advisors like McNamara, were always there with a plan which involved taking a further step towards escalation,' Charles later said.

Charles felt that Johnson should have put his foot down. But he didn't and, as Charles reported, the sense was growing that, as American casualties reached 90,000, no one was really in control and the country now was in a terrible bind. The options in 1968 were to step up efforts in the hope of winning the war, to let it grind on as it was or to start withdrawing troops, backing away from the conflict. As Charles summarised in one of his reports of the time: 'It's a big, bloody, costly, risky war.

Few Americans understand it. None know where it's leading.' President Johnson's War on Poverty was coming off the rails, his vision of the Great Society crumbling . . .

To make matters worse for Johnson, Robert Kennedy, entered the race for the presidency. With the prospect of facing the young Kennedy brother at the polls, overwhelmed by the escalating and inescapable conflict in Vietnam, as well as his ailing health, Johnson shocked not just the nation but most of his own administration by announcing, at the end of March 1968, that he would not run for re-election that year.

Charles recalled later how, a little blurry from sleep, he was asked to interpret events for BBC listeners: 'It was one of these famous two way-ers when the telephone rings at seven in the morning and I am in bed and it's William Hardcastle [a former BBC Radio *World at One* presenter] on the phone and he says, "Charles, why did he resign?"' Charles answered quickly that Johnson's decision was 'moral cowardice', feeling that, having taken responsibility for the Vietnam War, the least Johnson could do was to see it through.

But looking back on his own reporting of the time, and on that particular radio two-way, Charles later came to see his judgement of Johnson's decision not to run for re-election as 'cruel' and 'a bit of instant analysis'. His feeling that 'reporters should avoid looking into other people's heads' became all the more acute when he met Claudia 'Lady Bird' Johnson more than thirty years later, as part of a series of four BBC films that aired in 1996 called *Wheeler on America*. Charles interviewed the president's widow at the LBJ Library in Austin, Texas and she described to him her husband's inner turmoil at the time.

'It really was an agonising time. It wasn't the war he wanted to fight. It was a burr that you had to clasp, and you couldn't get loose from it,' she told him in her rich and rolling Texan accent, in what would be her final extended interview.

While he admired Johnson for his vision of the Great Society, Charles said he never felt the president was totally trustworthy. Indeed, Charles had learnt a lesson about the fallibility of the office of the American presidency at the start of his time in Washington.

The very first story Charles covered when he arrived in the United States in 1965 was in fact not in the US at all, but in the Caribbean. The Cold War, at the centre of his previous posting in Berlin, was also being played out there, on one of its peripheral stages around the world.

At the end of April 1965, Johnson had ordered 42,000 US troops – Marines and soldiers – to take on a perceived communist threat in the Dominican Republic, a small independent Caribbean state sharing the island of Hispaniola with Haiti. The fear in the US of 'another Cuba' loomed large and there were even rumours that Fidel Castro was pulling the strings. Soon after Charles and his fellow reporters arrived in the capital, Santo Domingo, the CIA briefed all the correspondents about the impending 'communist coup'. Even at the time, Charles noted that there was 'no evidence yet made public to support President Johnson's assertion that communist conspirators had taken over the revolt.' Later, he would recall in far more forthright terms: 'It was quite clear that the administration was lying. There was no question of a communist coup there.' By the autumn, the US had installed its own favoured conservative junta.

'That incident for me really formed my opinion of Lyndon Johnson,' Charles said. 'I thought, this man is really not telling the truth and he's the president of the United States. And I think my feelings about Vietnam were governed by this too.'

During the following eight and a half years of his Washington posting, Charles witnessed the increasing demystification of the presidency, culminating in the debasement of the office through Watergate. But he also saw the emergence of a stronger, more assertive Congress willing to take on the executive in ways not seen before, setting a perennial drama in motion that is still playing out today. It was a story that fascinated him and one he wanted to tell the BBC's international and British domestic audiences. At the centre of the action was the US Senate Foreign Relations Committee and its chair Senator J. William Fulbright, proving a thorn in the administration's side.

From as early as 1966, the committee had been asking uncomfortable questions about the cost of the Vietnam War in terms of American lives and dollars. Armed as he was with his White House press pass, the halls and corridors of Congress and Capitol Hill had become Charles's regular haunt, where he attended a series of public and televised sessions of the committee in the Senate caucus room. Airing eminent voices of dissent, like Professor John Kenneth Galbraith, a former policy advisor to President Kennedy and ex-US ambassador to India, the hearings gave a new legitimacy to the querying of US engagement in Vietnam. Charles saw in them not just a demonstration of American democracy by its elected representatives but a milestone in media coverage of war in a modern age. As well as transforming access to news and information from the battlefield, television was also allowing closer scrutiny of the decision-making by Congress. Charles described how in America's Vietnam involvement, 'the world is witnessing the execution of a war in a television age – in a society where information and scrutiny is expected, in a society which takes its conspicuous exercise of democracy seriously.'

The Foreign Relations Committee was also demanding to be told more about the circumstances behind one of the key events that had led to America's military involvement in Vietnam: the 1964 Gulf of Tonkin incident, where the North Vietnamese were charged with attacking the US Navy on two separate occasions, on 2 and 4 August 1964. This was, it was claimed, in response to covert raids on North Vietnamese military installations by South Vietnamese commandos that the Americans insisted they knew nothing about. It had led to the congressional green light for war in the form of the Tonkin Resolution – almost a carte blanche, members of the committee felt. A key staff member of the committee, later its chief of staff, was Bill Bader. Bader, who had also spent a short time with the CIA, was a brave and principled man. He became one of Charles's most valued sources in Washington and, along with his sculptor wife Greta, one of his and Dip's closest friends. Bader told Charles what he was discovering, not just about Tonkin but around issues that challenged the credibility of Johnson's war policy, from casualty numbers to troops committed, to the ability to win the war. President Johnson, concerned that leaks from the committee were fuelling criticism of his Vietnam policy, had asked Director of the FBI J. Edgar Hoover to investigate key staff members to find out who was responsible. Bill came to believe that he and Charles were both being tailed by the FBI but would later say that he never worried that Charles would let on where his background information was coming from: 'I had complete confidence in him. I never said to him, "don't ever tell anyone else what I told you". I didn't have a moment of worry.'

Bader and his boss, Senator Fulbright, were among the first to question the veracity of the two 'attacks' by the North Vietnamese on US Navy ships in the Gulf of Tonkin. They were convinced that Congress's approval for the Tonkin Resolution had been extracted fraudulently by the president and his defence secretary, Robert McNamara, based on misleading reports, with information deliberately concealed from the American people.

Thirty years after the events, Charles and his producer David Coxon Taylor unearthed material that showed how well-founded Fulbright's own misgivings had been. Sifting through newly declassified material from the congressional hearings and tapes of the president's phone calls from the Johnson archive, they were able to shine a light on facts surrounding the Tonkin incident. They unearthed a previously classified cable, relayed to the Pentagon by US Taskforce Commander Captain John Herrick. The cable had been mentioned in the Senate hearings of 1966, but until then it had been buried in the archive. It revealed that Herrick had reviewed the messages coming from the Navy destroyer USS *Maddox* when they had allegedly been attacked for a second time by North Vietnamese torpedoes on 4 August. His cable read: 'Review of action make many reported contacts and torpedoes fired appear doubtful. Freak weather effects on radar and over-eager sonar men may have accounted for many reports. No actual visual sightings by *Maddox*. Suggest complete evaluation before further action is taken.' But despite contradicting the official version of events, the message went unheeded and the administration pressed on.

As David and Charles would learn though, there were profound misgivings within Johnson's inner circle about continuing US engagement in Vietnam. Hawks were turning into doves. By 1968, McNamara was already coming to the conclusion that the war was lost, urging Johnson to halt the bombing and cut the number of troops. And yet, McNamara never even hinted at the extent of his doubts in his testimonies to Congress. In fact, as Charles recalled later, 'I spent many afternoons watching [the congressional hearings], convinced like everybody else that Robert McNamara was an unreconstructed hawk.'

In 1995, Charles and David Coxon Taylor had the chance to interview McNamara for their *Wheeler on America* series for the BBC. It was the first interview the former defence secretary had given in twenty-five years and, as he broke his silence, he may have been hoping that this was going to be a first easy stop on a penitent 'lessons learned' circuit of interviews on Vietnam. And things did start well, with a startling admission of the profoundly flawed approach of the administration. He told Charles, 'We misunderstood our enemy. We lacked an understanding of history – the history of Indochina, the history of Asia. We looked upon Ho Chi Minh as an associate and supporter of Stalin and Khrushchev where in fact I believe he was much more comparable to Tito. He was a nationalist. We were fighting nationalism. We thought we were fighting communism.'

Three years later, Charles and David went back for a second bite – this time for a Channel 4 film, *Playing with the Truth*, and this time they were armed with the recently declassified cables refuting the official version of events. In this rather extraordinary interview, Charles, now in interrogator mode, homed in on why McNamara and his fellow advisors also kept the public and Congress in the dark about their gravest doubts. He put it to him that there was from the outset a deliberate attempt to mislead Congress by the administration. 'No, no, no,' insisted McNamara, speaking over him. Charles then pressed him on the details of the Tonkin incident – specifically the Johnson administration's claim that the raid on North Vietnamese military installations that provoked the 'attacks' on the US Navy had been carried out by South Vietnamese commandos without the knowledge of the Americans and that North Vietnam's firing at the US Navy destroyer USS *Maddox* was unprovoked.

Watching the interview, I'm immediately aware that Charles is remarkably feisty, if not openly combative, as he gets stuck into McNamara. 'In every document and every transcript I've looked at,' he said, 'I have seen the raids that occurred at the same time as those destroyer patrols described as South Vietnamese raids. Every time you go before the Congressional leaders, you insist this is a South Vietnamese operation. You insist that the US Navy was not aware of it.

Now everybody knows that the bodies [the soldiers in the raids] were South Vietnamese. Everything else was American. Why could you not have come clean with the Congressional leadership in executive session?'

McNamara was clearly affronted by this onslaught: 'I think you are totally wrong. I just think you are totally wrong.'

'You didn't come clean. It's on the record,' Charles pressed.

'No, no, no, no. On the contrary. Read the testimony that [Dean] Rusk and I gave to the Congress,' McNamara parried. He told Charles that they had informed Congress about the South Vietnamese raids, which, McNamrara added, were just 'pinpricks'.

'That's not the point,' Charles retorted, but McNamara stopped him.

'Let me finish now. These were pinpricks by patrol boats or aircraft launched from South Vietnam, and, as you suggested, done with the knowledge and assistance of the US—'

'Controlled by the US, planned by the US,' Charles insisted.

McNamara, still on the back foot, replied that his testimony to Congress had been very clear on this. 'Now, you implied we deceived them. I don't think we did deceive them. I think the whole discussion on deception and whether I deceived the Congress is totally unreasonable.'

At this point, McNamara's voice had risen in volume, while Charles sounded calmer by the second, as he essentially accused the former defence secretary of lying to Congress to justify a war that would cost hundreds of thousands of American and Vietnamese lives. 'Mr McNamara, I'm reading from the record.'

'To hell with this,' McNamara said suddenly. 'I'm not going

to go on with the interview if we're going to handle it this way.' And with that, he pulled off his microphone and the team was ushered out.

The next day, McNamara was on the phone apologising for losing his cool. David made an offer to run a second interview but only if they could put the question again as to how much Congress – and the public – should have been told before the Tonkin Resolution received such impressive support from Congress in 1964, leading to the escalation of US involvement in the Vietnam War. But McNamara declined. As David put it, 'McNamara had clearly seen enough of the two of us . . . He felt we had unfairly ambushed him.'

While Johnson's inner circle hid their own doubts and divisions from the outside world, America's attachment to the so-called domino theory of communist expansion left many unconvinced, with the US more and more isolated. The logic behind trying to get the enemy to the bargaining table through bombing was also being questioned on the international stage – in the United Nations and even by allies Canada, France and Denmark. Britain was one of the few countries that was not openly criticising US involvement. But privately, Harold Wilson tried to advise the president against the bombing of North Vietnam. As Charles observed, this was a definite low in the 'special relationship'. Johnson never forgave Wilson for what he saw as interference – nor for his repeated refusal to deliver British troops to support America in Vietnam.

But opposition at home presented a much bigger problem for Johnson than international disapproval. Demonstrations against Vietnam were becoming a regular occurrence around the country. They started on the college campuses with strikes against the draft. The protests at New York City's Ivy League Columbia University (just three weeks after the murder of Martin Luther King) went on for a month and the police's disproportionately violent reaction against the white and Black students, radicals from the Black Panther movement and people from the Harlem neighbourhood drew national attention. Between January and June 1969, as Charles recorded in his notebooks and files on the Vietnam War, there were 221 major demonstrations in the US involving 34,000 students on 101 university campuses.

One of Charles's TV reports of the time came from the District of Columbia's Correction Center – an open prison cleared of its usual inmates to temporarily house some 600 anti-war demonstrators. A stream of very cheerful-looking protestors can be seen flashing broad smiles and peace signs at the camera. They'd been arrested and fined in temporary courts only to be bussed straight back to the city. But not everyone was amused. The backlash had begun – a few days later, counter-protestors set up in the capital too. Their placards, 'Cong burn better than flags' and 'Bomb Berkeley', made pretty clear what they thought of the protesting students and their cause. The fault line running through America was widening by the week.

As the death toll of US servicemen rose, Congressman Paul Findley, increasingly vocal on Capitol Hill, collected a list of more than 30,000 American soldiers who had been killed in Vietnam. Then, one by one, the protestors read them out on the steps of the Capitol. This sombre roll call of names, updated daily, became a focus for nationwide demonstrations during 1969 and was especially favoured by religious groups. Charles and his crew filmed the Quaker contingent's recitation, until the protesters were quietly led off by police. Catholic and Protestant clergymen and their congregations took up the baton in Massachusetts: 'Over 35,000 names they read – and they never paused, nor were they interrupted. It took them the whole of Sunday and, with torches, all of Sunday night. And they were still reading on Monday morning,' Charles related in his commentary.

The celebrity paediatrician Dr Benjamin Spock was addressing the crowd at another demonstration in D.C. Charles recognised him immediately, as Spock's liberal theories on child-rearing (treat them with affection and as individuals) had a keen advocate in my mother. Charles recalled how Spock had said if it weren't for the kids in America, he would have left the country some years ago. Charles identified with that position: 'I thought that I would say the same thing,' he said, speaking to the CBS reporter and friend Rod MacLeish in a special BBC report on correspondents in the field. He went on, 'I'm not just here for the money, not just here for professional enjoyment; I have to live here. I've lived here for several years, and I think the only thing that really keeps me in America is this constant ferment in the younger generation. It makes it a much more optimistic place to be than it would be otherwise.'

Charles had a natural and not very well concealed anti-authoritarian streak. The presents of bright paisley ties and jazzy 'bush shirts' brought by our aunts and cousins on their regular trips to D.C. from India were as close as he got to embracing the hippy fashions of the time, but it wasn't much of a stretch for Charles to imagine himself as part of an alternative, more radical future and certainly to sympathise with it. He had also developed a penchant for protest music and, by the time I was eight or so, he became my unofficial musical mentor, presenting me with my first LPs: Joan Baez, Mahalia Jackson, Judy Collins and Simon and Garfunkel's album *Bookends*. Our small private school, Sheridan, reflected different loyalties of the time: patriotic pilgrim fables, pledging allegiance to the flag every Wednesday. But we also sang along with gusto at assemblies to Woody Guthrie's 'This Land Is Your Land' and Bob Dylan's 'Blowin' in the Wind'. Mrs Denney, the music teacher, made sure I knew the words and the guitar parts to the standards of the protest movement of the time, such as 'Amazing Grace' and 'We Shall Overcome'.

In the spring of 1968, in a counterpoint to the increasing horror being broadcast nightly from Vietnam, flower power was in full bloom. Charles travelled to California to report on the emerging commune and hippy culture on America's West Coast. He was very taken with the self-sufficient community an hour out of San Francisco at Morningstar Ranch and the woodland hippies living there on the edge of the Russian River. 'Marijuana is smoked quite freely. Joints are passed around like pipes of peace . . . Unquestionably, many of them are amiable loafers but in a violent society, amiability may have a place,' he reported in his TV news piece from the 'ranch'. When I was older, and able to conceive of Dip and Charles as people with motivations that went beyond parenting my sister and me, he told me he had entertained the thought of staying on the commune and not coming back. I was never sure if this was an attempt to connect with my own hippy tendencies at the time or a genuine confession.

Charles arrived to cover the Chicago Democratic Convention the day before official proceedings started, in August 1968. The mood was febrile, many still heartbroken and in shock from the assassinations earlier in the year of Martin Luther King and Bobby Kennedy. It was no secret that the National Mobilization Committee to End the War in Vietnam (MOBE) had been planning a demonstration for several months. Rumours and paranoia pulsed around the city: of a hippy plot to lace the city's water supply with LSD; of an uprising in the ghetto being planned by Black militant leaders.

The convention centre itself, the International Amphitheatre on 42nd Street in the 11th district of Canaryville, was almost next door to the pigpens of the Union Stock Yards. Charles described the 'unmistakable stench of pigs and manure hanging over the convention site like a fog'. It was Mayor Daley's home turf, and he wasn't taking any chances. He promised the party a violence-free convention, mounting the strictest security operation in political history up to that point to keep the public out. In temperatures of 97 degrees Fahrenheit, some 6,000 National Guardsmen and state police assembled, anticipating trouble. Thousands of federal troops were also on standby. Charles filed a report describing an atmosphere of 'undeclared martial law'. He also reported that sixty Black soldiers from various units had conducted a non-violent protest against possible deployment for riot control in the city. After a pep talk from the general in charge, some backed down but forty-three did not. They were put in the stockade.

The result of these security measures was what the Walker Report, commissioned that December from the National Commission on the Causes and Prevention of Violence, called a 'police riot': indiscriminate and unrestrained violence by the forces of law and order aimed not just at the demonstrators and passers-by; members of the press too found themselves under attack from Mayor Daley's police force in a 'club-swinging melee'. Charles and colleagues had to run for cover into the hotel from where the BBC was broadcasting. On his return home to D.C., Charles told Dip what happened. I remember sitting on the edge of their bed listening to his account. The images he described are still vivid in my mind today: police running completely amok, truncheons raised, charging at demonstrators, delegates, residents and reporters alike, who all found themselves laid into, beaten and teargassed on the orders of Chicago's Mayor Daley himself. The ad hoc studio in a suite overlooking Grant Park, where much of the rioting took place, fortunately provided a safe haven as well as a vantage point for the BBC team – Charles and Gerry Priestland, producers and crew – and for other members of the press who were suddenly targets for the police.

The Chicago Convention anointed Vice President Hubert H. Humphrey with the Democratic nomination for the presidency – a man whose oratory style Charles wryly described as 'rousing stuff but more often than not rousing the speaker himself, rather than his audience'. But it exposed and deepened the rifts in the Democratic Party. Reporting from the floor of the convention hall, Charles and the BBC team stuck close to the candidate Eugene McCarthy and his anti-war New York delegation – they were singing 'We Shall Overcome', the anthem of the civil rights movement, even as Daley's police made history by moving onto the floor of the convention hall itself to clear them. 'The whole world is watching,' chanted delegates as their comrades were led off.

Charles painted the scene a few hours later for his radio listeners. 'At three a.m., after the convention had adjourned and Humphrey had been nominated, five hundred delegates caucused down here at the amphitheatre. The battle by this time had subsided but the delegates sat on the grass with the youngsters and sang songs of protest while the National Guardsman stood in a tight line within six feet of the group, with their rifles held pointing in the air.'

Charles didn't stop there – he worked straight through the night and into the next morning. In another radio dispatch, he concluded: 'The wounds the party has suffered in the past twenty-four hours are going to take far longer to heal than the gashes suffered by many of the demonstrators at the hands of the police. The Chicago paper now on the newsstands sums up the feeling of many people in this city in a banner headline: "Humphrey Candidacy a Shambles".'

Public opinion was not on the demonstrators' side. Sixty-six per cent of America supported the use of force against them and Richard Nixon, the Republican challenger for the presidency, jumped ahead right after Chicago with a 16 per cent lead. Scores of left-leaning Democrats deserted Humphrey after Chicago and many white working-class voters looked to the demagogue of the South, George Wallace, running as an independent. That disunity, as Charles reflected in his reports from the 1968 campaign trail, was to Nixon's great advantage. His supporters were already taking victory for granted and their rallies resembled victory celebrations rather than campaign stops, with defeat only the barest of possibilities. 'Local politicians here call him Mr President,' Charles reported.

In late autumn, the Republican lead suddenly started to flatten. Old loyalties were falling back into place and there were signs of a change in the administration's approach in Vietnam. Humphrey was actively courting the anti-war camp and Johnson was trying to sue for peace, attempting to change course and inviting the North Vietnamese to the negotiating table in Paris.

On the last day of October, Charles reported LBJ's announcement to the nation: a halt to all US air, naval and artillery bombing of North Vietnam. This, said the president, was due to real progress in the Paris talks, the prospect of a peaceful settlement and, as he put it, the 'essential understanding that we had been seeking with the North Vietnamese for some time'. Johnson announced that 'predictive talks' would take place the following week between all sides. But he added, 'I should warn you, fellow Americans, arrangements of this kind are never foolproof.' After five months of deadlock, the negotiating efforts of the Johnson administration looked like they were finally paying off, with an understanding from Hanoi that it would not exploit a pause in the US bombing by intensifying attacks against South Vietnamese cities.

Charles and the rest of the press corps reported Nixon's campaign trail declarations that 'peace, not politics, was the most important thing'. While Nixon had already earned his nickname Tricky Dicky two decades earlier during the 1950 Senate elections, none of the White House press corps suspected what was going on – and how hollow his words really were.

Behind the scenes an extraordinary drama of breathtaking deceit was playing out – one that would only become clear three decades later through painstaking research by Charles and David Coxon Taylor. With corroborating testimonies from Johnson's former advisors, Clark Clifford, who had taken over as secretary of defence, and William Bundy, assistant secretary of state for Far Eastern affairs , Charles and David pieced together a series of disjointed accounts and rumours to reveal a shocking story. With the US administration days from the beginning of meaningful peace talks with their allies in the south and the Communist north poised to meet each other in Paris, Nixon and members of his team were deliberately sabotaging these efforts. Their aim was simple: to ensure Humphrey gained no advantage from any diplomatic breakthrough and ultimately, of course, to avert Nixon's own defeat in the presidential race. The cost in lives lost in Vietnam was of secondary importance.

The interviews and conversations Charles and David carried out with Clifford and Bundy in 1995 for *Wheeler on America* convinced them that Nixon was engaged in his own back-channel talks, using an 'agent' called Anna Chennault, a Chinese-born Republican with links to the South Vietnamese ambassador. Clifford told Charles her main contact was none other than John Mitchell, Nixon's campaign manager, who as Nixon's attorney general later served time in jail for his part in the Watergate burglary and cover-up. Clifford said he was in no doubt that Madame Chennault, codenamed 'Little Flower' by the CIA, was 'intimately' connected with the Nixon campaign and that she was acting and speaking on Nixon's behalf. 'She was in almost daily conversation with the South Vietnamese ambassador and they were plotting ways to delay the peace talks before the election,' Clifford told Charles. 'The word was if the South Vietnamese would boycott the peace talks, they would get a much better deal from Nixon in the White House.'

David told me that at the time of their interview, Clifford was very frail. 'He was actually dying of cancer. We rented a hotel suite so he could rest during tape changes. Charles and I really had the sense that he wanted to unburden himself before he died and that's partly why he'd agreed to the interview.'

William Bundy, Clifford's deputy at the time, also went on the record to tell Charles and David he was 'categorical' that Nixon was personally involved in the plot. Bundy's 'source' told him Nixon had met with the South Vietnamese ambassador at his New York apartment in July 1968 to introduce Anna Chennault as his personal emissary to the South Vietnamese government. 'There is no question in my mind that the Republicans intervened to stop that bombing halt or at least to prevent the South Vietnamese to agreeing to it at once, and that Thieu [president of South Vietnam] accepted this in his own interest and also in the belief that it would gain him credit with the Republicans and with Nixon specifically if they were elected,' he revealed.

Three days before the election, Clark Clifford broke the news to Johnson that the South Vietnamese leaders had gone back on their pledge to take part in the Paris peace talks – and it had been because of the Nixon campaign telling them to stay away.

'Why didn't you blow the whistle?' asked Charles. The problem was, as Clifford explained, the Johnson team knew what Nixon had been up to thanks to their own dubious activities, including routine spying on US allies. They had been bugging the South Vietnam embassy's phone calls and intercepting the ambassador's cables to President Thieu in Saigon. They weren't sure they would be believed and proving it would mean airing classified intelligence assets. William Bundy warned Humphrey that outing Nixon could trigger a constitutional crisis. And so they stayed silent, hoping they would win the election anyway.

On 5 November, America went to the polls. Nixon won by a tiny margin, less than 1 per cent ahead in the popular vote. It was another four years before the sides got round the negotiating table again – costing tens of thousands more American and Vietnamese lives. Charles later called this deliberate sabotage of Johnson's peace efforts 'the dirtiest of Nixon's lifetime of dirty tricks – his worst crime, overshadowing Watergate in my view ... Watergate was a horror. It diminished the presidency, which has limped ever since. But at least it didn't cost any lives.'

In 1968 alone, nearly 17,000 American soldiers died in Vietnam, and, by the end of that year, 36,731 US soldiers had been killed there in total, with more than half a million US troops committed to the fighting. The last twelve months had also seen the assassinations of Martin Luther King and Bobby Kennedy, and the eruption of violence on American streets.

SHIRIN WHEELER

As the year drew to a close, the space race offered some respite from international humiliation and grief. While the Apollo moonshot missions had their critics, not least from civil rights activists who argued the money would be better spent alleviating the dire poverty of thousands of Americans, they also offered a different, more uplifting narrative for the times. It would be the first mission to take humans to the moon and back, transmitting live TV pictures of its surface and photographs of the earthrise from 'deep space'.

The BBC threw everything at it. Charles joined a platoon of reporters working around the clock for five days quartered at NASA HQ over Christmas to deliver blow-by-blow updates of the launch, the orbit, re-entry and splashdown.

Dip, Marina and I duly decamped from a snowy Washington, D.C. too, pitching up at a central Houston hotel. On Christmas Eve, the Apollo 8 astronauts Borman, Lovell and Anders watched a lunar sunrise and sent blessings down to Earth with a reading from Genesis. We listened from the hotel room and hung a few of our glass *kugels* (German baubles transported lovingly by Dip in egg boxes and tissue paper from Berlin) on a cactus-like miniature tree Charles had found somewhere near the airport. Marina and I hoped Father Christmas would find his way to Texas and avoid any collisions with the orbiting space capsule. He did, and we woke to find wrapped matching pyjamas under the tree.

Profoundly grateful for some distraction from the war as he prepared to leave the presidency, President Johnson awarded the three astronauts medals once they got back to Earth. In return, they gave him a photo of the beloved LBJ ranch (or at least somewhere nearby, as the ever-sceptical Charles reported), taken from space, and a miniature copy of the International Space Treaty.

*

As well as coverage of empire-building in space, Charles's beat during those years also extended to cover South America and the Caribbean. In the course of writing this book, I found in his papers sketches of section headings were he ever to attempt a memoir himself. 'Caribbean Interlude' includes a clutch of highly colourful stories he covered, including the US invasion of the Dominican Republic, the powerful presence of Vodou at the funeral of Haiti's dictator, 'Papa Doc' Duvalier, and the British military operation in Anguilla in 1969. The alarm in Britain over an apparent revolution in this tiny Caribbean colony was out of all proportion to what was actually happening on the ground. The British sent hundreds of paratroops and several Metropolitan Police officers, all of whom found they had nothing to do. Charles and an equally huge force of journalists were in a similar position. The American networks saw the whole thing as a farce and dubbed it 'The Bay of Piglets', but Charles's reports played it characteristically straight, letting the absurdity of the story speak for itself. Anguilla's very peaceful revolution and very pleasant palm-fringed beaches also offered Charles an enjoyable break from Washington life – at the BBC's expense.

In early January 1971, the kidnapping of Geoffrey Jackson, the British ambassador to Uruguay, saw Charles heading south to Montevideo. Once there, he found himself teaming up with his friend, the *Guardian*'s Adam Raphael; together, they interviewed the embassy's press people and pieced together the story. The ambassador had been en route to his office when his attackers rammed his vehicle, dragged out the driver and raced off with Jackson still inside. But once Charles and Adam had filed to their news desks there was little to add. They began to find the wait for briefings from the embassy increasingly tedious and came up with an idea to pass the time.

'Charles and I decided to re-stage the kidnapping,' Adam told me. 'Charles's car took the role of the ambassador's while mine was the Tupamaros kidnappers' car behind him, which came to a halt and whisked him off. It was a fairly elaborate reconstruction. Of course, we were promptly arrested by the Uruguayan secret police, as we'd been doing it in the exact spot where the kidnap had taken place.'

The two men were thrown into a cell and held by armed guards for six hours, then taken to be interrogated by the commandant. The commandant was so mesmerised by Charles's display of sangfroid, it seems, that, far from locking them up, he gave them an interview and a scoop on the kidnap. 'Charles was a splendid man to be held under gunpoint with,' recalls Adam. The matter didn't turn out so well for Ambassador Jackson, though, and the reporters were safely back in Washington long before his release from a damp dungeon eight months later.

One of the most emotionally charged stories Charles reported on during his time in America was the inquiry into the massacre perpetrated by US troops at My Lai. The world learnt of My Lai at the end of 1969. The unprovoked killing of hundreds of unarmed South Vietnamese civilians, including women, babies and the old, had been covered up for a year and a half. Charlie

Company, I/20th Infantry Battalion, 11th Infantry Brigade, was on the hunt for the Viet Cong, who had a stronghold in the area. They weren't in the village that day but the civilians who were were gang-raped, mutilated and murdered by American troops. The world had been given an even more horrifying glimpse into the darkness of the American mission in Vietnam.

Charles covered the Peers Commission Inquiry into the massacre and the alleged cover-up. Then came the court martial of twenty-seven-year-old Lieutenant William Calley, who had led members of Charlie Company into the village. He pleaded not guilty to the charge of murdering 120 people. Standing under a line of trees outside the unassuming courthouse at Fort Benning, the US Army's Infantry School in Georgia, Charles summed up the prosecution case.

His almost flat delivery, using the language of the military court, can't mask the horror of what he is telling us. In the report, he relays Calley's words to his soldiers: 'Why didn't you take care of these people? I meant kill them,' Calley said, before he ordered his soldiers to fire and picked up the gun himself when one officer refused. Children, babies, their mothers were put into an irrigation ditch and, under Calley's orders, executed. The jury heard that Calley made sure anyone still alive was finished off; an escaping child was thrown back into the ditch and shot and an old man beaten and killed by Calley himself.

The Peers Inquiry had recommended charges against twenty-eight soldiers but Calley was the only one ever convicted. The military had trouble even assembling a jury of objective soldiers, as most clearly wanted to clear the army's name even before the trial had begun, but they did find Calley guilty of murdering twenty-two people, sentencing him to life in an army prison. He barely served six months in total as President Nixon intervened to change his sentence to house arrest, allowing him to serve most of that time in his own apartment. The top brass of the US military were entirely absolved of legal responsibility for what happened at My Lai.

It was a depressing outcome and Charles felt it. The piece to camera that he delivered at the end of the inquiry is uncompromising in its condemnation of conservative America. Often reticent as he was, for a TV reporter, about appearing in front of camera, it's clear watching it now that Charles wants to say something here. He delivers an articulate outpouring on the state of America – simultaneously highly emotional and analytical: 'All wars blunt people's sensitivity and that may perhaps be especially the case when the enemy belongs to another race. Yet there seems to be more to it than this.' He goes on, 'One wonders if American society isn't more callous and more selfish than others who have grown out of the frontier stage. A very large silent majority didn't even blink when the police and the state indiscriminately gunned down negroes in Newark and Detroit two years ago. A large majority applauded the Chicago police for their brutality last year and came to the defence of the Green Berets. And yet there is another side to this. The more that the older generation clings to its outdated values, the stronger seems to be the urge of the younger generation to alter them and many young people are taking their elders with them. That is what is happening in America today. And for this ageing observer, it's an exciting thing to watch.'

*

Right: Charles aged 8, 1931.

Above: John and Charles at the Baltic seaside, c. 1928.

Left: Charles and his older brother John at RAF Stanmore Park, on John's last leave with the family before his death in April 1941.

Above: Charles aged 20 with AU 30 aboard German gun boat near Caen.

Right: Captain Charles Wheeler aged 21 with 'loot' taken from partly submerged German patrol boat at the Chantiers Navals near Blainville July 1944.

Below: Members of 30 AU with the Dubois family at the Liberation of Granville, Normandy in August 1944, from L–R: 'Bicoulette' Dubois, Mme Dubois, Marine Mike Wright, Lt Col Patrick Dalzel-Job, Charles (holding his kitten Ginette de St Sauveur) and René Dubois.

Charles covering the Bavarian floods, 1954.

A visitor from the Soviet Zone to the BBC Berlin office speaking to Charles – 1953 photo by Fritz Eschen.

Charles' first TV appearance, as a producer on *Panorama* reporting on the Hungarian Uprising in Sopron, November 1956. © BBC

Right: Interview for BBC News with future Prime Minister of India, Indira Gandhi, Delhi, November 1959. © BBC

Left: The Dalai Lama's first ever television interview – with Charles in Delhi for BBC TV, September 1959. © BBC

Right: Charles and Dip on their wedding day, Delhi, 29 March 1962.

Left: Charles with Dip, her siblings and their spouses in Delhi, March 1962. From L–R: Anup, Jagtar, Dip, Charles, Amarjit, Bhagwant, Satwant, Pritam.

Charles and Shirin, Berlin, January 1963.

Charles interviewing Martin Luther King after the Watts riots on 30 August 1965. © BBC.

Covering the Chicago Campaign for Fair Housing with Martin Luther King, September 1966 in Gage Park. © BBC

Left: Richard Nixon's visit to East Berlin, July 1963.

Right: Charles on location at the Senate Foreign Relations Committee, February 1966. © BBC

Below: Dip, Winifred, Shirin, Charles Senior, Marina and Charles in Dormansland, Surrey, Spring 1965.

Above: Charles in the BBC Brussels office c. 1975.

In 'no man's land' just outside Kuwait after the first Gulf War with stranded Sri Lankan and Indian workers, report for *Newsnight*, March 1991. © BBC

Kurdish refugees fleeing Saddam Hussein speaking to Charles on the Iran Iraq border – a report for *Newsnight*, in April 1991. © BBC

Charles on his 80th birthday, The Garden Cottage, 26 March, 2003.

Charles and Dip outside Buckingham Palace having received his Knighthood from the Queen, December 2006.

Renaissance portrait of Eleonara di Toledo by Alesandro Allori, given to Charles by an East German farmer in 1952, and returned to the Gemäldegalerie in Berlin in June 2006.

© *Heritage Image Partnership Ltd / Alamy Stock Photo*

Many of that younger generation Charles put his faith in were themselves counting on the senator for Dakota, George McGovern, as the change candidate in the 1972 presidential race after four years of the Nixon administration. I wasn't exactly the demographic they were targeting, but my own school ring binder was scrawled with slogans – McGovern for President! Dump Nixon! Peace signs and smiley faces ensured no one would mistake my allegiance.

McGovern's chief strategist was Frank Mankiewicz, who had been Bobby Kennedy's press secretary up until that terrible night in 1968 when he saw his candidate dying in the hallway of a Los Angeles hotel kitchen. He'd become a family friend to Charles and Dip. As the Wisconsin primary coincided with the Easter school holidays, he and his wife Holly suggested the whole family went along for the ride, as Charles would be covering the primary anyway.

We boarded a train for Milwaukee. The McGovern campaign had enlisted the help of singer Paul Simon in support of their candidate at an opening rally. I was so excited. I'd already learnt most of the lyrics off by heart from the LP Charles had given me. We had ringside seats and had dressed up for it: my mother in an orange and pink silk sari, and Marina and I in matching kilts from Marks and Spencer. McGovern won the primary and the Wheeler girls became even firmer fans.

Charles carried on with McGovern on the campaign trail – first they hit the rural state of Oklahoma, then Texas and the city of San Antonio, where Charles noted 'every third person seemed to work for the United States Airforce'. Faced with a potentially hostile crowd, McGovern's speech surprised Charles and the rest of the press corps travelling with him. Charles ran it in his piece for the BBC TV news that night: 'Some twenty-nine years ago I was in San Antonio as an Air Force cadet in the Second World War. I think all Americans at that time were proud of this nation and the role we were playing in the world. I want to see that pride in our country restored on the part of Americans, young and old alike. We cannot restore a sense of pride in ourselves or a sense of confidence in our government when we pick up the morning newspaper and see the spectacle of little children running burned with napalm from American planes.' The applause was loud, and Charles noted that for a moment it felt almost like Bobby Kennedy's 1968 campaign. 'Except for Wallace, no other Democrat can attract these crowds,' he remarked.

But the Wallace effect was drilling into Democratic support, splitting candidates and moving some of them to the right. The campaign trail had taken Charles to the Florida primary where there was a crowd of candidates standing for the Democrats, including Hubert Humphrey, Edmund Muskie, George McGovern, George Wallace, Senator 'Scoop' Jackson of Washington and John Lindsay, the mayor of New York. As Charles reported from the 'Sunshine State', the presidential process was becoming a war of attrition. 'This Democratic primary is probably the silliest of the lot,' he told viewers. 'Eleven would-be presidents, all of them Democrats, are driving themselves into the ground and spending literally millions of dollars in this state, competing against each other. Fortunately, some of them will do so badly that they will have to drop out of the race altogether. Meanwhile, two men are profiting.' One, he said, was Richard Nixon. The other was George Wallace, the extremist from Alabama who, paradoxically, 'seems to grow more popular as America grows more moderate'.

Wallace was holding four rallies a week in Florida, attracting 3,000 people each time with a message on racial segregation that seemed to please the voters, especially on the explosive issue of bussing. Charles and the team told the story of Richmond Heights High School in Miami-Dade County, where Black and white kids were learning and playing together with no tension or conflict, according to pupils and teachers there. Children were being brought in from other neighbourhoods to the largely Black Miami suburb by bus to ensure an integrated environment and a fair chance of a good education. Like any of today's avid culture warriors, Wallace swooped on the opportunity to make trouble and argued it was in fact a question of civil rights for the white community. Charles remarked that there was no issue until Wallace arrived and made it the core theme of his primary campaign.

Since the days of Selma and Montgomery, Wallace had expunged the ugliest words from his lexicon but, Charles noted, 'His message is the racist message of the old days, only the words have changed. And in bussing, Wallace has found a ready-made issue that only needs fanning to make it blaze from south to north, and from coast to coast.'

Charles had already reflected on Wallace's place on the political spectrum, and on his staying power. During a Wallace rally during the previous Presidential campaign one young, smooth-faced Wallace supporter in his boater hat and sunglasses was questioned by Charles about his candidate's appeal.

He replied, 'He's trying to bring America back to what it should be. He's tired, as is most of America. Tired of seeing these pseudo-intellectuals, as he calls them, these hippies and yippies and rioters burning and looting America. It's got to stop.'

It all sounds awfully familiar. As Charles said, 'Wallace is not a prepossessing figure but this, in a way, is the source of his strength. For millions of people who feel they have nothing in common with the top people that habitually run for president, he is one of us. Standing up for us against "them". Ask any Wallace supporter why he's a Wallace disciple and he'll probably tell you this: "what we've been thinking for years, George Wallace comes out and says in public".'

Wallace won the Florida primary with every county except Miami itself. But his presidential bid was soon to be cut short. In mid-May, he was speaking at a rally at the Laurel Shopping Center in Maryland. Charles called the camera crew, Eric Thirer and Bill Baglin, who were on one of their three-month stints from London: 'George Wallace is going to be in Maryland,' he said. 'We ought to go and look at that.'

Eric, then in charge of the sound, remembers driving to the shopping centre some forty-five minutes out of D.C. 'There was a huge crowd. We were standing in some kind of parking lot.' Earlier that day, Wallace had been pelted with eggs and tomatoes at a rally in Wheaton. But the atmosphere at Laurel seemed good-humoured. Wallace finished speaking from a bullet-proof podium that he carried around with him. He ended the speech and stepped forward to the edge of the platform, saluted the crowd with his trademark short motion and then took off his coat and walked down a couple of steps into a crowd of his supporters waving Stars and Stripes, many sporting Wallace straw hats. Someone shouted, 'George, come over here, I want to shake your hand!' Then, suddenly, there was a huge bang. Eric told me, 'And that was it. Charles said in a matter-of-fact way, "Oh, they've shot him. They've shot him." We just stayed there and carried on filming.'

Before the shooting, Bill and Eric had been filming from the roof of a van, which was actually full of refrigerated tear gas. The police told them it also held 500 shotguns. There were twelve Secret Servicemen and Charles estimated another fifty to sixty officers on the scene as well. As he put it, 'The security seemed out of all proportion to the need. But in fact, at that moment, no one was looking. It's the usual situation that the candidate is well protected when he's on the podium but when he moves into the crowd anything can happen.'

He recalled how he rushed forward to take a closer look as immediate panic swept over the crowd. 'There were people stampeding, women screamed, the MC called, "get back, get back" on the loudspeaker. The crowd pounced on a man. The police then pounced on the crowd, extricated the man and they carried him around the car park, five of them.'

It was Arthur Bremner, the would-be assassin – short, blond, crewcut, about thirty. He looked like a typical Wallace supporter: 'He was wearing Stars and Stripes socks and a Stars and Stripes vest under his shirt,' said Charles. 'He was badly knocked about. He had at least three teeth missing and there was blood running down his face. Meanwhile, Wallace was lying on the ground obviously bleeding – one could see roughly from the position of the lower rib cage on the right-hand side.

His wife kneeling beside him, crying.' The shooting would leave Wallace permanently paralysed from the waist down and in almost constant pain.

Within two hours, Charles was live on the line to London from the BBC studio in M Street in Washington describing the scene to the BBC audience. 'The police arrangements were in fact very bad. They carried the suspect around the car park almost three times looking for somewhere to put him and finally bunged him in a car and sat on him – the ambulance took five minutes to come.'

The minutes of the internal review meeting for BBC News that week record the opinion that the Wallace shooting was a key moment in television news. 'This was an extraordinary example of the global nature of television, with so many people around the world made so quickly aware of an appalling event at a minor political meeting in Maryland.' The minutes also remark on 'Charles Wheeler's astonishing capacity to be in the right place at the right time'.

The relentless election roadshow carried on. Next stop was Miami where, in July 1972, Dip, Marina and I rejoined Charles as the candidates converged for the Democratic Convention, an event that made very little impression on the American television-watching public. We had many hours by the pool at our base in the sprawling Fontainebleau Hotel on Miami Beach, some of it with Charles and the camera crew, Bill and Eric, who were fast becoming our honorary uncles. Jumping around in the water one day, I got chummy with a young blonde girl around my age called Janie-Lee. She introduced the tall man in a dark and hot-looking suit lurking around the edge of the water as her bodyguard and invited me up to play and get snacks in her hotel room. We entered a darkened, air-conditioned room, the blinds drawn. A man in a wheelchair sat against the window, dark hair, heavy eyebrows, pale. 'This is my daddy,' she said. I said hello. He asked my name and we had a snack: Hostess Twinkies and some orange juice. Though he'd seemed a little intimidating to begin with, he was very nice to me, and I felt sad about him having to sit there all the time in a wheelchair, in the dark.

Later that evening, Charles took me to a pre-convention gala meeting in the ballroom of the Sheraton Four Ambassadors Hotel, to which the press (and their tag-along daughters) were invited. I suddenly became aware of a child on the stage urging delegates to cast their ballot for her father and introducing his speech, saying, 'The reason my daddy should have the presidential nomination is that he has a lot of experience in government and even though he's in a wheelchair he can do most of things that he used to do when he could walk.' It was Janie-Lee, my new friend from the pool. And her father was George Wallace, governor of Alabama, presidential candidate, and known to most as an unapologetic racist and segregationist. Her entreaties came to nothing, and George McGovern was confirmed as the Democrats' presidential candidate.

Both conventions were held in Miami that year so, a couple of weeks later, the White House press corps was back in Florida to see the incumbent, President Richard Nixon, crowned with the Republican nomination and announce his running mate for vice president. Spiro Agnew was as oleaginous as his boss: a man Charles described as a 'northern, suburban George

Wallace . . . intolerant in his views, crude in his arguments, and indiscriminate in his choice of targets'. But for many in the press corps, the really entertaining story of the convention was an off-camera drama with Charles at its centre.

In its first term, the Nixon administration was remarkable in building up an impressive public relations machine. The aggressive White House press secretary, Ron Ziegler, earned a reputation for bullying and intimidating the press corps, dividing and then ruling them. The Nixon crew were slicker and more media-savvy than the Johnson people had been: many had a background in advertising, specifically at the ad company J. Walter Thompson. Thanks to Charles, they were about to have their feathers severely ruffled.

In the press area of the convention site, the BBC had set up camp in a tiny pasteboard cubicle, jam-packed with tables and recording equipment. Gas masks hung on the walls in case of demonstrations and tear gas in the city. Charles was leading a team of producers, crew and reporters, including a young, New York-based John Humphrys, future presenter of the BBC's *Today* programme. In contrast to the Democrats' shambolic event, which managed to be by turns tedious and dramatic, the Republicans' gathering was a far more stage-managed affair. But no one suspected that it was literally choreographed down to the last minute until a junior member of the Nixon team mistakenly posted into the BBC's pigeon-hole a detailed, word-for-word, minute-by-minute script of Nixon's acceptance speech and the proceedings to come, complete with stage directions. Charles must have been chortling with delight as he leafed through a pack of press releases and stumbled on this gem. It instructed Nixon and his support act, the Hollywood star and Republican stalwart John Wayne, exactly when to nod, pause and acknowledge applause. It set down that at 10.33 precisely the president would be nominated and there would be a 'ten-minute spontaneous demonstration with balloons'.

As the BBC team congratulated themselves on getting their hands on Nixon's own personal dope sheet, three messengers from the Republican comms team appeared and demanded the document back. Charles said it was out of the question, at least until he'd finished reading it and making notes. The hapless messengers returned a few minutes later with a woman from the Republican National Committee Press Center called Kit Wisdom, who snatched the script straight out of Charles's hands. As John Humphrys told me, 'Charles grabbed it right back and we were literally throwing it to each other around the cubicle. He was having none of it. He was definitely the hero of the hour.' Charles delivered a live account of the shenanigans for the TV and radio bulletins and the story was gleefully taken up by sections of the American press.

Charles had already been in full troublemaking mode earlier in the year over Nixon's famous trip to China – the first of any American president. The China visit was part of a pre-election strategy and foreign correspondents working for non-American outlets were not included in the plan. They would have to make do instead with pictures shot by one broadcaster and shared with the others via the agencies and US networks. Charles was highly irritated at the snub, and the night before Nixon's departure mounted an attempt at organised resistance over the exclusion of non-American correspondents. As

Timothy Crouse, reporter for *Rolling Stone* magazine, relates in his book, *The Boys on the Bus*, 'Charles Wheeler tried to organise a boycott of a cocktail party the White House was giving for correspondents who weren't going to Peking. "My God," Wheeler said later, "they had made space for parish newsletters with circulations of seven hundred and fifty, but they weren't allowing any foreign correspondents to go. And then they tried to buy us off with a cocktail party. So I phoned around and said I didn't think we ought to go to the party. But several people went anyway just for fear that they might miss something."'

The machinations of the president's men paid off, initially, anyway. There were already rumblings around a burglary in June 1972 at the Democratic Party Campaign HQ at the Watergate building but they didn't put so much as a dent in Nixon's performance at the polls. That was even though the connection with CREEP, the Committee to Re-elect the President, had already been made by the reporters Bob Woodward and Carl Bernstein at the *Washington Post* well before the election, suggesting the break-in was linked to a wider plot of spying and illegal bugging by the Nixon campaign team. The extent to which the president's inner circle was implicated in the break-in and the elaborate cover-up that followed would only gradually emerge after months of congressional hearings, eventually leading to a constitutional crisis and the resignation of Nixon himself.

Four days before the voters went to the polls on 7 November 1972, Charles noted that 'the Democratic candidate George McGovern appears to have little chance of being elected'. He was right. Nixon won the election with a historic landslide, taking forty-nine out of fifty states. McGovern had paid the price of raising real issues in the campaign, Ted Kennedy, younger brother of John and Bobby, told Charles during a post-mortem interview on the BBC's *Friday Talk* programme, chaired by Charles and his colleague Robin Day. All through the '72 campaign, Nixon had refused to engage in any kind of debate while McGovern had attempted to tackle thorny topics like race, accessible health care and eduction and the Vietnam war. 'How is it that an incumbent candidate is able to campaign for weeks and weeks without taking a single question from a voter or a journalist? How does he get away with it?' Charles had asked, rhetorically. Kennedy conceded that this was a blow for liberalism and that 'the American people have become more insensitive to the brutalisation of the war in South-East Asia as well as the contamination of the political atmosphere in the United States.'

Kennedy retained some optimism, however. Despite what he listed as the Nixon legacy of 'secrecy in government, the intimidation of the press and media . . . the dual standard of justice . . . and the corruption in government', the Democrats had kept control of both chambers of the Congress and even increased their senators by two (including a young Joe Biden for Delaware). He added, 'I'd say in the Watergate scandal [with regards to the involvement of Nixon], we'll just have to wait and see. But there's no question that . . . the high White House officials were involved in it up to their ears.'

He wasn't wrong. In the following year, the combined efforts of press and Congress, with its Democratic majority, would help to expose the involvement of Nixon's closest aides, demonstrating a determination to uncover and investigate the Watergate Scandal, culminating in impeachment proceedings against the president.

Fifty years on, it's hard not to be amazed, given his strong showing in the polls ahead of the election, that Nixon and his aides ever even entertained the notion of the Watergate burglaries, bugging the headquarters of the Democratic campaign and then constructing the cover-up that followed. It seems beyond reason. Charles believed Nixon's psychological flaws led to these decisions: 'His personal insecurity and fear of defeat at the polls did drive him to extremes, as his choice of political associates and his cover-up of Watergate eventually revealed.'

What really struck Charles about Watergate in hindsight was the extent to which public servants who had no direct involvement in the buggings or the burglaries were persuaded to become 'accomplices' in the cover-up: Richard Helms, director of the CIA, who apparently agreed to block the FBI investigation because it was colliding with a CIA investigation; FBI director Patrick Gray, who prevented his own agents from pursuing their inquiries.

At the start of February 1973, the Senate voted unanimously to set up a special committee to investigate Watergate. North Carolina Democrat Sam Ervin was appointed as chair. Meanwhile, a trail of clues and semi-confessions from some of the burglars who had been caught in the act at the Watergate building was leading federal prosecutors inexorably to the White House. Judge Sirica, presiding over the trial of the Watergate burglars at the District Court for the District of Columbia, was also flushing out more information that pointed to the involvement of government officials.

John Dean, Nixon's special counsel, who had been tasked with heading an 'internal' investigation and cooperating with FBI investigators, broke ranks and started to cooperate with the federal prosecutors instead. As the Nixon political balloon started to lose altitude, the president threw Dean out of the White House and accepted the resignations of his chief advisor, John Ehrlichman, and chief of staff, Bob Haldeman.

The Watergate Hearings were broadcast live, beginning on 17 May. The drama was beamed into TV sets across the country, then re-broadcast in full every evening in primetime slots. Inevitably, the BBC went big on the story too. Charles sat in the press seats of the Watergate committee most days, along with John Humphrys, who'd been sent to D.C. as things hotted up.

Charles's reporting of the Watergate scandal and the hearings suddenly became a regular fixture for television and radio domestic audiences in Britain. The BBC carried live coverage and analysis of the goings-on in the Senate committee on special programmes like *Midweek* and in the news bulletins. One of those glued to his set was then fifteen-year-old Mark Thompson, a future director general of the BBC and CEO of the *New York Times* and CNN. He told me, 'As a young teenager, I became enthralled by Watergate and stayed up night after night to watch the Senate hearings and Charles's reporting of them on the BBC. He was one of the main reasons I decided to become a journalist myself, some six or seven years later, and devote my whole life to the thing.'

Among the first to appear before the seven senators was John

Dean. My mother had brought the small TV set into the kitchen at home so she could watch the hearings while she prepared our after-school snacks without missing anything. I still remember the sight of Mo, Dean's ice-cool wife, sitting behind him in the committee room. Her smooth blonde hair was pulled back, her face so composed it barely moved, as her husband named his former colleagues Haldeman; Erlichman; John Mitchell, the attorney general; Jeb Magruder, deputy director of White House communications and, of course, Nixon himself as complicit in the cover-up. It was gripping stuff. The Watergate conspirators were family men, clean cut, and yet 'seasoned liars', as Charles put it. We knew some of them as neighbours and fellow parents at school. Gail Magruder dropped her daughter Tracey, Marina's best friend, at the house on the day her husband, Jeb, testified to the committee so she could be by his side. That was the only day in those weeks that the TV was switched off, to spare Tracey the sight of her father being grilled by members of Congress. But I knew he was in trouble, and it was hard to square the idea of this friendly father, whom we'd met at home with his family, now in the news facing grave accusations.

On 29 June, Charles was granted the first exclusive interview on Watergate with John Ehrlichman, President Nixon's former chief advisor on domestic policy. It was two weeks before Ehrlichman's own testimony before the Watergate Committee. Listening back to the interview, what emerges clearly is the sense of the special advisor, known today as a 'SPAD', who appears to feel no loyalty to anyone but his boss. Like Robert McNamara, who as an unelected official felt firmly and solely accountable to Johnson, with no compulsion to inform Congress about the progress of the Vietnam War, Ehrlichman was staunchly one of the president's men. 'I wasn't there to make friends, I was here to support the president,' he told Charles.

'Do you ever have the slightest feeling that you might have been abandoned in your hour of need by the White House if it was a question of saving the president or the presidency?' Charles asked him.

'Well, that's a good cause, you know,' he sparred, 'if you need a cause for abandonment.'

In the recording, it sounds like Charles is employing his old wartime interrogator's skills. He started off the interview as if it were a friendly chat, putting his victim at his ease: 'I heard you were in England during the war. Tell me about that.'

'I was in the Eighth Air Force,' Ehrlichman replied. 'I was a navigator and we were up in Suffolk. Very nice.'

But before long, the gloves came off.

Charles steered the interview to the subject of dirty tricks, the absence of any meaningful internal investigation into the burglary and to John Dean's credibility. Ehrlichman told Charles he wouldn't comment directly on Dean's testimony ahead of his own appearance at the committee but, in what feels like a kind of dry run ahead of that appearance, he seemed to clearly be trying to pin it all on Dean, although the suggestion that this relatively junior member of the inner circle could have masterminded a cover-up that none of his bosses knew about was already looking distinctly threadbare.

This is the line of questioning Charles pursued: 'Now, at what level in the White House could such an elaborate operation have been conducted and maintained for so many months without people as omnipresent as yourself and Mr Halderman, [who] had their fingers on virtually every operation of major importance, knowing about it?'

'It did,' replied Erlichman. 'How it happened I think is that everybody in the place was looking to Mr Dean as the person responsible for collecting the information concerning wrongdoing.'

'So, there was a Dean investigation?'

'I am satisfied that there was . . .'

'[Dean] also says that because he was part of the cover-up, he couldn't have been doing an investigation,' Charles countered. 'So Dean, in plain English, is lying to the committee.'

Erlichman was not willing to go there. 'Well, that's what you said – I didn't say it.'

'I said it. What sort of a man is he? From your knowledge of him?' Charles asked.

Erlichman was less than complimentary. 'He's a very inexperienced young man . . . a very low-powered chap.'

At this point, Charles pounced: 'Was he capable of organising a cover-up, being the principal figure in a cover-up, in an administration of this type, in a White House with so much talent around him?'

Erlichman replied, 'I think the facts speak for themselves on that.'

'The facts?' jabbed Charles.

'Yes sir,' answered Erlichman.

Within twelve months of that interview, Ehrlichman was convicted of charges that included perjury and obstruction of justice. He served seven months of a one-to-three-year sentence.

The minutes of the weekly meeting of BBC bigwigs record the 'scoop' and it is evident that they were cock-a-hoop that the BBC had 'cracked him first'. Re-reading the full transcript of the interview, I can't help but feel that, after going several rounds in the ring with Charles, there's no definitive point where Ehrlichman is down and out for the count. He is guarded, his performance is pure equivocation, and he deploys his full lawyerly arsenal to obscure and confuse. But the fact is, Charles lands several telling blows and his questioning draws out answers that ultimately make it difficult to believe a word Ehrlichman says. And so, while there was no clear knockout victory, an impartial judge might well have concluded that Charles won on points.

In July, the testimony of Alexander Butterfield, former presidential appointments secretary, revealed the existence of presidential tapes with recordings of conversations and telephone calls since 1971. A request to hand them over from the Senate Watergate Committee and the special prosecutor Archibald Cox was denied by Nixon himself. A few months later, the tapes were subpoenaed, and the committee, prosecutors and Judge Sirica had the smoking gun they'd been looking for. Nixon was facing impeachment.

Looking back, Charles believed that America had learnt valuable lessons from Watergate – that it had forced the American public to recognise the need for more effective checks on those in power. As he put it, 'it shattered the myth that the office of the president somehow ennobles the incumbent'. But he did question whether Nixon may just have lowered the bar and injected a new cynicism from the electorate.

But despite the Ehrlichman interview and the years prior to that spent focusing his quizzical gaze on the Nixon presidency, Charles was deprived of following the story to its natural conclusion – the denouement of Nixon's resignation in August 1974. The US presidency was facing its biggest crisis and, after eight and a half years in the US, Charles was being moved. The BBC wanted him to take up another posting just as the story was in its final, intensely dramatic stage of unravelling. John Humphrys was to take over in Washington. John Osman, who had become the BBC's radio correspondent when Gerry Priestland returned to London, told me how Charles 'left kicking and screaming'.

'Whichever way you look at it, it was an insane decision,' John Humphrys said when I asked him about it. 'To pull your chief reporter right in the middle of the story. Not one of us could understand it. All kinds of wild rumours started flying around, some propagated by the BBC Washington bureau itself. The only reason we could think was if Downing Street thought there was some use in him going to Brussels from an intelligence perspective. Because there was no apparent journalistic reason.'

In fact, the reasons were probably a lot less cloak and dagger than that. A new chapter in the UK's history was beginning. Europe beckoned. Britain had officially joined the Common Market – the European Community – at the start of the year, alongside Ireland and Denmark. And the BBC decided that a new post of chief correspondent in Europe would send the right signal to the Heath government that the corporation was serious about its coverage. Quite simply, they believed that Charles was the man for the job.

7.

REMAKING EUROPE: THE BRUSSELS YEARS

It is not just a question of whether Britain values membership of the community, it is also a question . . . of what price the community should pay to keep a reluctant Britain in the club.

Charles Wheeler, 'Britain and the Community': *From Our Own Correspondent*, BBC Radio 4, 20 March 1974

In July 1973, the Wheelers said a final farewell to Washington. We sailed from New York harbour and our family friends, the Stevensons, came with us from the capital to see us off. The night before leaving, we took in a showing of a recently restored version of *King Kong* and had dinner in Chinatown. The next day, after a tearful goodbye, we boarded the SS *France* bound for Southampton.

Charles arrived back in England to find he had become famous. I remember boarding a train for London with him that summer and being surprised when he was recognised by a couple who greeted him as if he was a celebrity. It began happening fairly regularly. In fact, his coverage of Watergate and the dramatic undoing of the president's men had made a far bigger impression on British viewers than he'd realised. During his time in Washington, he had appeared on television night after night, coolly analysing and interpreting the extraordinary events taking place in there for a domestic audience. But he wasn't at all comfortable with this new celebrity status, and was known to sometimes mutter, 'I think you mean my brother,' when asked in the street if he was Charles Wheeler, 'off the TV'. Although with his distinctively bushy eyebrows and shock of thick, by now nearly fully grey hair, these sort of distraction techniques probably didn't work.

For all the success and acclaim he was enjoying in his career, however, leaving the US had in many ways been a watershed moment for Charles. Approaching the age of fifty, he'd been feeling anxious about life for longer than most people who knew him were aware. He was restless, both professionally and emotionally. In the previous two years, he had lost both his parents, first Charles senior to leukaemia and then Winifred, who died in her sleep not long afterwards, a month before she was due to come and live with us in America. What's more, the back problems that would plague him for the rest of his life began, something of a blow for such an energetic person. I remember one day after school bounding up the stairs when, unusually, I heard Charles's voice in our parents' bedroom – he would normally be at work. But my mother shooed me away and closed the door, telling me, 'Fa needs to be left in peace.'

As the Washington posting had come to an end after eight years, Charles had found it hard to see the obvious next step in his career. It felt like some in the BBC were pushing him towards a management role to which he felt unsuited. 'I don't enjoy working among sharks; I dislike responsibility for the performance of others; I don't really enjoy responsibility at all,' he wrote in a letter to his former BBC colleague Dick Walker a year before he left for Brussels.

Dick was Charles's senior by some fifteen years and had been the correspondent based in Bonn when Charles arrived in Berlin in 1962. In fact, Dick had got to know Dip much better and, as he pointed out to Charles, the two men 'had barely exchanged more than a hundred words' back in Germany. And yet now they had struck up a correspondence and here was Charles taking the older man into his confidence, expressing the anxiety that the next move, especially if it meant one into the world of management, could not be as exciting and as important journalistically as his time in the United States had been.

'I'm nearly fifty and should learn to behave like an adult and not like an ambitious child,' he went on. Dick's reply offered an intriguing horticultural metaphor to assuage Charles's self-doubt: 'You and I, and our like, are hollyhocks – the rest of them are tomatoes,' he wrote.

And yet Charles was distinctly nervous about being sidelined or missing the right opportunity. While still in Washington, he'd been urged by the head of news and current affairs to apply for the editorship of *Panorama*, but in typically byzantine BBC management style was at the same time made to understand that he probably wouldn't get the post. At a time of exceptional unrest in Northern Ireland, it was also proposed that he might like to head the BBC's operations there as 'controller'. I am not sure he was really tempted, but in the wake of the fatal shooting of fourteen Catholic marchers in the city of Derry by

British troops at the start of 1972 – an incident that would be remembered as 'Bloody Sunday' – Dip deployed her veto to definitively jettison the plan.

The flood of accolades he had been receiving for his reporting in Washington was perhaps in some way adding to the pressure. Charles was now regularly described in internal reports as the corporation's 'pre-eminent correspondent'. In one memo, a manager gushed that 1972 had been 'the Year of Wheeler'. In fact, despite Charles's fears about the direction his career would take, the BBC were clear in their intention that this correspondent was 'of a calibre which requires the corporation to build appropriate posts for him, rather than require him to fit into the present structure. His creative reporting potential must continue to be fully and exclusively exploited, without burdening him with any but the minimum administrative duties,' stated one letter.

And then came the call to Brussels. In January 1973, Britain had joined the European Community, alongside Ireland and Denmark, in the community's first enlargement. Finally shoehorned in after six years of trying, having suffered two successive French vetoes under Charles de Gaulle, this was regarded as a major political win by Edward Heath's Conservative government. With a more receptive leadership in Paris under President Georges Pompidou, the UK government was now ready for a European love affair and, especially, a warm Anglo–French embrace. By moving their chief correspondent to a new posting in Brussels, the BBC was signalling the necessary commitment to the new direction in which Number 10 was steering the country.

Although it lacked the heightened political theatre of the US, Brussels would soon be pitched into a drama of its own. In October 1973, the community was hit by its first international crisis – a global energy shortage triggered by conflict in the Middle East. For Britain, there was to be no honeymoon period, no relaxed getting-to-know-you sessions with her new partners in the EC. The devastating impact of an oil embargo imposed by Arab nations through OPEC, the Organization of Petroleum Exporting Countries, was the first major story Charles would report on in his new post.

Among the Europeans, OPEC's actions were particularly targeted at the Dutch, accused of supporting Israel in the Yom Kippur War against Syria and Egypt. Petrol prices soared, production slowed and, within weeks of our arrival in Brussels, Belgium followed the Netherlands in banning Sunday driving. That meant a new freedom for me and my sister Marina who, like most of the kids in the neighbourhood, were delighted that we could now whizz around the streets on our bicycles, undisturbed and unthreatened by distracted weekend drivers, free to explore our new home, the residential commune of Woluwe St Pierre and its chief delight: the Fritkot (chip hut) in Place Dumon. But that was about as far as the upside went.

One of the most severe effects of the petrol crisis was to take the unity out of the European Community. While most member countries looked for solidarity in the face of oil shortages, perhaps through a fuel-sharing scheme or, at the very least, a common statement, the British and French were arguing that any display of solidarity would make matters worse by provoking the Arab States, who had already explicitly warned the other EC members against sharing oil with the Netherlands. And it didn't go unnoticed that, thanks to their special relationship with ex-colonial Arab countries in the region, France and Britain also felt the oil embargo would hurt them very little.

In Charles's view, the first warning that the nine countries of the EC were heading for a crisis came from the European Parliament. Back then, the parliament seemed more like a gesture towards democratic representation in the EC rather than the real thing and it's fair to say that Charles didn't have a high opinion of it, calling it 'that much maligned talking shop'. By the time I arrived in Brussels in 1995, some twenty-two years later, as BBC political reporter for the Nations and Regions, the community had become a union and the European Parliament was well on its way to taking on the mantle of co-legislator with national governments. I confess I found reporting on the business of this institution – as I did regularly for the BBC's *Record Europe* – extremely interesting, whereas Charles had said, 'I admit I don't go there very often because it is in fact an extremely boring place to go to.' But on this occasion, he found that a debate on energy policy held by MEPs in Strasbourg provided a useful way of gauging political opinion across the community. While the Germans and the Dutch asked (as Charles put it), 'If European industry is going to grind to a standstill, hadn't we better decide that we are all in the same boat and go on to make policy from there?', the British Conservative appointees to the parliament voted against the rest. They rejected a fuel-sharing scheme and any 'equality of misery' that the Dutch were looking for. But by the time the vote was called in the chamber, Charles noted, the French members, ostensibly comrades-in-arms, had gone to bed, leaving their British friends to defend the position alone.

As Charles explained in a *Panorama* special on BBC1 at the start of December, the Anglo–French stand was seen as 'selfish' and proved very unpopular. In private, British diplomats were telling him the UK position was getting harder to defend and out of sync with 'continental' public opinion. A distinctly anti-British sentiment was building in some quarters of the European press, which, improbable as it might seem now, saw the UK as unduly influenced by the French. 'The press in more and more countries are beginning to say that Britain is holding up the unity of Europe and might even destroy it,' Charles observed. In the end, the lights did not go out in the Netherlands due to the 'under the counter' efforts of the oil companies. But the EC's self-respect had taken a battering: 'In a common crisis it had taken up a position of appeasement while two of its larger members, Britain and France, raced each other in pursuit of a special relationship with the oil producers. And it was a gift to the cynics, who were able to say that the community was little more than a rich man's club, and that when the going got rough its members would put their own best interests first.'

By the time the leaders sat down at the summit roundtable in Copenhagen on 14 December 1973, they were more divided than ever. With national interests to the fore, quarrels soon broke out. Although they hadn't officially tabled the topic for discussion, the leaders in Copenhagen 'found oil spreading all over the agenda, like spreading poison', as Charles put it. It clogged up every decision they attempted to make. This was the first summit of European leaders (soon afterwards to be given its own title of European Council) that Charles would cover. I can see the raised eyebrow, hear the hint of impatience in his voice, as he delivers his radio commentary: 'There must have been moments late last Saturday night when the heads of government must have wished they'd postponed the whole tiresome exercise. There they were, miles from the nearest fireplace and without so much as a sandwich, arguing about words . . . This was the darker side of the EC, as hard a bargaining session as you'd expect to find at an encounter between East and West at Helsinki, or Vienna or Geneva.'

That gloomy assessment of the summit was shared by many of the participants themselves – Edward Heath later wrote in his memoirs that it was the worst summit he had ever experienced. Heath desperately wanted some tangible goodies to show an increasingly disenchanted British public, but, with the bill getting larger with every hour of negotiation, the Germans pulled the plug, fed up with the growing sense that the 'Community was a bottomless pit for their Deutschmarks'. In retaliation, Britain also blocked making progress on monetary union.

One of the problems Charles identified was that the loftier ambitions of the EC were getting bogged down by both an obsession with minutiae and a lack of political vision. 'They've been too busy running a market – inexorably devoting whole days and nights to things like coffee powder and pineapple chunks,' he wrote in one dispatch.

Derisory mentions of pineapple chunks pop up fairly regularly in Charles's reports of the time from Brussels. One can only deduce that, while there were undoubtedly some dramatic moments, Charles was not totally gripped by his new brief and was at times exasperated by it. The cost of butter since membership, Franco–German wine wars, not to mention a later conflict over cod, all featured on the menu of stories that Charles was serving up to his audiences. And dominating all of this was the disproportionate size of Britain's budgetary contribution to the community, something that would fester for the next four decades. An internal BBC memo on Charles's first year in the post records, 'There was an inevitable period of settling in, which Charles employed to good effect by mastering all the complex details of EEC procedures. He was soon producing highly informative material on every aspect of Community Affairs, although he did give the impression at times that a certain zest had gone out of his reporting.'

In a dispatch reflecting on the disastrous summit in Denmark's capital, Charles suggested that its inherent weakness began with its conception. 'It was the product of an ambition suddenly to speak out and create a foreign policy and become a force in the world. It can't be done of course between October and December, not by governments that set out common institutions, a parliament in Strasbourg, a commission in Brussels, only to forbid them to make even trivial decisions lest they tread on somebody's national interest.' These kinds of concerns were of course the grist for later historic decisions on European integration. But for the time being, in their intergovernmental club, a prime source of disquiet in the ranks remained the domination of the community by the French and British. As Charles reflected, the Pompidou–Heath axis that Britain had to build to get into the community 'has now become a fact of community life'. For the smaller countries, though, it also resembled 'a bludgeon'. Germany's chancellor, Willy Brandt, who remembered Charles from his time in Berlin, wondered out loud to him how it could be 'in the community's interest that it should be dominated by its two least European-minded partners'. A change in that dynamic would come within a decade, though, with Britain under Mrs Thatcher stepping back from a leading position in Europe while the ultimate power couple, Helmut Kohl and François Mitterrand, headed the charge towards European integration.

At the same time as this very un-communal wrangling was taking place in Brussels, nearby in the grounds of an old chateau in leafy Uccle, Marina and I had joined some 3,000 other young guinea pigs for a fascinating experiment in European cooperation. We entered the new *'section anglaise'* and, alongside other British and Irish children (the Danes had their own small section too), were the latest recruits to the European School. The school was reserved mainly for the children of EC functionaries and diplomats but a few outliers like us with parents in the press corps also snuck in – and Charles and Dip much preferred the idea of a multinational environment to the very expat surroundings of the British School in Tervuren. I was delighted at the fantastic possibilities for friendship and teenage romance that lay before me. To my young eyes, this alternative European Community had a lot going for it, especially with the young Romeos in the Italian section. This was our own community, which, apart from the occasional stone-throwing in the playground between the younger Dutch and German boys, was a far more heart-warming manifestation of European harmony than that on display over in the frosty chambers of the European Council.

At the start of 1974, barely a year after Britain had joined the European Community, Charles was advancing the view that the existential question of Britain's membership was no longer just a domestic issue but had taken a central place in the minds of her European partners as well: 'The question should Britain stay in or get out can no longer be called a spurious issue invented by the British Labour Party to embarrass Mr Heath ... Other people, many dedicated Europeans among them, have now picked up the cue. Some are suggesting it really is time that the British made up their minds for once and for all, whether to stay with the nine or go.'

Labour's knife-edge election victory in February 1974 provided the opportunity for that decision to be taken by the British people themselves. Harold Wilson was back in Downing Street as PM for a third term, though now as leader of a minority government (a second general election, in October, would see the Labour Party returned to power with a wafer-thin majority of three). A return to the council table to try to improve on the entry terms negotiated earlier by Edward Heath's Conservative government was a core element of the Labour Party's famously short election manifesto, as was the promise, insisted on by the anti-marketeer left of the party – figures like Tony Benn and Peter Shore – to put those terms to a vote by the British people in a 'yes' or 'no' referendum. High on Labour's shopping list for renegotiation were the Common Agricultural Policy, the UK's contribution to the EEC budget, the goal of economic and monetary union and the question of parliamentary sovereignty when it came to regional, industrial and fiscal policies. Life was about to get a little more interesting for the BBC team in Brussels. As one BBC manager put it, Charles suddenly seemed to be 'imbued with a new enthusiasm'. This may have been wishful thinking – or it might have been because Charles had detected an enlivening whiff of trouble in the air.

In early spring of 1974, 'Sunny Jim', as Britain's rather bluff foreign secretary James Callaghan was known, was able to reassure his European partners, spooked by Labour's anti-marketeer rhetoric before the election, that Britain was not looking for a confrontation and that renegotiation was not a 'code word for withdrawal'. There was praise for Callaghan's measured tone in his speech to the House of Commons on this issue on 19 March and his politically astute 'studied vagueness', as Charles saw it, which was taken as a sign that Britain would 'feel its way forward, instead of staking out positions that community governments will feel compelled to challenge in public before negotiations begin'. Charles reported that, by and large, it had gone down well in Europe, though Sunny Jim didn't quite put the lid on lingering reservations. As Charles wrote, 'At present, they [Britain's EC partners] are by no means sure that such a thing as British commitment to Europe exists. And their doubts are bound to make themselves felt in the coming negotiations.'

But before the question of membership could be put to the British public, Charles suggested there was another, more immediate question for Britain's European partners: 'It is not just a question of whether Britain values membership of the community, it is also a question, and this dates back to the Conservative Party's final months in office, of what price the community should pay to keep a reluctant Britain in the club.' Nonetheless, as Charles observed, 'The fact is, nobody among the eight wants a divorce in the family . . . the constant debate among the British whether or not to consummate their European marriage is distracting for the Europeans. They would like to see the issue settled and the sooner the better.'

Jim Callaghan's first physical encounter with his EC counterparts took place at the beginning of April. Charles and his crew made the two-hour journey down the motorway to Luxembourg, where the Council of Foreign Ministers meeting was being held. Here, the more bruiserish side of Sunny Jim's style was on display, as he demanded a renegotiation of the UK's Accession Treaty in fairly blunt terms. In his book, *Reluctant European*, Stephen Wall, later UK permanent representative to the EU, cites Michael Palliser, Britain's permanent representative in 1974, who told him that Callaghan 'behaved with gratuitous and embarrassing roughness'. Following the more conciliatory speech to the Commons the previous month, it looked like the foreign secretary was playing both good and bad cop all by himself. Of course, as Wall comments, there was in this 'a bit of theatre'. As would be the case for the next forty years, audiences had to be played to on both sides of the Channel.

Charles's own first encounter with the new Labour government would also prove to be far from cordial. As he recounted to me over a birthday supper a couple of decades later, a large scrum of journalists was waiting outside the room where a press conference was to be held in Luxembourg at the Council of Ministers. The press were impatient and flustered by a delay in starting. When the UK government team turned up, everyone began jostling and pushing to get in. At this point, Charles said, one of the people with the team – a burly Labour Party minder, he assumed – shoved him aside. As a former Royal Marine, Charles wasn't going to take that lying down and, fighting his way in from behind, gave the minder a sharp kick on the ankle. *That must have hurt*, he thought to himself. But he was surprised to see the man limping up to the main table and taking his place alongside Fred Peart, the minister of agriculture. 'Who's the one next to Peart?' he asked a fellow hack. 'It's Roy Hattersley,' was the answer. Charles had just assaulted the new minister for foreign and Commonwealth affairs, later deputy leader of the Labour Party. Luckily, Hattersley never saw the face of his attacker and, as far as I have been able to ascertain through my research, Charles managed to avoid kicking any more of Her Majesty's ministers during his time as chief European correspondent.

The run-up to the referendum of June 1975 brought a national debate and new didactic programming from the BBC on the European Community. That included a special programme called *The State of the Union* Charles made for the Open University, a new British institution brought in under Labour at the end of the previous decade to widen access to higher education for people from all backgrounds and ages. In fact, in 2006 Charles himself would be the proud recipient of an honorary doctorate from the OU, which, considering that at the age of seventeen he had joined up to fight in a world war rather than attend university, made him especially chuffed.

Echoing a central theme in his dispatches of the time, Charles concluded in the programme that two questions arise: 'The first is familiar – do the British want to stay in Europe? The second is becoming more frequently heard – is British membership good for the community? At present, no one seems sure.'

It was not just a matter of what Britain wanted, Charles was pointing out – the usual focus of how the British press reported the UK in Europe then and for the following decades – but the position of her partners. And barely a year into the UK's EC membership, some were already losing patience. There were deeper issues at play as well, boiling down to what proved to be a perennial British anxiety, perhaps exaggerated as Charles later suggested, but nevertheless occupying a central position in the minds even of the so-called pro-marketeers: 'The real issue is sovereignty, and so far, it hasn't been faced. The fact is that most continental members of the community have committed themselves to a gradual if limited transfer of sovereignty to a still undefined European power, and they see all community progress as movement in that direction.' It is a prescient analysis and a foretelling of a deep ideological rift between Britain and her partners that would eventually come to a head in the Brexit vote of 2016.

Referendum Day was fast approaching. But as Charles stood in front of Dublin Castle at the end of the first week of March 1975, he registered a change in mood among the other eight leaders of the European Economic Community gathering inside the grand St Patrick's Hall. This was a momentous occasion for Ireland, which, as a new member, was taking up the reins of the EEC's six-month rotating presidency for the first time. But the real event was the last lap of Britain's renegotiation before the 5 June vote by the British people on EC membership. As Charles explained to television viewers in his piece to camera, it was well within the ministers' capacity to solve the remaining two issues: the demand for privileged access for New Zealand butter to the common market (a curiously emotional issue, which for many in the UK represented a test of commitment to traditional Commonwealth partners) and Britain's contribution to the community budget. But the atmosphere was sour. There was distinct irritation in the air: 'Among the other eight, a feeling has grown up that Britain's demands for special treatment from the community may be unending – that long after renegotiation is over, Britain may come back for more and that the limit to what ought to be conceded to keep Britain [in] has now been reached,' he told viewers of the BBC TV news that evening.

Right up to that final round in Dublin in March 1975, the Wilson–Callaghan renegotiating team kept their cards very close to their chests. According to Stephen Wall, in 2016 David Cameron undermined his own negotiating credentials by giving 'the impression of a man who had made up his mind that, however unsatisfactory the EU might be, Britain's overwhelming interest was to remain part of it. That was in stark contrast to the tactics of Callaghan and Wilson in 1974/75, when their position was that they would only decide what recommendation to make once the renegotiation of the terms of UK membership had been completed.'

At the final press conference on 11 March in Dublin, after two days of talks and a year of negotiations, Charles and a young John Simpson, later the BBC's world affairs editor but at this point Charles's number two, joined the assembled press in the UK briefing room. They were treated to the Harold Wilson quip, 'Final outcome – Leeds 1, Ipswich 1 . . . On the renegotiations, we have now taken the discussions as far as they will go, and we know where we stand.'

Speaking to Charles after the press conference in a live insert for the *Midweek* programme on BBC1, Wilson stressed that he and his foreign secretary James Callaghan would be reporting to the cabinet in detail, and only then would a recommendation be made – on behalf of the cabinet – to the British people for the referendum. Wilson admitted to Charles that, 'The country is divided, every party is divided,' including his own. And he reflected that people would have to judge not just on the success of each item negotiated but on the character of the community itself: 'Many people feel . . . the theory, the bureaucracy – the overstaffed bureaucracy – that this is very alien to our British way of life. What we have found in the last year has been on practical questions like what do you do about the beef mountain . . . [that] despite this theology and this legalism . . . we've been able to get . . . a very pragmatic approach.'

Charles put it to Wilson, 'Would you say that if the referendum ended in a British decision to stay in, it is likely that no British government would ever raise the question of withdrawal again, or is this always a possibility?'

Wisely, Wilson didn't claim the art of divination, but he hazarded a guess anyway: 'I think our decision will one way or the other decide the future of Britain in relation with the Market. I can't see any change in that . . . in the foreseeable future.'

From Britain's partners in 1975, as Charles reported, there was undoubtedly real concern at the impact a British departure might have, just as countries like Spain, Portugal and Greece were starting to knock on the EEC club door for encouragement as they embarked on their democratic transitions from dictatorship. 'I think the community would have to go through a period of agonising, with an appraisal of its own institutions and perhaps we might get a totally different Europe arising from the kind of chaos that Britain would initially produce by leaving,' said Charles.

Britain emerged with a package that Harold Wilson and his team felt they could sell both to the British public and, crucially, as compared with the next make-or-break negotiation in 2016, a largely pro-common market press.

A few days before the referendum on 5 June, Charles was invited to speculate on the possibility of a no vote for a special programme on BBC radio. He didn't think it was likely. The 'great centre of British politics' was in favour of staying. Predictions of disaster from pro-marketeers – that is, from a largely united Conservative Party – were exaggerated, as was the argument of the anti-marketeers about 'things like sovereignty and the powers of the commission'. Exaggerated perhaps, but, as would come to pass forty years later, these same arguments – even in a vastly changed Europe – would prove the springboard for both sides of the debate.

Charles left Brussels to join Robin Day, a very young-looking David Dimbleby and election expert David Butler in the BBC studio in London to make sense of the results for BBC1's live 'talk-in' referendum results programme. One by one, well into the early hours of 6 June, the results came in from around the country and it soon became clear that the pro-EC membership camp was heading for a resounding victory. The contrast with the Brexit vote of 2016 wasn't just in the final result – 67.2 per cent in favour of staying in the EC – but in voting patterns across the country. Scotland's Western Isles and Shetland were the only parts of Britain to vote no, and West Sussex recorded the highest yes vote in the land, with a stonking 85 per cent.

Unlike in Washington – especially under the Nixon administration – where Charles and the BBC team had fought for space as a foreign news organisation on presidential visits like Nixon's trip to China, in Brussels he and the BBC were very much in demand. John Simpson, who had just turned thirty when he first arrived at the BBC Brussels office, told me, 'The people in the European Commission, the top characters, tried to include Charles in their thinking. They were wooing Charles in a way that they wouldn't have wooed him in Washington.' I'm not sure this really flattered Charles much, though. He was desperate to get away from the magnetic field of the Berlaymont and Brussels in pursuit of other types of stories.

He found them in the tremors of international conflicts that were making themselves felt even in the most apparently sleepy corners of northern Europe, such as the Dutch seaside resort of Scheveningen.

In October 1974, twenty-two people were taken hostage

by inmates during an evening service in a prison chapel on the edge of the town. Their four armed captors included a Palestinian serving time for the hijacking earlier in the year of a British Airways flight from Beirut diverted to Amsterdam's Schiphol airport.

When the story broke, we were just starting our autumn half-term from school, planning a family trip away from Brussels. Scheveningen wasn't quite what we had in mind but, when Charles got the summons, he proposed that Dip, Marina and I came along too. He set us up in a hotel near the beach and from time to time we ventured out to pace up and down the promenade in the drizzle. Meanwhile he and the BBC team camped outside the prison along with dozens of other journalists, from where a very cold and windswept-looking Charles filed a dawn TV dispatch, reporting that a good Dutch breakfast of coffee, ham, bread and butter and cheese had been delivered to both hostages and hijackers. By this time, the number of hostages was down to seventeen, with more children freed by the convicts overnight and mobbed by the international media as they exited the prison. And then the Dutch Marines' crack team stormed the prison chapel armed with Uzi machine-guns. No hostages were hurt and the hijackers were all captured alive. It later emerged that they had got their guns courtesy of a Benedictine monk who had become friendly with one of the hijackers. Needless to say, the monk soon joined his friend in prison.

It wasn't just breaking news that took us to Holland. One day, Charles proposed we take a trip to Keukenhof to see its famous tulip fields. Stanley Johnson, an old acquaintance from Washington, now a head of division at the European Commission dedicated to cleaning up Europe's polluted air and beaches, was coping with four rumbustious children on his own. Dip, great friends with his artist wife Charlotte, who had left Brussels for medical treatment in the UK, took pity on him and invited the family to join the excursion. Marina and I were at the European School with the mini-Johnsons and knew them well. As we walked through the Keukenhof that day, Alexander (later better known as Boris), Leo, and Rachel took it in turns to pummel each other and trample around the flowerbeds as Charles, Dip and Stanley carried on ahead pretending they didn't know them. I watched the mayhem with a kind of appalled admiration. Later that afternoon in Amsterdam, we found ourselves wandering through the red-light district. Passing a billboard advertising a live sex show with silhouettes of couples in various impossible positions, one of the Johnson children innocently asked what they were doing. 'They're doing gymnastics,' Dip said, firmly shutting down the conversation with a stern look that managed to silence even that unruly bunch.

Charles was keen to get on the trail of the ailing tyrants and crumbling dictatorships in the southern part of the continent. The previous year had seen the Carnation Revolution in Portugal, with the overthrow of the Estado Novo and the dictator Salazar, who had been holding on to power since 1932. Three months later came the collapse of another military dictatorship, the Greek junta – the Regime of the Colonels – immediately raising hopes that eventual membership of the

European Community would help end the two countries' isolation from the rest of Europe and avoid civil war.

Some eighteen months after the Portuguese revolution, Charles went to Lisbon to observe how the route to democracy was looking there. His first impressions were of a city 'smelling of anarchy and decay', but he soon realised that these were, if not wrong, then only partial observations – 'For what is significant about Portugal,' he concluded in his dispatch for BBC Radio's *From Our Own Correspondent*, 'is the way its people are managing to live with political and economic chaos without becoming violent.' Next door in Spain, when the Franco regime dissolves, what will happen? he asked. 'The Portuguese . . . [are] inclined to listen to their opponents instead of bashing them over the head. As old hands among the foreigners here are always saying: "In this country, they don't kill the bulls."'

Charles would occasionally read his radio stories to me before he phoned them through to London, and I vividly remember this one after his return from Lisbon. I am not sure he expected a very profound understanding of the issues from me, then aged twelve, but rehearsing his short sentences and punchy thoughts out loud to another human, however small, always helped him iron out the final script. And he would also say that if I didn't understand the words and phrases he was using, he was doing something wrong. The whole exercise made me feel important, sitting on the small sofa in his study at our rented house on Avenue des Grands Prix, and I felt I was playing a significant part in delivering this important broadcast. But looking back, it also gives me an insight into what I think was a largely instinctive journalistic technique, where clarity and precision were always paramount.

Charles's question about what would happen when Portugal's neighbouring regime ended was about to be answered. Spain's dictator was already gravely ill and the prospect of an end to four decades of his iron-clad rule was attracting legions of critical international journalists to the country for the first time since the civil war in the 1930s. Among them were Charles and the young Europe correspondent for the Australian Broadcasting Corporation, Malcolm Downing, whose office was along the corridor from the BBC at the International Press Centre. Charles and Malcolm (who would later defect to the BBC) had travelled to Madrid to report on what turned out to be General Franco's last public appearance at a rally in Madrid's Plaza de Oriente on 1 October 1975. They found themselves in the middle of tens of thousands of Franco supporters, mostly bussed in from outside the capital, having been given the day off or been forced to attend the rally by their employers. Judging from the report that aired on BBC News that night, the cameraman was mesmerised by the sheer number of fascist salutes around him, hands all angled towards Franco on the balcony of the royal palace. His appointed successor, Juan Carlos, grandson of Spain's last king, Alfonso XIII, stood beside him.

Most of the demonstrators were there in support of the National Guard and in protest against the international condemnation that had followed the execution by firing squad of five political opponents of the regime charged with the killing of policemen and civil guards. More than a dozen European countries withdrew their ambassadors from Madrid. It was these proceedings that formed the focus of the international coverage. 'The accused were not told they were to be tried until the evening before the trial. The defence lawyers were given four hours to prepare their case. When they objected, they were thrown out of court. No defence witnesses were allowed. The trial took less than half a day,' Charles filed in his report. During the demonstration, in other parts of the city, three policemen were shot dead by gunmen in revenge.

The mood of the crowd was volatile and turning ugly. Malcolm told me that Franco's denunciation of foreign governments and a 'leftist Masonic conspiracy' left him and Charles in an extremely vulnerable situation: 'Sections of the crowd near us were chanting, "*Abajo la prensa extranjera!*" (Down with the foreign press!). Apart from the peasants dragooned along for the occasion, two contingents stood out – scary, leather-jacketed skinheads and posh older ladies in fur coats who told the boys to behave themselves and to leave us alone. It was clear they badly wanted to beat us up. So Charles and the crew and I stayed as close as possible to the fur coats.'

They were all spared a beating but, that day, Charles was briefly arrested around the Puerta del Sol. He was released in time to meet Malcolm for dinner that night but, as Christopher Tulloch, a journalism professor in Barcelona, described in an essay on the role of the international press in Spain at the time, the arrest was part of a pattern of reprisals being taken by the regime against the foreign press. *Newsweek*'s correspondent had been forced to leave Spain 'in an incident interpreted by many as a warning shot to the foreign press corps' and, ten days before Franco's death, Spanish radio withdrew technical support to the BBC, alleging that its recent programmes were an 'intromission into Spanish internal affairs'. In fact, a Basque source was quoted in *The Times* as saying the BBC coverage and criticism of Franco's regime was reminiscent of the coverage it gave during the Second World War to the resistance to Nazism.

When Franco died the following month, on 20 November, a few weeks after slipping into a coma, Charles returned to Madrid to cover the story. For two days in the royal palace, Franco lay in state, his open coffin on the catafalque, dressed in the uniform of the supreme commander of the armed forces. It reminded Charles of seeing the tyrant Papa Doc Duvalier's corpse in Haiti – a story he had also covered. But, he said, the 'best' one was Franco, whose long velvet cloak, Charles recalled, was covering his whole body, running down from bier to floor.

'I was allowed in there with just a cameraman and a police guard,' Charles told me once over a late-night glass of whisky. 'The cameraman mentioned he'd heard that Franco's legs had been amputated because of gangrene and then suddenly said, "I'm going to see if it's true." He went over to the body and began feeling around the velvet covering. The policeman came straight over, ordered him to stop and then handcuffed him to a railing. "Call the consulate and tell them I've been arrested, will you, Charles?" the cameraman said.' For once, Charles was not the one in trouble with the authorities and was able to oblige by contacting the necessary official and helping to secure his release. But as for the scoop on Franco's missing legs – it seems that Charles's colleague had been defeated by the sheer weight and quantity of velvet covering the body and was unable to confirm or deny if they were there, and so Charles never did find out whether the story about the dictator's limbs could be stood up.

It was now the duty of the new king to introduce democracy to Spain but, as Charles commented in the report he filed on the day of Franco's death, he 'may not succeed because Franco has made him wait so long. Post-Franco Spain is now for Juan Carlos to guide but it is not an enviable inheritance.'

Charles would return to Spain six months later to record the first faltering steps towards democracy. Unlike in Portugal, there had been no revolution and progress was slow. But the sight of crowds around a thriving news kiosk, and the men and women now emerging as the champions of a free press, did testify to some change: 'News, real news, as opposed to government handouts, is still a novelty in Spain and papers and magazines have been having a boom since Franco died,' he reported.

Newspapers still had to show every edition of anything printed to the censor. But for the editors of *Cambio Doblon* and the new political daily *El Pais*, the game was to sail as close to the wind as the government would allow, remarked Charles, himself a long-standing adherent of the sailing-close-to-the-wind school of journalism. 'Dissent can be profitable in this new Spain,' he concluded, pointing to *Cambio*, which had started underground three years before Franco's death and now had a burgeoning readership. Charles found its young and enterprising editors impressively brave. One of them, Juan Tomas de Salas, told him how the news team had been threatened, prosecuted, closed down and sent parcel bombs in the post. He described growing right-wing violence and the torture of suspects by police. The journalists' position was still highly ambiguous and fraught with danger. And yet de Salas explains that government is 'tolerating' the expression of ideas in the paper that were unthinkable even six months ago. 'Evidently, we have almost total freedom of the press now – almost. But always subject to the decision of a minister whose job consists of seizing newspapers.'

Countries like Spain, Greece and Portugal were looking to the prospect of membership of the European Community to support them in their journeys away from tyranny and dictatorship. But within the community itself, there was a growing sense that there was more dividing its members than uniting them. 'The nine member states have to do something, something new, to save the European Community,' Belgian Prime Minister Leo Tindemans told Charles in an extended radio interview from the BBC office in 1976.

The EC was going through one of its periodic identity crises and Tindemans had been tasked by his fellow leaders with preparing a report on what the whole enterprise meant – and thus what direction it should take. There was a sense that the community needed future-proofing. Tindemans had spent a year canvassing opinion in the capitals, gauging the views of politicians in power and in opposition, as well as trade unions and employer federations, on how the EC could get itself out of its present rut. Beyond the recommendation for direct elections to the European Parliament, his conclusions were not especially radical but his job was to recommend a course that all nine members would find palatable – including the avowedly non-federalist Great Britain and Denmark.

Tindemans conceded that, 'Great Britain may not have the same dynamism in favour of Europe.' And then back to that old chestnut – sovereignty: 'You have a very strong tradition, a democratic tradition, but the idea of sharing sovereignty in common with the other states is a very difficult one to accept in Great Britain.' But he ventured to point out that the concept of pooled sovereignty had always been part of the project from the very beginning. 'When you approved the Treaty of Rome you accepted it in a certain way because the abandonment of a part of national sovereignty in order to exercise it in common is in the Treaty of Rome.'

Tindemans really believed that the solution to the community's economic problems was economic and monetary union, but he told Charles that his conversations with bankers, ministers and businesses were so 'contradictory' that a common proposal proved impossible. 'That's the reality – there are two types of member states.'

Charles pressed Tindemans on what became known in Brussels-speak as the 'democratic deficit' – the way in which laws were being made behind closed doors in council meetings. 'Surely, one of the things that distinguishes democracy from a dictatorship is that laws are made and discussed, and the process of lawmaking is carried on in public. Once you delegate and you give more powers to bureaucrats, to ambassadors, to officials, aren't you making the community less and less democratic, and isn't that in fact what is happening?' Charles asked.

Tindemans did not disagree. 'We must have a government and we must have a parliament controlling the government just like it is a tradition in our own countries.' But at this stage, he'd have 'no chance' of getting that through. Instead, his more modest proposal was for a directly elected European Parliament. Later, the Maastricht and the Amsterdam Treaties delivered what Tindemans may have been thinking of, granting the European Parliament an equal say in making and rejecting EU laws, with new powers to hold the European Commission to account as well.

By early 1976, covering the EC story from Brussels had come to a natural end for Charles and he was on the verge of a big decision. The family was weary of the peripatetic life. From my sister and me, Charles was facing open revolt at the idea of seemingly endless moves and more lost friendships. He and Dip also felt that, if we were ever to go to school in England, it was now or never.

A BBC memo recorded, 'Earlier this year, Charles gave notice of his wish to return to the UK. While his work as chief European correspondent, based in Brussels, had been fruitful and inevitably marked with his own special distinction, one had the feeling that he was no longer entirely committed to the role of a foreign-based correspondent.' His bosses in London took note. The removal van duly arrived at our house on Avenue des Grands Prix on 19 July 1976, to take our belongings – gathered up across three continents and, the inventory records, including Charles's trusty Adler typewriter, rugs from Kashmir and Afghanistan, the still-unidentified portrait of a woman in Renaissance clothes that he'd been given in East Berlin in the early 1950s, and the painting of a Vodou ceremony he'd picked up in Haiti – to our new home outside Horsham, Sussex. Charles was to take on the role of chief correspondent in a country in which he hadn't lived for almost twenty years and had barely covered in his entire career. The question for this now veteran foreign correspondent was, how foreign would it seem to him?

8.
HOME FRONT: FRIENDS AND NEIGHBOURS

*Wally Brown, British by birth, but partly Black . . .
encounters just as much prejudice and racism as any newly
arrived immigrant from Bangladesh or anywhere else.*
Charles Wheeler: 'Race: Where Do We Go From Here?',
BBC1, 19 September 1977

When Charles was on leave in England in the spring of 1961, a year before his marriage to Dip, he wrote to her: 'My cousin buys up old cottages and rebuilds them for renting or selling and this morning I went off to see a row of four going for £600 for the lot. I would have bought one for us as a country cottage there and then . . . but they had been taken. I suddenly thought it would be nice to buy us a house, even if we couldn't live in it.' Ten years later, home from Washington for a summer holiday, Charles and his father spotted a parcel of land with some outhouses for sale in West Sussex. A few thousand pounds sealed the deal. Charles had at last secured his little patch of England.

The Garden Cottage, as they named it, was more garden than cottage. The house was, in effect, a large clapboard shed.

What Charles prized was the outdoor space it offered: a walled garden on one side, an old apple orchard on the other and, at the front, a yard, at that point littered with multi-coloured broken crockery. The land had once served as the kitchen garden for the far grander Elizabethan house next door, also up for sale.

Charles senior oversaw the initial transformation of shed to house while his son was away. He also planted shrubs and trees: forsythia, acer, roses, clematis, wisteria and espalier pears against the wall. Work allowing, we'd spend every summer at the Garden Cottage, Charles outside digging like a demon, creating his garden, from first thing in the morning, coming in only at last light, covered in stings and scratches. After we moved there from Brussels in 1976, he would spend almost all his free time outside, as everyone who came to visit would soon realise. He took on the demands of a large garden with all the energy and focus he gave to his biggest news stories. He put in more fruit trees – peach and plums – and, so there would be colour all year round, planted Japanese anemone and quince, sedums, viburnum and winter jasmine. To achieve all of this, he called on the services of the 'rotavator' – a beast of a garden tool designed to plough up the soil in preparation for more planting – which made such a racket it nearly drove Dip mad.

His father was no longer there to see the result. But after his parents' deaths, Charles had collected some yellow poppy seeds from their garden, wrapping the dried heads in envelopes and then crunching them into the newly laid flowerbeds. They were in bloom that summer when we arrived. In fact, they had self-sown and the little flecks of yellow were visible everywhere.

Whereas the garden was coming along nicely, Charles himself was not so settled. With the title of chief correspondent, Charles was now presenting 'Foreign Report', a new ten-minute daily segment within a BBC2 programme called *Newsday*. As presenter-cum-correspondent and editor, he covered stories that were, in the main, studio-based. He would take the train to London, then the tube to TV Centre in White City – but he wasn't exactly enjoying the experience. 'I am just a suburban commuter,' he joked with a reporter from a local paper in 1977, betraying a creeping fear that things might be getting just a bit too predictable.

His restlessness was slightly assuaged by a trip to Germany to cover the general election, and to Spain, to report on the country's transition to democracy. He even managed to revisit India, in March 1977, in the aftermath of an election that saw Prime Minister Indira Gandhi and her Congress Party voted out of office, punished severely at the polls for the Emergency, where she had ruled by decree for almost two years and initiated a highly controversial programme of mass sterilisation. Charles sent back a well-received report from a village in Haryana in northern India where the local MP had been ousted as part of what Charles saw as an impressive example of Indian democracy at work. Back at home, he provided the commentary for the Queen's Silver Jubilee celebrations and the ceremony at Westminster Abbey, a rare foray for him into the world of outside broadcasts and the grand state occasion, normally the preserve of the Dimbleby dynasty and well out of his comfort zone.

But Britain in the late 1970s did give Charles the chance to revisit some of the big themes he had first encountered in the

US a decade earlier. The new Race Relations Act came into force in 1977, and with it the establishment of the Commission for Racial Equality. The Act introduced new legislation to confront racism at work, in education and housing, and even with regards to social life. At the same time, Enoch Powell, the former Conservative minister for health, now an Ulster Unionist MP, was preaching about the threat of 'racial civil war'. The BBC asked Charles to present and report a special three-part series on race in Britain, looking at the make-up of Britain's multicultural society and the challenges facing it. It went out in September and had a prominent slot on BBC1.

'You should have seen the mailbag from our viewers,' Charles announced during the live discussion after the second episode aired. The mailbag was full, though this time not with the accustomed accolades. It seemed the viewers had taken particular issue with a statement from Charles that multiculturalism was here to stay. 'Why do you accept this?' many asked. Charles was taken aback. When a Camden councillor called Nirmal Roy (later a prominent campaigner against racism and apartheid) sent a note to praise the programme, Charles gratefully replied, saying he was one of the only people who had made positive comments about it.

Making the series was an eye-opener for Charles, who, as a foreign correspondent, had covered the civil rights campaign in sixties America, the right-wing backlash and the Black fightback in US urban centres. Now he was in Whitechapel in London's East End, speaking to members of the Bangladeshi community there who, he observed, 'face bigger problems of adjustment to British society than any other immigrant group'.

He found Bengali families at the bottom of the list for council housing, many squatting in empty properties and some who had been living without electricity for six months. The whites who were getting rehoused in the newer flats complained that the Bengalis lowered the tone of the neighbourhood. Tension and all too often violence was erupting.

Charles heard testimonies from newly arrived immigrants, second-generation Asians and, in Liverpool, members of a Black community whose heritage dated back hundreds of years. And yet, as Charles told the viewers, they all found themselves in a hostile environment. He met Wally Brown, a youth worker living in Toxteth – 'British by birth, partly Black, [who] encounters just as much prejudice and racism as any newly arrived immigrant from Bangladesh.' Driving through the neighbourhood, Charles took in line after line of derelict tenements, rows of houses with boarded-up and broken windows. This was, he said, a decaying corner of the city, in decline for decades, where the community had not been able to move out because they had been 'kept in their place'. He recognised the unmistakable stamp of neglect: he had seen it ten years previously in America's northern cities, like Detroit.

Charles spoke to one young mother who was clearly grateful for the friendliness of her white neighbour, unlike her previous place where she had to keep her children indoors to avoid the racist abuse. But, said Charles, 'Locally born Liverpool Blacks want more than neighbourly tolerance; they want equality of opportunity, a fair share of whatever jobs this depressed area has to offer.'

Wally Brown, who would become a well-known educator

and deputy lieutenant of Merseyside in later years, told Charles that many Liverpool employers had discriminated against the Black community for so long that the practice had become an accepted fact of life. One of the problems in Liverpool, he maintained, was that a myth had grown up of a harmonious multiracial community dating back over a century. But, he said, 'The reality is otherwise. The issue of opportunities, patterns of discrimination, the presumption of discrimination is such that there is no point in applying for a job.' As far as Wally Brown was concerned, it was time for a policy of positive discrimination.

Charles would return to Toxteth four years later, in 1981, to report on the aftermath of the riots there. There were several uprisings across England that year, but Toxteth's was seen as one of the most significant in modern British history. It went on for nine days, with several hundred police and rioters injured and huge destruction to property. One man died. Prime Minister Margaret Thatcher swept into Liverpool to meet police officers and members of the Black community. One of them was Wally Brown. He told Charles, 'I've never seen anyone attempt to listen so hard . . . She hung on every word.' But he was in for a shock when, at the end of the meeting, she summed up the main issues as she saw them. 'We talk about the alienation of the Black community from society,' said Brown. 'By gum, she was alienated. She didn't even begin to address what we'd been talking about.'

Local Toxteth residents insisted that this was not just about housing or unemployment. 'Lots of people involved in the rioting had jobs,' one young woman told Charles. It was, in fact, also about the relationship with the police. Ted Watkins, who Charles had interviewed after the riots in Watts back in 1965, came to the UK that year to advise on community relations with the police. Now chairman of the Watts Labour Community Action Committee, he spoke to Charles after several visits to Britain: 'The progress of Blacks here, economically and politically, is about twenty years behind the progress in the United States.' He warned of 'open warfare'. For Ted Watkins, and for Charles, the parallels between Toxteth and the US in the tumultuous era of the 1960s were all too clear.

At the end of September 1977, Charles resigned from the BBC. It wasn't quite the bombshell moment it sounds, though. He'd decided to give up his staff status and go freelance – though the very next day he accepted a contract to report for BBC News. As he would discover soon enough, this new status meant he had less job security than before, but it would also give him a new kind of freedom to work where he wanted within the BBC and outside it as well if he wished.

Shortly before taking this decision, he'd been offered the editorship of *Panorama*. He'd turned it down, as he had once before in the late 1950s, on the grounds that he didn't want to be responsible for anyone but himself. I suspect that he saw it as another BBC ploy to move him into management, a place inhabited by the 'sharks', as he'd called them, and, feeling that he would find himself being steered in that direction if he stayed on the staff of the BBC, felt he needed to go freelance in order to prolong his journalistic shelf-life. And so it was that in November 1977 he became *Panorama*'s main presenter, rather than its editor.

He didn't stay long in the job. Charles was frustrated by having to introduce and comment on other people's stories, on topics he hadn't covered himself and felt he wasn't equipped to discuss. And maybe that same fear of being simply a 'commuter' going up to London to front the programme was getting to him. After a year, he stood down and returned to reporting. This allowed him to make some in-depth films of his own for *Panorama*, the highlight being a trip to China in March 1979, a country he was fascinated by and had wanted to visit ever since being denied a place on the groundbreaking Nixon trip seven years earlier.

China was now in the first stages of a rapid industrial and military modernisation under Deng Xiaoping. Charles went there with the secretary of state for industry, Eric Varley, and a large British trade mission that was hoping to cash in on the Chinese government's opening up to the West. The fifty-minute film he produced provides a remarkable snapshot of what looks like a fairly poor country just embarking on a journey to becoming a twenty-first-century superpower. Charles also turned his sceptical gaze on the legions of British, American, French and German businessmen swarming around what they clearly saw as a golden opportunity. And he identified the West's willingness to turn a blind eye to actions taken by the Chinese that might otherwise have been condemned – in this case, the awkward fact of China's invasion of Vietnam a few weeks before the British delegation landed in Beijing.

Back in the UK, however, *Panorama* was still not quite working for Charles. The fact was, whether presenting or reporting, he felt that the programme had lost its buzz since he'd been one of its legendary group of producers and reporters in the 1950s. As he told an interviewer on Radio London in 1988, 'I think *Panorama* was better then than now, partly because you could do so many new things on television. There were so many things that had never been done before . . . We were sailing as close to the wind as you possibly could – all the time. And Broadcasting House in those days had less control over what went on in television than they do now.'

And then came what he would describe later as 'the revolution I'd longed for'.

Newsnight, the programme with which Charles would become most associated, was launched by the BBC in January 1980 with the intention of providing audiences with more analysis and investigation in its news coverage. It offered an alternative to the breathless two-minute reports aired on the news bulletins, with films that might last for fifteen minutes, an emphasis on style as well as content, and a sometimes irreverent approach, with interviews and discussions in the studio around the issues of the day. Like the early *Panorama*, *Newsnight* was set up to challenge the current orthodoxy on news programming and break down the separate silos of news and current affairs. It gave reporters the opportunity for longer-form reporting, to share their expertise and analysis, and provide a more considered take on the stories of the day.

George Carey was the programme's founder and first editor. He credits Charles with helping him get the new programme signed off by the bosses and a very sceptical management, who gave it a year at most, betting that the audience's appetite for even more news would not stretch to a programme past 10 p.m., let alone one purporting to be – as they saw it – more highbrow. George had first seen Charles back in 1972 reporting from the Republican Convention in Miami, making merry with the script he'd happened upon that choreographed not just Nixon's acceptance speech but all the fandango before and after. He was blown away: 'When Charles appeared, saying something like, "I'm not going to tell you what happened but what *will* happen" live into the news, it was a revelation to me, busting apart preconceptions,' he told me. '*Newsnight* was a kind of approach that a younger Charles had already started to pioneer: news with context, succinctly told, combining the journalist with the historian and academic. Immediate and human – on the ground and pacy. He really started the *Newsnight*-type of thinking about ways of reporting.'

Initially, though, instead of being out on the road reporting, Charles was to be part of the presenting line-up, alongside John Tusa, Peter Snow and Peter Hobday, later joined by Linda Alexander. He was clearly not in his natural element, ill at ease with technical hiccups and unwilling to provide the live patter required to fill uncomfortable silences when things went wrong.

George described to me what might be called the final chapter in this particular part of Charles's career: 'One day, the film went down, as happened so often on the set in those days. We had a technical problem. We turned to Charles to cover. Except he didn't. He slapped his hands on his knees and said, "Well, we'll just have to wait." The silence that followed probably lasted thirty seconds, which feels like an eternity on live television.' George blew up at Charles after the programme. 'You just can't do that!' he told him. Charles could only mumble in response.

It was mutually agreed that he – and the programme – would be better off if he got back on the road. George said he could almost see the burden being lifted from Charles's shoulders. 'Later, he would laugh and tell me, "You're the only person who ever sacked me, George." I really think I did him a favour, though – this would become his heyday.'

As a reporter on *Newsnight*, Charles pretty much had free rein. He covered some UK stories, but he was now spending a good part of the year travelling overseas, often across the Atlantic. Colleagues in the Washington bureau always knew when he was in town, as Steve Selman, the bureau chief in those days, recalled: 'Edit rooms were strictly no smoking but a deal was struck with Charles . . . that he could stand just inside the doorway with his arm and cig extended into the corridor. His hand hovered over a waste-paper bin into which he periodically tapped his ash. He never missed, no matter how much he was absorbed in the editing.'

Charles's new patch for *Newsnight* gave him the opportunity to renew an old presidential acquaintance. In 1982, Richard Nixon was touting his new book, *Leaders*, a collection of reminiscences of political and military bigwigs from across the globe he'd met during his career. At first, Nixon's people turned down the bid for an interview with the BBC. Then, *Newsnight* producer David Coxon Taylor let it be known that Charles was the journalist who had shown Nixon round East Berlin in late July 1963 and it was the memory of that evening in Berlin that clinched an interview with the former president.

This was a man who held an extreme fascination for Charles. Despite covering his presidency as well as two election campaigns during the Washington posting, he'd not actually interviewed Nixon before. But like many who had observed Nixon's political manoeuvrings over the years he had strong opinions about him in private – namely, that he was a profoundly dishonest and at times downright bizarre character. Back in the early 1970s, Charles bought a Halloween mask of Nixon from Murphy's, our favourite five-and-dime store in downtown Washington. It was truly grotesque, and we were terrified, especially when he put on the mask and pranced about making strange hand movements, and we would beg him to take it away. Eventually he conceded, though he never threw it out. When we moved to Brussels, he lodged it in one of the upstairs bedrooms, peeking out from behind the curtains. He said it would keep any burglars away.

Charles and David flew to New York to do the interview in Nixon's office. They were confronted by a Richard Nixon who was highly focused and immensely articulate. From Chairman Mao and Zhou Enlai ('two revolutionary leaders, one a destroyer, the other a builder', as he pithily described them), to the Russian leaders Khrushchev and Brezhnev, Charles was deeply impressed by the depth of Nixon's knowledge of foreign affairs – particularly in contrast to President Reagan's ignorance, he told David afterwards. And the post-Watergate Nixon was now presenting himself in a softer light: 'I hope a time will come when we can build a world not just free from war but built on more cooperation. That may seem sappy coming from an old hawk like me but that's what I believe.' Charles said it was one of the most interesting interviews he ever conducted.

David Coxon Taylor told me that for him the best part

was the pre-interview session that went on for almost an hour. 'They actually enjoyed each other's company. In the taxi going back to the hotel I remember Charles saying he still thought Nixon was a crook but now saw him more as a tragic figure who could have reached greatness had it not been for his self-destructive personality.'

After the recording, Nixon pulled out a copy of his book and inscribed on the inside cover, 'To Charles Wheeler – with pleasant memories of events we shared together over the years – From Richard Nixon'. For all their newfound bonhomie, the dedication always greatly amused Charles, who, after all, had been prevented from sharing the famous trip to China with Nixon in 1972, and was so appalled by him after that day in Berlin together that he had remarked to Dip that he was quite mad.

A few years later, with the hijacking of TWA Flight 847 in June 1985, Charles also got the chance to interview Nixon's former sidekick Henry Kissinger. Charles once said, 'The choice of Henry Kissinger as his foreign affairs advisor was the one inspired appointment Richard Nixon ever made. Kissinger was brilliant and highly aware of his brilliance. He was secretive and loved publicity. And he could be ruthless. He had an uncanny ability to influence people and to shape the course of events.'

Now Dr Kissinger was weighing in from the sidelines on an intense national debate, five days into the crisis. A young US Navy diver had been murdered by the Hezbollah hijackers and another forty hostages were being held. Pressure was building on President Reagan from the public and the media to end it. President Carter's former national security advisor Zbigniew

Brzezinski was urging restraint and negotiation, and Dr Kissinger was telling the networks President Reagan should be tough. That meant no negotiation and rejecting the hijackers' demand for the release by Israel of 700 Shiite prisoners.

'Innocent Americans cannot become the subject of blackmail in order to influence American foreign policy,' Kissinger told Charles on *Newsnight*.

'But what does he have against "finessing a settlement", using the Red Cross to mediate as is being suggested?' asked Charles.

'[If the prisoners are released] in any timeframe related to this hijacking, if whatever kind of finesse as you call it is invented, the consequence will be that hijacking will have paid off,' Kissinger replied.

Charles had a final question up his sleeve: 'If you were secretary of state and managing this crisis, would you be happy about the number of former secretaries of state, national security advisors and others who are publicly taking issue with each other about what America should now do?'

Dr Kissinger's face went blank. He was not someone known for being often lost for words but in the recording it's two seconds before any sound comes out of his mouth and another four before he forms a sentence. 'Well . . . uh . . . that's a very interesting question . . . uh . . . I would think that I should do what I think it is right to do. I'm not aware that former secretaries of state are publicly taking issue—'

Charles interrupted. 'You and Dr Brzezinski, for example, are taking publicly quite opposing positions. Do you think this helps President Reagan or not?'

The *Newsnight* team in London couldn't disguise their glee.

Ever fond of sporting metaphors, the BBC's deputy foreign editor John Mahoney declared in a note to Charles, 'What a scorecard: Kissinger clean bowled on the last ball of the over! The look on the good doctor's face after that final dismissive Wheeler crack will live in the memory for a very long time. I wonder if he'll ever do an interview with you again?'

He did. They met in person in December 1986, when Admiral Poindexter, Reagan's former national security advisor, was to testify before the Senate's intelligence committee investigating the Iran–Contra affair. Arms had been sold secretly to Iran in exchange for the release of hostages and to finance the anti-Communist Contra guerrillas fighting the Sandinista government in Nicaragua. Admiral Poindexter pleaded the fifth amendment, as did his subordinate, Oliver North, 'just like Mafia godfathers have done for years at congressional hearings on organised crime,' Charles told *Newsnight* viewers acerbically. 'So much for the president's assurance that he and his staff would cooperate fully with Congress.'

But what of the president himself – how much did he know? Was he telling the truth? Charles put these questions to Kissinger, hardly a stranger to political scandal himself. Kissinger came very close to saying that Reagan was too dim or at least too unengaged to know what was going on around these 'bizarre events'. 'His basic personality is not sympathetic to the nitty gritty of foreign policy,' he told Charles. He added, 'I don't believe they are holding back on the truth . . . I would be astonished and deeply disappointed if a new category of misdeeds or evasions appeared.'

In fact, several members of the Reagan administration

including Poindexter, North and Caspar Weinberger, secretary of state, were indicted, and only spared a possible prison sentence because they were pardoned by Reagan's successor, George Bush Snr, before they could even stand trial. In spite of a congressional hearing and a special commission, the extent of President Reagan's and his circle's complicity in the Iran–Contra affair has never been fully established.

Charles reported on every US election for *Newsnight* in the 1980s. On returning from covering President Reagan's second election victory in November 1984, he was told out of the blue that *Newsnight* proposed to cut his days by a third. The life of the freelancer may suddenly have seemed a little less sweet. Charles felt slighted and fired off an unhappy letter to a contract manager at BBC News and Current Affairs.

'When we talked a year ago, I told you that when BBC television wanted to get rid of me, I should not hang about arguing. I still mean that. But I am under the impression that what is happening now is not due to a lapse in standards on my part but to the need for economies.' He added, 'All this is more in sorrow than anger. It has been a busy year and I feel that with the American election out of the way, I'm being gently waved towards the door. Could we please all think again?'

Somehow, they found a compromise. It was clear they didn't want to get rid of him quite yet. And the BBC internal letter that, luckily, Charles never saw, still manages to be both insulting and crass, a reminder that even the BBC's most valued employees can be subject to the cold winds of change: 'Now that the election is out of the way, I want to reduce my Wheeler holdings,' wrote the editor at the time. 'I do not wish to cut the old boy loose in any shape or form. I would like *Newsnight* to go on employing him as long as he can get to the airport.' But, he continued, pruning back Charles's input 'leaves *Newsnight* with certain amounts of Wheeler cash to try out potential new stars . . .' At this point, the 'old boy' was only just coming up to his sixty-second birthday and had more than twenty years of work in him. And just around the corner were a string of awards from BAFTA and the Royal Television Society for his coverage on the BBC of the momentous events in Eastern Europe.

Charles often described himself as the British-based US correspondent for *Newsnight* but over the next decade he would be equally active behind the Iron Curtain in the Soviet Union and its satellite states like Poland, reporting on the emergence of a new world order and the collapse of the Soviet empire.

It began in Gdańsk's Lenin Shipyard – 'where the ice started to crack', as Charles would describe it later. In August 1980, *Newsnight* reported on the emergence of an 'irresistible force' in Poland as workers in the shipyard went out on a strike that rapidly spread nationwide: ports like Szczecin joined in, then the mines in Silesia. Just as in East Germany in 1953, when Charles had covered the uprising of construction workers against the Communist government, a workers' uprising was challenging a regime in theory dedicated to their welfare. Poland's Communist leader Edward Gierek responded with a conciliatory gesture, the Gdańsk Accords, a set of demands by the strikers that paved the way for the founding in September of Solidarność (Solidarity) under its leader, the electrician Lech

Walesa. With around forty regional unions also uniting under the banner, Solidarity was the first independent trade union to be recognised as such in the Soviet Bloc, and it soon became clear that it was far more than just a union. It was, in fact, rapidly emerging as an anti-communist political movement and attracting international attention.

This new openness proved to be short lived. Just over a year later, when Charles travelled to Poland for what was to be the first of several trips to the country for *Newsnight* over the next decade, Gierek had resigned and been replaced by the hardline General Wojciech Jaruzelski. Solidarity was not backing down. The calls for a general strike were getting louder. Solidarity's Warsaw branch claimed the union now had more supporters than the Communist Party. As Charles reported, the night before a nationwide strike, Polish state TV ran a documentary about the Hungarian Uprising, a story Charles himself had covered in 1956. The film had never been shown in Poland before. The images of Russian tanks on the streets of Budapest were hardly a subtle warning. But just in case viewers had missed the point, the narrator signalled the 'historical parallels' and underlined that 'the Soviet Union intervened in Hungary because misguided workers demanded the right to dismiss and appoint the managers of factories'.

Meanwhile, Solidarity was also upping the ante. Outside factories across the country, posters plastered the walls: '*Strajk Do Odwołania*' – 'occupation strikes'. Charles and the team filmed inside a textile mill where, instead of staying at home and risking arrest, the mainly female workers occupied their own factories. Solidarity's proclamation that week declared:

'It is our programme to have a self-governing republic' – in other words, without Russian interference. Tensions were running high, but an even more immediate worry for Solidarity's leaders than retribution from the Russians was the approach of winter. The strikes had meant that the usual shortages of food and fuel were even more acute. Lech Walesa's right-hand man, Bronislaw Geremek, would later become foreign secretary in a Solidarity-led government. But on the day Charles first met him, he looked every inch the academic that he was – heavily bearded, wearing a tweed jacket and sitting back in an armchair in his study with books spilling out of the shelves behind him. 'It should be understood as a very dramatic sentence – that the country is not prepared for the winter. It means we have no food, no heating, and, if the winter is hard, life will be very hard,' Geremek said, gravely.

He remained upbeat about the chances of finding an agreement, however. 'I think it's impossible that the government can refuse talks with Solidarity,' he insisted. Yet within days, the Communist authorities had banned the union altogether – and within two months, Geremek himself had been interned, released for a short spell, and would then be detained again for a year.

Behind the camera for those *Newsnight* stories was Witold Stok, a cinematographer who had been involved in the Solidarity movement. Witold told me, 'I was astounded by the force of Charles's journalism. Working with him was a very positive shock to me, a very big influence.' He remembers watching Charles through the lens: 'Those eyes under the thick eyebrows. I saw his technique of interviewing people like Geremek.

SHIRIN WHEELER

He could get anything from anyone. He had an immense gift for listening.'

After that first visit to Poland, Charles was deeply moved by what he'd seen and heard. Bronislaw Geremek's warning of the consequences of a cold winter worried him and he was determined to try to do more. He offered support to the Ockenden Venture, a charity that had been fund-raising for the resettlement of Vietnamese 'boat people' in Britain and was originally established to support displaced German families after the war. Charles and my sister Marina together launched an appeal for shoes for Poland and set up shop at the old bandstand in Horsham, our local market town. They collected more than 5,000 pairs and then started raising money for baby food and medical supplies. In November, Charles and a camera crew headed for the Laski Home for Blind Children just outside Warsaw. The Laski Institute, like the Catholic Church as a whole, played an important role in sustaining Solidarity in the resistance to Communist rule. Located in woodland a few miles out of Warsaw, it was run by nuns and a formidable woman called Maria Morawska. There, one dark evening, with the rain pouring down, she and the nuns were filmed receiving the much-needed consignment from Horsham. Unusually, Charles's own actions had become part of one of his *Newsnight* reports.

The hardship was set to continue. Martial law was declared in Poland on 13 December 1981. Charles called it inevitable but it was no less heart-rending for that. With it came the severe repression and persecution of Solidarity's leaders, their families and sympathisers. Around 6,000 people were interned; others decided to leave the country. Among them were cameraman Witold Stok and his wife Danusia, a translator. With the crackdown on Solidarity and the media they made the decision to go to England to join Danusia's mother. 'We were partly in shock, partly there was a euphoria at having got out,' he told me. Then the Polish authorities made it clear they were not welcome back. Within three weeks, with Charles as a referee, Witold obtained his British passport. They spent Christmas that year with us at the Garden Cottage. The atmosphere around the dining table was sober and restrained. Then the subject turned to Ronald Reagan.

As a supporter of CND and someone who, the following year, would become a regular at demonstrations against plans to expand the American stockpile of nuclear weapons at Upper Heyford, near Oxford, I was ready to go into battle against what I saw as the warmongering machinations of an extreme right-wing president. In the circles I was mixing in at university – and, it must be said, at the Garden Cottage – I could usually rely upon a certain agreement on this aspect of the man in the White House if nothing else. But now, over the Christmas turkey, things became surprisingly heated. Witold and Danusia, it turned out, would hear no bad word against the current incumbent of the Oval Office. For them, like many Poles, Reagan's virulent anti-communism was a mark of his true friendship for Poland. Charles bit his tongue; my argument was beaten back – and Witold and Danusia carried the day. It didn't change our opinion of Ronald Reagan that much, but I learnt a valuable lesson about the positive way that countries under Communist rule viewed the United States – something that would be reinforced when, as a BBC correspondent in Brussels, I covered the accession of several former Eastern Bloc countries into the European Union in 2004.

The day after General Jaruzelski lifted martial law in July 1983, Charles was back in Poland. There were no celebrations. The general, wearing his trademark, slightly sinister, tinted glasses, warned of dire consequences for those engaging in anti-state activities. Lech Walesa was one of the few Solidarity leaders not in prison. But it was hoped that the leaders of Solidarity and other political prisoners would be released in what had been billed as an amnesty. Charles and a small posse of other foreign journalists waited outside Rakowiecka Prison in Warsaw's Mokotów district for the political prisoners to come out. But it seemed Solidarity supporters and other dissidents were condemned to a longer stay. At the time, Charles reported that, according to the Church, between 130 and 150 people were serving jail sentences, with another 1,200 in prison and awaiting trial. People like Jan Rulewski, Adam Michnik and members of KOR, the Workers' Defence Committee who, Charles reported, were among the most feared by the regime. They'd published books and even tried to set up an underground university. They possessed something that made the regime nervous, but that Charles could particularly identify with – the power of the word.

It would be another five years before Charles went back to Poland. In mid-May 1988, in the wake of an unsuccessful general strike, he found a new generation of protestors out on the streets. The first person he looked up and interviewed was Adam Michnik, just released from prison. Charles asked him,

'Have you lowered your objectives since the high days of 1980 and 1981 when it seemed you were hoping you could replace the Communist government of Poland?'

Michnik insisted they were not seeking to replace the government but to make it come to terms with changes it could not reverse. He said, 'There was more hope then; we were more naive. There is less hope today. After so many years of repression, of persecution, of ignorance, we have little hope that this government is capable of dialogue. In simple terms, what we have in Poland is a totalitarian state, co-existing with a developed and pluralistic society. People are not afraid; they speak their mind – the truth is told in churches, and no one is afraid to tell foreigners what they think of the government. Totalitarianism in Poland has rotten teeth. It cannot bite as it did thirty years ago.'

At the centre of that state was a member of the Polish politburo, Mieczysław Rakowski, a former journalist, true believer in the Communist cause and right-hand man to General Jaruzelski. Charles was excited to get an interview with him, obtained through a contact in Jaruzelski's office. Rakowski would become prime minister of the country in a matter of months. He was part of the crew described by the historian Norman Davies as Polish servants of St Petersburg and Moscow – 'Pliable Greeks in a world ruled by cruel Roman savages, whom they serve with infinite regret and infinite agility.'

It was a quietly combative interview. Charles put it to Rakowski that, while there may be Glasnost and freedom of speech in Poland, the Polish leadership had not tackled fundamental political reform. Rakowski turned the question back on Charles: 'Do you think that only the existence of Solidarity would be an example that we have political reforms in Poland?'

'No,' replied Charles, 'I would say that you have political reform when you start questioning the leading role of the party – and the monopoly that the party enjoys of political power.'

Rakowski insisted that now was not the time to question the leading role of the party and that they were listening to the opinions of others.

'Why arrest the leaders of Solidarity then?' Charles challenged.

For his part, Rakowski resorted to making parallels with Britain's arrest of IRA members and the treatment of striking miners. 'Solidarity belongs to the past. It is a closed chapter of our history,' he retorted, with ultimately misplaced certainty, as if saying it made it true. In fact, less than a year later, in April 1989, Premier Rakowski and Lech Walesa would break the deadlock with the Round Table Talks between the ruling Communists and the opposition to lay the foundations for a transition to democracy.

Many of Solidarity's leaders had believed that a full transition to democracy and independence in their country ultimately depended on a major change in the Soviet Bloc's political and military masters in Russia. Such a change had been slowly seeding itself as the 1980s progressed. In 1986, Soviet General Secretary Mikhail Gorbachev adopted a new political slogan of Glasnost, or openness. Perestroika, the movement to reform and restructure the economic and political system, had been born. Although it might not have been obvious at the time to

Solidarity members like Adam Michnik, the Russian empire was beginning to disintegrate.

British Prime Minister Margaret Thatcher famously declared that Gorbachev was someone she could do business with. That was at the end of 1984, when he was chair of the Foreign Affairs Committee of the Soviet legislature, tipped as a possible successor to Chernenko and earning a reputation as a reformer. By the time she met him in Moscow during her landmark five-day trip there in March 1987, he had risen to the position of Soviet leader.

Charles was in Moscow too, covering the visit for *Newsnight*. After the first day of the visit, he spoke to the prime minister outside the British embassy. She told him, 'I think we all put our views very, very frankly. I think it says a great deal for the relationship between the Soviet Union and Great Britain that [Mr Gorbachev] took the trouble to allocate a whole day to discussions.' She was looking remarkably fresh and energetic at the end of a day that had seen seven hours of meetings and a long banquet. But, she told Charles, she was now two hours late. 'We went on and there wasn't time to come back to change for the evening's dinner. It really has been a most interesting and valuable day.'

Extraordinarily, Thatcher had been given the freedom to meet opponents of the ruling Communist regime, including Christians and Jewish refuseniks, and was at liberty to expound to those who cared to listen her views on the nuclear deterrent. Among those she spoke to was Dr Andrei Sakharov. Exiled to Gorky for seven years, beaten by KGB men and force-fed when he went on hunger strike, he had been released the previous year. After his meeting with Mrs Thatcher, Sakharov, who was encouraged by Gorbachev's reforms, told Charles that human rights featured prominently in their conversation: 'Pressure on this issue cannot harm Gorbachev. On the contrary, it will give him another argument to use in his steps towards a more democratic society.'

To Charles's surprise, on the last day of the visit, Thatcher herself agreed to an interview. It was to be the first of several about the Soviet leader. 'For the first time ever she said yes,' Charles would recall, having tried unsuccessfully on several occasions to get an interview with the Iron Lady. 'She'd spent something like ten hours with Gorbachev, something nobody else had done at that point. Here was a chance to ask somebody who'd actually been talking to the man, exploring his mind, what he was like. So I said to her, "Mrs Thatcher, you've spent ten hours talking to what is probably the most interesting man in the world, what do you think of him?"'

As Charles put it, she just opened up, and she talked and talked. 'He can discuss anything, debate in a very interesting way, a lively way, in a very direct way, no jargon,' Mrs Thatcher told Charles. 'That suited me because I like to debate in the same way. You can be absolutely direct with him, and he with me, without there being any offence taken.'

He asked her if she thought Gorbachev was 'honest'. She answered with a resounding yes. 'I think as a leader, all these things matter. What matters infinitely more than all that is that he's had the fantastic courage to say, look, this system isn't working properly, we've got to change it, and this is the direction in which we are going. That's difficult in any society.

In a society as rigid as Soviet society, it is utterly outstanding and remarkable.'

Charles was asked to reflect on that interview with Margaret Thatcher in the following year for a programme on BBC London radio. 'It was a good interview because she actually had something to say,' he told the presenter, Roger Clark. 'I wasn't trying to make a point or bully her. And I'm sure if I'd tried to bully her she'd bully me back, and she would win anyway. But I was trying to find out what she really believes. That's what an interview should be like. It's curious how rarely you can do that with politicians. They habitually think you're trying to get at them.'

Before the Thatcher visit, Charles had also found himself able to travel around the Soviet Union, from Tallinn to Tbilisi, seeing what Perestroika actually meant in practice. What he encountered was a hugely enthusiastic entrepreneurialism, whether manifested by the hairdresser who had turned his cellar into an independent boutique or the owner of Russia's first fast-food cafe who had thrown away the menus proscribed by the Ministry in Moscow in favour of a homemade meat pie that was now the talk of the capital.

Charles returned to Russia the following year and was amazed at how much had changed: in one letter back home he wrote, 'When I was last there in March '87, people were beginning to stick their heads over the parapet, talking relatively freely but still uncertain whether the changes would stick. Now one can even have completely open conversations with middle-ranking party officials.'

Charles also found the altered attitude of the Russian press astonishing. The purpose of the trip was to do daily pieces of up to seventeen minutes at the party conference called to make Perestroika irreversible. There was no access for the foreign press into the building where the conference was held, so they were dependent on the TASS agency and Soviet television for material. After a very hesitant start, Sovtel got into the spirit of the thing and gave Charles and the crew the clips they wanted of delegates either arguing with Gorbachev or denouncing Gromyko and others in the Politburo as relics from the past who should be purged, and even an argument between the arch-conservatives and the ultra-reformist ex-chief of the Moscow party. 'All rousing stuff,' Charles thought, and saw it as Glasnost in action. Meanwhile, on the streets, brave individuals were holding up placards saying: 'Dissolve the KGB' and then being taken away by the police. A group of men expelled from the Communist Party under Brezhnev had formed a 'popular front' to fight the anti-Perestroika wing of the party. They were greeted by a Saturday afternoon crowd of a thousand people with shouts of 'power to the people'. This time there was no police interference.

Charles once told me that of all the people he'd encountered, Gareth Peirce was the one he most admired. To most people, she became known as the lawyer who helped overturn the wrongful imprisonment of the Birmingham Six and the Guildford Four. In the 1993 movie *In the Name of the Father*, based on the book by her client Gerry Conlon, one of the Guildford Four, she was played by Emma Thompson. But Gareth Peirce is intensely private – and the work was distinctly unglamorous. That was partly what Charles liked so much about her, he told me – that and her gutsy resolve, sharp intelligence and passion for justice. When they first met in the spring of 1986, Peirce – a solicitor – was based in a small community practice.

She told me, 'I would have said to Charles, you should be looking at what the police are doing in Notting Hill, as well as the resistance to their constant racist activity. And there's a trial going on at Knightsbridge Crown Court . . .'

Peirce had already been acting for civil rights campaigners in west London, like Darcus Howe and Frank Crichlow. They were well known as part of the Mangrove Nine, accused and then acquitted of inciting a riot following protests at repeated police raids of Crichlow's restaurant The Mangrove, in 1970. Now, Peirce had taken on the cases of several men accused by the police of assault and possession of cannabis – whereas in fact they were the ones beaten up by officers, all from one police station in London, Notting Hill, renowned in the community for planting drugs on Black youths on a routine basis. As Charles's report for *Newsnight* in May 1986 would detail, these cases had several elements in common: all the arrested men were Black, all were charged with offences involving cannabis and assaulting police and all were acquitted of the main charges by juries.

'In this report, we are not saying that large numbers of London policemen are vicious. What we are saying is that the number of assaults by policemen on citizens is growing and that the police commissioner's own highly publicised objective of policing by consent is in jeopardy and perhaps is in some places breaking down,' Charles's opening commentary laid out.

In the film, Peirce tells Charles about the cases in Notting Hill: 'There is an intense feeling that it's almost impossible to ever ensure that a police officer who commits a crime will be brought to book for it. People are without recourse when it's the police who commit crimes.'

Vincent Lee and Hughgine Wilson were among those pursuing civil actions against the police at Notting Hill for wrongful arrest and assault. Wilson, a soft-spoken accountant, described the evening he was arrested: the officers stamped on his thumb, then kicked him in the head. They had 'found a bulky packet of cannabis in his tight-fitting trousers'. He showed Charles how preposterous that was. It seemed the jury at Knightsbridge Crown Court agreed, and he was acquitted. As Frank Crichlow, head of the Mangrove Community Association, tells Charles in the film: 'Young people are habitually threatened, searched and humiliated. This is provocation. It happens all the time – it's improper policing.' Later, Crichlow himself, represented by Peirce, would make legal history, receiving £50,000 in compensation from the police on the grounds of false imprisonment, battery and malicious prosecution.

Charles may have seen in these cases a further echo of the stories he had covered in the US in the 1960s: he now learnt that Peirce, seventeen years younger than him, had lived in New York before she took up the law and had followed Martin Luther King, writing for local papers and magazines on the civil rights campaign. But when she heard Enoch Powell's dog-whistle 'Rivers of Blood' speech in 1968, she decided there was a battle to fight back in Britain and signed up to study law. 'I thought lawyers packed more of a punch,' she told me wryly.

WITNESS TO THE TWENTIETH CENTURY

Armed with details of the cases from Gareth Peirce, Charles confronted Assistant Commissioner of the Metropolitan Police Colin Sutton about the goings-on at his station in Notting Hill. Sutton refuted the charge that there was a general breakdown in the police structure. Instead, he told Charles it was the attention of the 'media and politicians' on what he called these 'remote' cases that 'saps' public confidence. But following the programme, the Police Complaints Authority ordered two inquiries, one in 1987 and another in 1989, into allegations at Notting Hill. Lee and Wilson, and several others, did receive compensation and settlements, and officers at Notting Hill were severely admonished. None were ever convicted.

Four years later, in May 1990, Charles reported on another apparent miscarriage of justice. Winston Silcott, Mark Braithwaite and Engin Raghip, who became known as the Tottenham Three, were serving long sentences for the horrific murder of PC Keith Blakelock during riots at the Broadwater Farm Estate in London in October 1985. The riots followed the death of Cynthia Jarrett after police had searched her home. The case had been extremely sensitive and emotively covered in the press, but the evidence against the men, solely based on confessions extracted by the police, increasingly appeared unreliable. It eventually went to appeal, with Gareth Peirce representing one of the convicted men, Engin Raghip.

The programme 'Beyond Reasonable Doubt', for the *Inside Story* series, recreated parts of the original trial, employing actors in the role of prosecution and defence counsel, the jury, defendants and judge, with Charles occasionally walking into the specially built TV courtroom to deliver pieces to camera with the actors behind him. It's not his usual style but, with a starkly dramatic edge to it, the programme was highly compelling.

'The purpose of this film is not to ask and certainly not to answer the question: did these men take part in the killing or not? We do not and cannot know. What we are questioning is whether society should continue to tolerate convictions based on nothing more than what defendants are said to have said to police in the isolation of an interviewing room. In the absence of any independent corroboration, we ask whether Silcott, Braithwaite and Raghip should ever have been found guilty beyond reasonable doubt.'

As well as exposing the flawed process, the film was also presenting new evidence, some of it public for the first time. As Gareth Peirce told me, this required her to trust the journalist she was working with. She admitted that, having seen the devastating legal consequences of 'instant, prejudiced, corrosive journalism', she had an instinctively wary approach to the media. But in certain cases, working what she described as 'strategic pressure points' with the right journalist could be a valuable approach, especially when a home secretary is needed to review a case. Charles – who, in her view, was endowed with 'an intelligent, informed understanding, huge energy and determination to find out more' without pressuring her to divulge more than she could in the interest of a quicker story – was such a journalist.

'He was a highly politically educated guy. Integrity shone out of him,' she said. 'My view was if Charles is interested or engaged in the fact of a wrongful conviction and wants to have it explained to him, so he can do something – well, then it's a happy marriage . . . The tiny pieces that might be put together to achieve the reopening of a wrongful conviction are fragile and need understanding. It can be a very slow and accidental process. You need to find a journalist you can talk to, who can comprehend, with whom you don't need to go through any long process. And unless you trust the person you are talking to, you can never share or open up in the way that you have to in order, for example, to persuade a minister to reopen a case. It is a shared endeavour in that sense.'

As well as the lawyers, the film also interviewed psychologists and witnesses in the original trial. One was thirteen-year-old Jason Hill, who had accused Silcott of being the ringleader of PC Blakelock's murder. He had made a 'confession' after hours of police questioning, stripped down to his underpants, with no solicitor, parent or even social worker present.

In Sharon Raghip, Charles had found a forceful and highly articulate advocate for her husband. Engin was described by one doctor appearing in the film as 'very close to being classified as mentally handicapped . . . equivalent to a mental age between ten and eleven. He's also illiterate,' his ability to read and comprehend being like that of a six-year-old. And yet, as Peirce told Charles, her client was detained without a solicitor for nearly five days in a police station. 'The police obtained a signature from him to the effect that he didn't want a solicitor, even though he can't read or write, and they continued questioning him until they coerced from him what was later construed as an admission to murder.'

The decade had seen miscarriages of justice revealed in the

case of the Guildford Four, the Birmingham Six and the four men convicted of the murder of the newspaper boy Carl Bridgewater. In all of these cases, the media had played an important role. In his review of the programme in the *Observer*, Richard Ingrams commented, 'Once again, the "Beyond Reasonable Doubt" documentary was a necessary coming together of lawyers and journalists, because of the failures of the judiciary.'

But others were less enthusiastic about the idea of television journalists setting themselves up as judge and jury. Melanie Phillips wrote in the *Guardian*, 'Following trial by television, we now appear to have arrived at Court of Appeal by television . . . Is it really much of a surprise that in such a climate television, which has played such an important role in fostering this breakdown in public confidence, should now claim that it can step in where the judicial process has failed?'

The general verdict, though, was that the argument was persuasive and that this was a necessary piece of journalism. *The Times* reflected: 'You begin to wonder how it is that TV researchers are able to dig out such material, but not, apparently, lawyers who were defending the accused at the time.' The *Sun* reviewer concluded that: 'There is no doubt in my mind that Silcott – who had already been convicted of killing a friend – is evil. But despite that, Wheeler threw a shadow of doubt on whether he actually led the Broadwater butchers. A disturbing, gripping piece of television.'

Charles sent a copy of the programme to David Waddington, the home secretary, to put the case and the new arguments about it on his radar. The reply he received from the Home

Office read: 'The Home Secretary has undertaken to look at the matters raised in your recent film, and he will consider very carefully whether there may be grounds which would justify his intervention in any of the convictions.'

Meanwhile, supporters of the Tottenham Three, the Broadwater Farm Defence Committee and Bernie Grant, MP for Tottenham, cranked up their efforts. Even Environment Minister Michael Portillo, MP for Enfield Southgate, took up the case of his constituent Engin Raghip. On 5 December 1991, the Court of Appeal formally quashed the convictions of Winston Silcott, Mark Braithwaite and Engin Raghip as unsafe, regretting the 'shortcomings of the criminal process'.

In 1988, with Ronald Reagan's presidency drawing to a close, Charles was back on the road covering another US election campaign, bashing out regular reports for *Newsnight*. Until now, he'd written his scripts on his trusty Adler typewriter. I have a picture in my mind of him from our time in Washington and Brussels, typing at speed, using his two index fingers, in classic newsman style. The clacking of the keys and the ding and zip of the carriage return are important riffs in the soundtrack of my childhood. But in 1988, in time for the American elections, he abandoned the Adler and invested in a Tandy 200, one of the earliest laptop computers on the market. As he waxes lyrical to his goddaughter in a letter written on the plane to New York: 'It's smaller than a typewriter and works off batteries . . . I much enjoy the luxury of being able to have second and third thoughts and changing things.' It occurs to me that for someone of his generation, who'd even once had to file a story by Morse code, Charles was always delighted by new technology, from satellite TV to the internet, particularly when it made his job as a journalist easier.

George Bush, Reagan's vice president, was the party's favourite but he was lagging behind Democrat candidate Michael Dukakis in the polls. (Reviewing a 'relentlessly long' book about the 1988 election, Charles would later write: 'That the neurotic, humourless, insecure Dukakis should have risen to become the party's standard bearer was a measure of the Democrats' decline.') The Republicans were holding their convention that year in New Orleans, and I asked Charles if I could join him. It had been nearly ten years since we'd managed a trip on our own; some father–daughter bonding was in order. I was twenty-five and had been on a path that could not have been more different from my father's: performing with a travelling music and theatre company, playing in bands and writing songs. Charles had never encouraged me to follow in his footsteps, but I was starting to think that journalism might suit me. I was working at a local paper in Oxfordshire where the goings-on at the crown court and the coroner's office already had me hooked. Charles said I would have to clear it with the producer, so I wrote to David Coxon Taylor and asked if I could come along and make myself useful. Perhaps my most significant contribution to the operation was buying an eyebrow pencil for David Dimbleby, who was presenting the BBC's live coverage of the convention.

Just as everyone was settling down to what seemed to be a fairly predictable news story about George Bush's anointment as candidate, a last-minute announcement was made. Bush had chosen the ultra-conservative, and somewhat callow, Senator Dan Quayle from Indiana as his running mate. The surprise news panicked Republican insiders but pleased the right wing of the party. Charles spoke to the right-wing televangelist Jerry Falwell, who told him delightedly that Quayle was even more conservative than he was.

And then it emerged that Dan Quayle had in 1969 managed to join the Indiana National Guard – the US equivalent of the Territorial Army – 'the favourite refuge of men who didn't want to fight' and, it was alleged, thereby avoided the draft for Vietnam. The Republicans pulled him off all the breakfast shows. Charles spoke to the chief political commentators from the *Washington Post*, *LA Times* and *Baltimore Sun* that evening, 17 August 1988, who all predicted potential catastrophe for the campaign. But by the end of the convention, Quayle appeared to be weathering the storm. As Charles remarked in the report from the convention floor, his speech was 'suitably banal and encouragingly belligerent'. He had struck the right tone and confounded the critics. 'It may eventually go away,' Charles predicted – correctly, as it turned out.

Later that evening, the BBC teams gathered for the traditional end-of-convention meal and then carried on to Bourbon Street, which offered live music for every taste. First stop was Charles's favourite, the old Preservation Jazz Hall. I left Charles there and, along with Martin Bell and a few others, made for Ryan's – an Irish bar with a house band called Innisfree. Somehow, I ended up joining the band on stage for a number, and then the Belfast-born lead singer and I spent until dawn combing the bars of New Orleans, talking about 'home' and what it meant to us. When the sun came up it occurred to me that I'd better phone my father. 'I'm fine by the way,' I told him. 'I've had a great time. I think I've fallen in love, though. I might stay here in New Orleans for a bit.' The reaction was less explosive than it might have been. 'What do you think I am going to tell your mother when I get back to London? That I've left you in New Orleans with some Irish musician?' He had a point. I capitulated. New Orleans wouldn't become my new home.

In 1989, Charles took time off from *Newsnight* to undertake the mammoth task of completing an eight-part documentary series, *The Road to War*. He'd begun working on this almost three years earlier and the series would be a central part of the BBC's commemoration in September of the fiftieth anniversary of the outbreak of the Second World War. Charles was generally very wary about long projects. As much as anything, it was the fear of being stuck with the wrong producer for a long time. Occasionally, the chemistry was just right but, more often than not, the relationship could be decidedly spiky. Emerging from one long project, Charles wrote to a colleague, 'In my world . . . any project four years and more in gestation imposes a huge burden on its authors. If it doesn't prove a major success, it's a disaster. From the outset it's a major act of faith. You have such faith. I do not, alas.'

Perhaps it was because of his personal interest in the subject, but for *The Road to War* he made an exception, even if that road proved pretty rocky. The consultant to the series was the historian Richard Overy. Charles later told the *Observer* that he had 'bitter' disputes with Overy, especially about Chamberlain and appeasement, while writing the script. 'Look Charles, I've read the books,' Overy would say. 'Yes, Richard,' Charles would reply, 'but I was there.'

Rather than cover the events of the war itself, each episode focused on one of the seven main participant nations in the years leading up to the conflict, the final programme pulling the different threads together as the world tipped into war. One of Charles's main aims in structuring the series in this way was to view each country's path to war from its own perspective, rather than an Anglo-centric one, using archive footage and interviews with veterans, politicians and civilians from the relevant country and thus drawing attention to how the actions of all the main protagonists played in their own way into the coming conflagration.

A reviewer in the *Daily Telegraph* was 'bothered' by this and felt that Charles was suggesting that all the nations covered in the series 'bore equal guilt', which was undoubtedly over-egging it. Mostly, though, the series was well received by TV critics, who collectively appreciated the crisp commentary and authoritative voice Charles brought. An 'exemplary analysis', commented Max Hastings, also in the *Daily Telegraph*; a 'beautifully researched and presented series', said the *Sunday Times*.

For a history series on BBC2, the programmes had healthy viewing figures, almost reaching 3 million for some episodes. One viewer, Molly McEwan from Kirkby Lonsdale in Lancashire, wanted Charles to know how much she had appreciated the programme. 'I hear younger people say when I mention this series "Oh, we want to forget all that" – it frightens me . . .

It is only by showing people what war is all about that we can prevent it. I am too old (85) to worry one way or another – it is the young people I think about.' She signs off, 'Please do not trouble to reply.' Of course, Charles did reply, and he filed her letter along with many others from listeners and viewers that he kept all his life.

In October 1989, while *The Road to War* series was still airing on the BBC, Charles travelled to Georgia, in the wake of what became known as the Tbilisi massacre. He wanted to tell the story of what had happened outside the palace in the city's main square earlier that year, when, in stark contrast to the advent of Perestroika that he had reported on two years before, Russian troops had attacked peaceful demonstrators with spades and trenching tools, injuring hundreds and killing twenty-one people, most of them women.

The *Panorama* film 'Reaping the Whirlwind: Bloody Sunday', a joint production with Georgian TV, described the scene on 9 April as 10,000 people gathered in the square. They were there to demonstrate in favour of Georgian independence and to support a hunger strike that had begun five days earlier by students protesting against Soviet rule in general and anti-Georgian separatists in the Black Sea region of Abkhazia. There was a festive atmosphere, with singing and dancing to traditional Georgian music.

For all that, the first secretary of the Georgian Communist Party, Jumber Pastiashvili, had called for Soviet troops to come in and help restore order. Aware of the approaching danger, minutes before the attack, still in the darkness before dawn, the patriarch of the Georgian church pleaded with the crowd to come into the church or leave the square. Nobody moved. Instead, the cry went up, 'We swear, we swear, we swear' – the people were swearing an oath to stay and waited in absolute silence. That silence was broken by the sound of armoured troop carriers and the Russian 'special' troops advancing on the demonstrators in the square.

Eyewitnesses and survivors described their ordeal to Charles: 'He sprayed gas into my mouth, kicking my head, breaking my teeth,' one woman said. 'It was sheer savagery,' said another. Translating these harrowing testimonies for the BBC was Maya Kiasashvili, a Georgian academic and writer with whom Charles stayed in touch afterwards – one of many friendships he cherished and forged while reporting on intense moments of personal and political change. On her thirty-ninth birthday, Maya wrote, 'Lots of us knew the hard times were coming, but to live through them really takes all our courage ([of] which I have plenty) and hope (none whatsoever!) . . . every time there's trouble brewing in Georgia, I've a faint hope you might come for a story.'

The night shots of the massacre were captured on a VHS camera by a local freelancer who wouldn't let the BBC team use more than five minutes. But that was enough. It shook many who watched it for the first time. The *Panorama* film won the Royal Television Society award for the best international documentary of the year. It was picked up around the world. The *MacNeil/Lehrer NewsHour*, the flagship TV news programme on the American PBS channel, ran a cut-down version of the film.

SHIRIN WHEELER

The events of 9 April, which took place even as Russia was pushing ahead with the drive towards greater political openness, galvanised opposition to Soviet rule in Georgia. And there's a certain irony that it was because of those same reforms that an official inquiry into the terrible events of that day was held soon afterwards. This found blame with the Georgian government in asking for troops, with the Russians for sending them, and with the Soviet military for attacking civilians. There were still many questions about the sequence of events that were not clear. Galina Staravoytova, a member of the Soviet Duma, told Charles that she believed that behind the Tbilisi massacre were anti-Perestroika forces that could still carry the day, believing that unless nationalism was stamped out, the Soviet Union would break up. 'The process taking place now could either strengthen the sovereignty of the republic through the Soviet Union or it could lead to the disintegration of the Soviet Union. Neither possibility can be excluded,' she told Charles, somewhat prophetically.

Staravoytova, a defender of ethnic minorities in Russia, would be gunned down nine years later outside her apartment block in St Petersburg. Once a trusted advisor to Boris Yeltsin, she had fallen foul of him and other dangerous men once she started criticising the intelligence services and the Chechen War.

Another long-standing conflict would flare up again that year: the one between Charles and the BBC's top management. Two years earlier, John Birt had been brought in from London Weekend Television as deputy director general. Birt was not only known as the producer of London Weekend Television's hugely successful David Frost interviews with Richard Nixon but also creator of the politics programme *Weekend World*, with a reputation as a hyper-efficient manager who would now 'reform' the BBC's News and Current Affairs department. In July 1987, he summoned the news teams to Lime Grove to hear his plans for a revamp according to his vision of news – more 'analysis', along with more management controls, systems and audits.

His presentation over, Birt fell victim to Charles's forensic questioning: 'When you say analysis, when you use such words, how soon are you going to define what you mean? Because we can't define it – you have to do the definition. When are you going to do that? Because we've been analysing on *Newsnight* for about six years.'

'I never suggested you haven't,' said Birt.

'Well, when you say you want more analysis, can you spell out precisely what form that should take and how it should contrast with what we're now doing?' Charles pressed.

Birt became a little prickly. 'If you listened to what I said, when I talked about more news analysis, I used it in the context of the news, not in the context of *Newsnight*, which very plainly as you say has been in the news analysis game.'

'I wrote it down, actually,' said Charles. 'You said you thought that *Newsnight*'s role should be more tightly defined and that you were thinking primarily of news analysis of stories of the day and the past few days.'

Birt was visibly uncomfortable with this onslaught. One of those present at the meeting was Tim Gardam, soon to be editor of *Newsnight*. 'You could just feel the ice coming from the platform,' he remembered. Accounts of the confrontation spread rapidly through the BBC. According to Gardam, Charles was voicing the feelings of many in the room and out of it, upset at the 'purge' of colleagues who had, it was charged, been moved sideways to make room for Birt's own people and unhappy at being lectured on how to do their jobs by an outsider. These days there's no hint that John Birt harbours any resentment about the episode: 'If that kind of thing upset me, I would not have lasted very long,' he told me, 'I only ever admired Charles – I'm not sure the feeling was mutual though.'

At the time, the confrontation was the expression of a deep-seated culture clash. As a later BBC director general, Mark Thompson, described it, 'If John Birt was the Roundheads' Roundhead, Charles came across as a Cavalier hero – passionately committed to the primacy of the individual correspondent's witness and judgement, deeply suspicious of any attempt to hedge that autonomy and personal responsibility with systems or checks and balances.' Thompson, who was one of the young producers fast-tracked into senior management by John Birt, told me that he eventually came down 'firmly' on Birt's side in the argument: 'You could believe in the Birt agenda and still recognise that many of the best journalists, including Charles, were fully paid-up members of the awkward squad and bound to be suspicious.' But the fact that Charles, someone he respected deeply, was so critical definitely made him pause. Ultimately, though, Thompson believes BBC journalism was in need of reform – 'I never heard anyone, and certainly not John Birt, ever criticise the quality of Charles's work . . . But the fact is that in the 1980s, not every BBC journalist was operating anywhere near Charles's level . . . A majority of my colleagues were quite sure that John's plans would be the death of independent journalism. In the event, it grew stronger and more ambitious.'

Before long, Charles and John Birt were crossing swords again. At the end of April 1989, the unions BECTU and the NUJ set up a picket outside TV Centre. Charles was among them. As he told the *Sunday Times* reporter, and later bestselling novelist, Robert Harris, 'I'm going to join the strike in protest at the action of the director general and his deputy in giving themselves a thirty per cent pay rise, while arguing they can't afford comparative increases for their staff. Half a dozen previous DGs must be turning in their graves.' Charles said he didn't actually believe in journalists striking for pay but his sense of fairness was offended. Michael Checkland and John Birt's 30 per cent pay hikes had been at the centre of the unions' campaign for industrial action for several months, and had already been reported by several newspapers unchallenged. But perhaps because it was Charles, one of the BBC's most respected correspondents, who spoke out, the *Sunday Times* article caused a massive rumpus. By Monday morning, the BBC press office had released a statement saying the claims of high pay increases for 'top BBC people' were 'misinformed'. The salary levels of the DG and his deputy had been reassessed and fixed by the board of governors – crucially, they hadn't been self-awarded. The BBC's lawyers, acting for Checkland and Birt, were soon in touch with Charles to demand an apology.

The atmosphere at home was getting stressful. Dip was anxious; Charles was belligerent. She pleaded with him to apologise publicly. But when the BBC demanded Charles put his name to a blanket apology on the *Sunday Times* Op-Ed page the following weekend, he declined. He explained in separate personal letters to Birt and Checkland that the apology covered assertions he had not made, and he'd been left with no time to negotiate an alternative wording. But he conceded that he had been inaccurate and 'careless, even offensive' in saying the men had 'awarded themselves' the massive rises. As he wrote in his letter to Birt, 'When you telephoned me last Sunday, I volunteered to try to correct the misinformation of which you complained. I did so in an interview with ITN on the picket line the next day.' This didn't do the trick.

Another letter arrived from the BBC solicitor demanding a public admission from Charles that he'd got it wrong or they would take 'further action'. They proposed an article in the *Listener* magazine in June with an apology. But the draft that Charles agreed to send in advance wasn't what they had in mind. The apology was there but Charles had presented a detailed examination of the circumstances leading up to the strike, dissecting the annual reports and concluding that none of the 'denials and explanations issued on behalf of the senior managers have done anything to dispel the strong feelings that led to so many – not habitually militant – BBC people to make the only protest available, to demonstrate.' He concluded, 'the BBC is applying different standards – one on the quarterdeck, another before the mast', which was an ex-Royal Marine's suitably nautical tilt at the preferential treatment enjoyed by the high-ups in charge of the vessel.

The BBC decided to cut its losses. The lawyer wrote to

Charles to say although it wasn't the redress they were looking for, his draft article did at least show he had 'taken steps' in the right direction. The article was withdrawn from publication and the matter was closed. But Charles had the pleasure of knowing that, although it was a fine-run thing, the bigwigs up on the quarterdeck hadn't really won this particular battle.

Things were moving fast as the new decade arrived. The Soviet empire was on the point of collapse, hastened by the Gorbachev reforms and by the unstoppable force that had begun in Gdańsk, that early flap of the butterfly's wings. By the end of August 1989, a Solidarity-led coalition government had been formed and Charles would attend the final congress of the Polish Communist Party in Warsaw. The following year, Lech Walesa would be elected president.

On 3 October 1990, Charles joined Jeremy Paxman in Berlin to mark the moment of German reunification, barely one year after the Berlin Wall came down. This was a place that had been the symbolic heart of the Cold War. And now the country where Charles had been born, had fought in during the war and had covered as a journalist when it was split in two was at last about to be peacefully reunited – though, as Charles was about to find out, 'peacefully' might not have been exactly the right word.

The BBC had managed to get a position right in the middle of the square near the Brandenburg Gate. But what they hadn't banked on was the million or so drunken revellers also in attendance and the huge fireworks display that took place. The noise was deafening, and Charles and Jeremy were struggling to hear each other. Charles's body language in the recording says it all – shifting from side to side, hands in pockets, turning his back to the camera, raising his eyebrows and grimacing.

'I'd like to be down there instead of up here,' he shouts to Jeremy.

'You will be in a moment, Charles, just bear with us for a moment, though,' says Jeremy. He doesn't seem entirely happy with Charles's response.

'Jeremy, this is pure Monty Python – having a serious political discussion in the middle of a fireworks display.'

Curiously, Charles's wry response to the proceedings at this anarchic ushering-in of a new era became one of the best-known and most quoted moments in his TV career. The BBC didn't come out of it quite as well. According to Paxman, the whole debacle was later described to him by the managing editor of BBC TV as the 'worst outside broadcast in the entire history of the organisation'.

But as the Cold War reached its pyrotechnical, Pythonesque conclusion in Berlin, another war was about to take place on a different continent – and Charles would be there to witness the far grimmer conclusion to that one.

9.
VOICES FROM THE EDGE

Five million people are on this mountain ... Our houses are destroyed ... They see this, but they don't talk. Why? We are human like you.

KURDISH MOTHER ON THE IRAN–IRAQ BORDER
SPEAKING TO CHARLES, BBC *NEWSNIGHT*, 15 APRIL 1991

'Must go to the local graveyard and try to talk to gravediggers. All my love, C x.'

Charles was looking for bodies. He was writing home from Kuwait City in the aftermath of the Gulf War, in March 1991. Saddam's forces had been driven out of Kuwait, but the US-led coalition decided not to pursue them to Baghdad. At which point, the international press retreated. The story looked like it was over. But Charles insisted there was something else that needed telling.

Reports had been coming out of Kuwait of violence and detention of members of the Palestinian community and other non-Kuwaitis, accused of collaboration with the Iraqis during the occupation. The PLO leader Yasser Arafat had sided with Saddam Hussein, believing he was the best hope for Palestinian statehood, and, while many among Kuwait's Palestinian community disagreed with this position, revenge was being taken. Human rights groups like Amnesty International, where Dip had now taken up a job and was working on the Middle East desk, were growing increasingly worried. The head of Amnesty's team responsible for Kuwait and Iraq, Hania Mufti, was planning to investigate and gather testimonies. Dip suggested that Charles might find a story for *Newsnight* in it too.

During the occupation, the Kuwaitis suffered hugely at the hands of the Iraqis. Hania worked on the Amnesty International paper published at the start of December 1990, which is said to have contributed to the decision by the US and others to intervene. The paper carried accounts of human rights abuses, such as hundreds of extrajudicial executions, widespread torture of people in custody, and the arbitrary arrest and detention of thousands of civilians and military personnel. After the Iraqi retreat, Hania went back to the region. She told me, 'We went to Kuwait to investigate both the Iraqi abuses and those of the returning Kuwaitis. Once on the ground, we found ourselves overwhelmed by the sheer number of cases being reported of arbitrary arrests, torture and killings being committed by the Kuwaitis, who had quickly turned from victims to abusers. The majority of these victims were foreign workers – Palestinians, Sudanese, Egyptians and others – targeted as suspected collaborators with the Iraqi occupiers. We spent some two weeks working day and night, recording terrible testimonies from those who had initially been held in secret detention facilities for several weeks and then released into the mainstream prison system.'

Charles managed to persuade Tim Gardam, the editor of *Newsnight*, to give him a camera crew and a producer. *Newsnight*'s deputy editor, Eamonn Matthews, also went to help produce the films. They flew into Saudi Arabia, then headed out to Kuwait City, where they settled into a small hotel next to the bombed-out Hilton. It was pretty basic, with limited food supplies and no hot water. But compared to conditions in the city's Palestinian district of Hawalli it was luxurious. Before the Iraqi invasion, around 400,000 Palestinians were living in Kuwait. That number had more than halved, with many now facing expulsion and persecution. Charles found the Hawalli neighbourhood 'ghettoised'. The Kuwaitis had taken charge. Self-appointed gun-toting guardians of law and order were operating checkpoints. Piles of wrecked cars barred any entry to or exit from the neighbourhood.

'What marks out Hawalli,' reported Charles, 'is an air of insecurity, not to say fear.'

They spent four days in Hawalli. During that time, they were constantly approached to meet victims of interrogations, beatings and worse. One young man, his face masked by a red-and-white Palestinian scarf, recounted his ordeal to the camera. He had been taken by ten men from his parents' home, held for five days in a police cell, beaten with rubber and metal piping and burnt with electric wires to extract a confession that he had collaborated with the Iraqis.

Alongside the Palestinians incarcerated in detention centres and makeshift prisons around the country, witnesses told the BBC there were dozens of others in the cells – Sudanese and Egyptians – all accused of collaboration. Charles heard the charge that people were killed in custody, including a thirteen-year-old boy whose body was delivered to a hospital with a bullet wound to the head. The atrocities were taking place in police stations but, 'We also know that the military have taken over schools to use as detention centres,' Charles reported.

He wrote to Dip: 'Darling, I love you and miss you all – but I'm glad I came out: the aftermath of the war needs reporting – especially from a human rights angle and not enough people are ignoring the barrage of Kuwaiti government propaganda and getting at the plight of the Palestinians and others. There are rumours that the government is to clamp down on journalists – give us minders and stop us taking unofficial guides through checkpoints.'

In case the clampdown happened, Charles and the crew worked fast. Hence the trip to meet the gravediggers. The visit to the al-Rigga cemetery on the edge of town brought no information at first. They were told that unidentified victims of Iraqi atrocities could be buried in multiple graves. 'Have any non-Kuwaitis been brought here for burial?' Charles asked the grave manager. 'No,' he replied, 'they are all Kuwaitis.' But later a younger gravedigger approached the BBC team to tell them that, in the last few days, a third row of graves had been dug. The mutilated bodies of Palestinians, about twenty of them, were brought in and recorded as martyrs. 'Shot in their heads, cigarette burns on their body, cut with knives,' he told Charles.

Charles gently confronted the grave manager at al-Rigga again with what they had been told. Under Charles's questioning, he admitted he saw cigarette burns on some of the bodies and conceded that they may be victims of interrogation. And then the team got a tip-off that torture victims were being admitted onto a ward in Kuwait City's main hospital – Ward 18.

In the film they made at the hospital, a nurse, her face concealed, tells Charles that two teenage Palestinian boys had been brought up through the basement to the surgical ward. They had been tortured. She says: 'There was injury to the legs, stab wounds on the back, bruises around the eyes, cigarette burns on their bodies.' The boys were treated by military doctors, kept in for twenty-four hours and taken away again. A few days later, she says, they brought a nineteen-year-old Palestinian, with cuts on his hands and head. 'We stopped the bleeding and we stitched the wounds. Then one Kuwaiti officer saw us and said there was no need to stitch his wounds because, he said, "We will torture him again and maybe we'll bring him back only for you only to wrap him."'

'Only to wrap him?' repeats Charles. 'Meaning?'

Meaning they will have killed him, she tells him, and that she will be wrapping his body in a winding sheet. The camera films Charles as he strides down the hospital corridor in search of Ward 18. Two armed men in uniform bar his way. A nurse arrives. 'Nobody is allowed in here,' she says. 'Orders of the army. Talk to the medical director, Dr Ali.'

Dr Ali looks a couple of decades younger than Charles. Frowning, he's clearly not quite sure what to make of this persistent Englishman who says with calm authority, the camera filming over his right shoulder, 'We want to go in because we understand that you have two severely injured Palestinian men.'

'We have injured patients, different nationalities. No Palestinians came as patients. There are no Palestinians in Ward 18,' comes the definitive answer.

Charles has caught the whiff of a lie. He presses on: 'Is this absolutely sure? We've heard that some of them have been brought in by the police. Do you think you could check?'

And then Dr Ali divulges that some injured men have been brought in but were discharged again with just bruises – 'maybe because of a fight'.

'Just bruises. Possibly beaten under interrogation?' Charles hazards.

Dr Ali erupts under the barrage of questions. 'Why,' he rails, 'has no one cared about what the Iraqis did to the Kuwaitis during the occupation?'

'Doctor, I promise you, that has received extensive coverage by the media,' says Charles.

And then, from Dr Ali: 'If we treated them badly, they deserved it.'

The silence lasts for three heartbeats. 'Are you speaking as a doctor?'

'No, not as a doctor, as a Kuwaiti citizen.'

Another dramatic silence, then Charles turns to leave, and the crew follows.

The film is gripping television. Eamonn Matthews told me, 'It was all very fluid. Brian Hulls, the cameraman, was just stuck to Charles in an as-it-happens kind of way. Charles was treating the camera like a kind of companion. Today we would call it unmediated television. In those days television was rather staid – you'd write the piece to camera and memorise it. I think those films were very influential in terms of how we could do foreign affairs coverage.'

An MA student who later wrote to Charles for help in her thesis on multilingual exchanges in journalism wondered if non-native speakers like Dr Ali had been put at a disadvantage. 'I don't think Dr Ali was at a linguistic disadvantage,' Charles replied. 'His problem was that he was lying and was aware that I knew it.'

The 'liberation' of Kuwait had deprived thousands of foreign workers in Kuwait of their freedom to travel and earn a living. Kuwaitis captured by the Iraqis or fleeing the war had been allowed back into the country after the Iraqis had dumped them on the border, but thousands of non-Kuwaitis were not. They were regarded as a security risk, but also the economy had shrunk since the war and the Kuwaiti government wanted to reduce its dependence on foreign workers. Charles met about 600 of them near a town called Safwan, in a barren patch of no man's land on the border of Iraq and Kuwait. He found them hungry and confused, sheltering under corrugated steel sheets, treated like 'third-class citizens'. There were Egyptians, Palestinians, Sudanese, Indians and Sri Lankans. They'd been told they could not return to Kuwait where they had been employed alongside the hundreds of thousands of other non-Kuwaitis who effectively served as the backbone of the economy, not just in its service industry but in keeping its administration and hospitals functioning. Their families, living abroad and reliant on their monthly remittances, had received no news of them.

Charles became especially friendly with a group of Indian and Sri Lankan workers. Among them was a young man called Paranthaman 'Paran' Somasundaram. After several months in an Iraqi prison, he had grown thin, his hair wild and his beard matted with dust. In the report Charles filed for *Newsnight*, Paran told him that he had been working as a waiter at the Pullman Hotel in Kuwait City. Shortly before the ground fighting began, he and several other Sri Lankans and Kuwaitis were arrested by Iraqi soldiers and transported to Basra. When anti-Saddam rebels liberated the prison, they walked around fifty kilometres south as far as the border. But the Sri Lankans were refused permission to re-enter Kuwait.

Charles took up Paran's case and travelled to Kuwait City to see if his former employers could be of any help. The Pullman was still in one piece and Charles asked its manager, Alam Al-Kazemi, the camera rolling, 'He's going to be hungry, he's very thin, he doesn't have many clothes. Are you going to help him?' The hotel manager quickly produced a 'to whom it may concern' letter that testified to Paran's previous employment with a promise of another job on his return.

The route back from Kuwait City to the settlement at Safwan took Charles and the crew down Highway 80, the so-called 'highway of death', the camera taking in the hundreds of charred and smashed-up trucks, tanks and buses, the result of an Allied aircraft attack on a boxed-in traffic jam of Iraqis retreating from Kuwait towards Basra. Back at the makeshift camp, Charles presented the letter from the Pullman to the Kuwaiti 'commandant' of the camp. He was a young, tall man with a distinctly American twang when he spoke. But he was unimpressed, barely glancing at the letter. Buttoning up his jacket and pulling down his baseball cap, he donned a pair of sunglasses and told Charles, 'This is not their land. This is our country, our border. We had enough trouble. You should be speaking to the government.'

So, it was back on the road to Kuwait City to see Suliman Mutawa, Kuwait's minister of planning. 'In the film, it's clear that Charles has the bit between his teeth. 'It must be a bureaucratic problem,' the minister insists. He tells Charles on camera that there is no policy of discrimination: 'I am not asking for forgiveness but . . . we are learning and remedying every single moment.'

Later that afternoon, the British ambassador told Charles that the Kuwaitis had put a new policy in place since the invasion to slash the number of their foreign workers by half. That left several hundred thousand, including the workers near Safwan, facing grave insecurity.

'The Palestinians and the foreign workers here need protection. The Allies planned the war, they didn't plan the peace,' Charles told his audience. 'If the Kuwaitis do expel several hundred thousand of these people, where are they to go? And what about the stability of the Middle East? The Kuwaiti government needs help. But surely also some degree of international supervision. At the very least a United Nations presence. After all, this was a United Nations war.'

Charles had to inform Paran and his friends that, for now, he didn't have good news – except for one man. In Kuwait City, Charles and the crew tracked down Mrs Sadvi Rajakambalam, a staff nurse whose Indian husband was at the camp after three months in an Iraqi prison. They brought her to meet him – along with their eleven-year-old son. They ran to each other. As she broke into loud sobs, burying her face in her husband's dusty jacket, her son started to shout. It was like a scene from a Hollywood movie, only it was real. The camp commander felt moved enough to relent and the family was allowed to cross back into Kuwait.

'Sadly, reuniting this family was our only success. For the time being, the Sri Lankans had to be left behind,' runs Charles's commentary. But the story didn't end there. Before he left Kuwait, Charles told the International Committee of the Red Cross and the British embassy about Paran Somasundaram and his friends' predicament. He wrote to Paran's parents: 'Your son and I became good friends. He is cheerful and well, in spite of the frustrations of living in a makeshift corrugated iron hut without much water and no sanitation.'

The next month, he received a reply from Paran's father, writing from Sri Lanka's capital Colombo through a scribe, who couldn't resist the chance to employ a few rhetorical flourishes: 'The whole family was highly worried and prayed to the Almighty God day and night for the safety of Paran . . . On receipt of your letter, we find that the Almighty has answered our sincere call. It is Mr Charles Wheeler who has appeared as the God's Representative and helped our son.'

Charles rather typically never mentioned the letter to us, and I imagine he might have winced slightly at his promotion to the Lord's emissary. He and the team received a Royal Television Society award that year for the film *Kuwait: The Forgotten Prisoners*, but I suspect that a second letter from

Mr Somasundaram was just as welcome: 'Now we are happy to inform you that we received a letter from Paran on 23:4:91 through the Sri Lankan embassy, Kuwait, that he is okay. I hear from him that he is now working as a cleaning supervisor in the Kuwait health ministry.'

A few days after he left Kuwait, Charles travelled to US-occupied southern Iraq with the *Newsnight* team. His reports from the region carried horrifying accounts from witnesses to the failed uprising against Saddam Hussein in the south: charcoal-coloured corpses hit by napalm; the tell-tale signs of chemical weapons on the woundless dead; unburied bodies eaten by dogs and hundreds of rebels executed, some hanging from the gun barrels of tanks, others tied to lampposts and left for days.

Encouraged by rhetoric coming out of Washington after Saddam had been pushed out of Kuwait, in March, Iraqi rebel army units joining the Shia in southern Iraq and the Kurds in the north had both staged uprisings against the Iraqi regime. But Saddam's forces had crushed the resistance by early April. The reprisals were brutal, and tens of thousands of people died in the slaughter.

Across the region, around two million people were on the move, fleeing Saddam's fury, battling the elements, trying to stave off starvation. In mid-April, Charles returned to the region with another *Newsnight* team to report on the plight of the Kurds. They flew into Iran. After two days in Teheran, Charles, his producer Jim Gray, the crew and fixer slipped their official government minders and headed into the Zagros Mountains.

Armed with papers that allowed them only to move within

Iran, they reached the border with Iraq. Charles and Jim looked at each other. 'Oh, bugger it,' Charles said. They took a quick straw poll with the camera and sound man and kept going, past the townships and the villages, into the mountains. They were confronted by an astounding sight. Coming from the opposite direction, on this road from Kurdish Iraq to Kurdish Iran, were hundreds of thousands of people, many in vehicles, most on foot – Kurdish families, exhausted, hungry and cold.

Watching the BBC report again, I am struck how, as he often did with the people he interviewed, Charles moved to a position so as to physically accommodate them and be unthreatening, in this case at the feet of a young Kurdish mother sitting on the ledge of the mountain, holding her small child close to her. The camera is behind him, hovering over his right shoulder. Here, on the Iran–Iraq border, at 6,000 feet up in the mountains, the woman he is speaking to accuses the world of forgetting about them and abandoning them to Saddam Hussein's bombing and persecution. The Kurds, refugees in their own land, were under attack. She had been walking for two weeks, 100 miles from the city of Sulaymaniyah in Kurdish Iraq. She was desperately tired. But she wanted to speak.

'Five million people are on this mountain, in this cold, wet place. Who is responsible for this? Our houses are destroyed . . . Mr George Bush is responsible for all of this. He could destroy Saddam and his army but he doesn't try. All this because he doesn't want Kurdish and Shia to be leaders in Iraq . . . Why did he do that? We could live in peace. The war is finished. Kuwait is one million. He does this whole war for one million. We are five million. Saddam Hussein is bombing with helicopters to destroy us. They see this, but they don't talk. Why? We are human – like you.' She sobbed into her scarf, exhausted.

When Charles and the crew descended into the valley, they found thousands in the settlement below. There was more bewilderment and anger. In the film, we see a woman standing in front of Charles, calling out her litany of suffering. Slowly, she moves the backs of her hands against his chest in rhythm with her cries. He stands there, unmoving, looking down, listening. 'We seem to have been the first Westerners here and felt the blast of much pent-up bitterness,' Charles later recorded in his commentary.

He and the whole crew were deeply affected by what they had seen. People were dying – babies, the old and the infirm – on that crowded single-track road where barely any aid trucks could get through. Charles found his producer giving away some of their provisions, stored in the back of their car, to the children. 'I understand why you're doing it, Jim, and it's good,' he said. 'But we have to finish the assignment and get back to tell the story.'

Jim Gray, who became head of BBC TV Current Affairs, said as a news producer it was the most formative and arduous story he was ever involved with. He told me that when he first learnt he was to work with Charles on the Kurdish story in Iraq, he was distinctly nervous. They'd never worked together before, and Charles had a reputation among the producers on *Newsnight*: 'I had heard he tested people – I wouldn't say test them to destruction but was fearsome in asking you to check things and for putting you through the mill. Eamonn Matthews, who had just got back from the Kuwait story with

Charles, told me, "When you come out the other side – and I'm sure you will, Jim – it's all sweet and a great strong bond." And sure enough, that is what happened. The first couple of days – you felt the weight of his experience. He was seeing how I operated and then it went away because we were simpatico.'

Tim Gardam, editor of *Newsnight*, which put the story out, later said: 'Looking back at my years in journalism, this remains the one piece of journalism that matters most to me.' For his own part, Charles said this was the most moving story he'd covered in his career. As he later commented, 'The only time in all the fifty years that I've been a journalist when I felt that [I've] been able to help bring about change was when the Kurds were suffering after the Gulf War. And I think for once the pictures moved the politicians to take action.'

British Prime Minister John Major had been lobbying hard for militarily protected safe havens for the Kurds but the proposal was encountering resistance, especially from the US. Soon after the story ran on *Newsnight* and the BBC's *Nine O'Clock News*, Tim Gardam wrote to Charles: 'I am told by the Foreign Office that your first report was extremely important in galvanising the British effort.'

The *Newsnight* team had pushed the story hard. In the US, ABC's *Nightline* programme picked it up and it ran on several other American networks on 15 April. Two days later, John Major was on the steps of Downing Street welcoming a decision by the US to support his initiative. And by the time Charles was filing his second report on the Kurdish refugees in Iran, *Newsnight* was reporting that the first British troops were flying out to northern Iraq to set up safe havens for the Kurds.

The focus was now shifting to Iran where, despite Iranian efforts, international aid was not getting through. Charles encountered harrowing scenes. 'There is nothing but mud and water,' he reported from the town of Piranshahr in Iran, where he found thousands of refugees. It had been raining for days and, underneath makeshift shelters, families were shivering, barely keeping dry.

A nearby mosque had become a haven for the women, children and the older men, rammed inside to escape the rain. 'All these people are hungry, there's no milk for the children – they are drinking Coca-Cola. These mothers, after two weeks in the mountains, are struggling to keep their children alive. Some of these women seem to be in shock; they sit staring into space. The air is foetid,' he reported.

There was no proper tented refugee camp for miles and no sign of aid. Refugees coming down from the mountains told Charles that people were dying on the side of the road. One man told him he'd lost two of his children. Another, speaking from under a shroud of plastic to keep off the rain, said, 'We need life. This is no life. We live here like animals.'

Charles was not so much shocked as profoundly angered by what he saw. Looking bedraggled and standing in a sea of mud, he told viewers in his piece to camera: 'You spend five or ten minutes in this weather and no matter how many clothes you're wearing, you're soaked, and you're wet, and you're miserable. These people have been here for two weeks. Two weeks since they left the Kurdish towns. The road is closed, the town is full, the Iranian authorities can't cope. There's a big green plain here. This is a valley, a high valley. It should be possible to drop tents, to drop food, from aircraft. It wouldn't be too difficult – it doesn't rain all the time, there aren't high winds all the time. What these people cannot understand is why they're still sitting here and why so little aid is coming from outside.'

Later, Charles would reflect that this was not a time to aspire to any kind of detachment as a journalist. 'I got terribly wrapped up in it. We all got terribly wrapped up. I got angrier and angrier; nothing was being dropped. Nobody was even dropping small packets of food. I watched it happen. Looking at that crowd of Kurds, wet, hungry, miserable, ankle-deep in water, in diarrhoea, I was terribly angry. Objectivity flies out in situations like this.'

Editing the material and then getting it down the line to London was always going to be a challenge. The crew travelled to a small pension house to edit the films, but they could only feed them to London from back in Teheran. A band of Peshmerga guerrillas, young men carrying AK47s, had been engaged by the fixer to guide them down and keep watch at night. One time, they'd bedded down, with straw bales on stone floors for mattresses, when Jim woke from a fitful doze to the sound of banter and laughing. 'It was Charles and the guerrillas.' The fixer was translating between them. 'You'll never believe it, we're playing a guess-my-age game,' Charles told Jim. They thought baby-faced Jim looked way younger than his thirty years and, as for Charles, the 'vintage gentleman with the craggy face and shock of white hair', as Jim put it, once they heard his age, they insisted he shouldn't be chasing up and down mountains.

That was not Charles's approach to life, though. In fact,

he'd spent his sixty-eighth birthday one month earlier in a smashed-up hotel in Kuwait City. There was no electricity and no hot water. Worse, there was no booze, though that hadn't dampened his spirits. After a candlelit supper of rice and beans over their camping stove, he said to cameraman Brian Hulls and his producer Eamonn Matthews, 'I can't believe how lucky I am to be here. Something awful might have happened to me – like retirement.'

For a journalist who had never held the title 'war correspondent', war – the lead-up to it, its aftermath and its human cost – coloured Charles's journalism from the very start. As a veteran of the Second World War, he'd also emerged as a kind of de facto 'world war correspondent' for the BBC. And so, as the fiftieth anniversary commemorations of D-Day approached, Charles found himself in demand for a series of documentaries and projects that would return him to his own past as well as that of the nation. The two-part series *D-Day: Turning the Tide* and *The Battle for Normandy* in June 1994 brought together former British and German servicemen, as well as French civilians, to tell their stories of the landings and the bloody campaign that followed.

As Charles recalled in the opening programme, which charted the first twenty-four hours of Operation Overlord, 'Most of us guessed quite early in 1944 that we'd be crossing the Channel that summer but what we never imagined and scarcely believed as we saw it all coming together was the sheer scale of the thing.' Unlike *The Road to War*, which Charles had completed some five years earlier, the programme was almost entirely based on the testimonies of those who were there. 'This is a film entirely about veterans,' he said. 'There are no historians, no pundits. All the people in the film, including me, are Normandy veterans.'

Using the testimonies of the men who lived through it, *The Battle for Normandy* charted the terrible human cost of the campaign: the implications of the failure to take Caen in the first days of the landings, the devastating bombing of the city, the carnage wreaked on British troops by the German Wehrmacht during Operation Goodwood and Operation Epsom, caught out by the sunken roads and hedgerows of the *bocage*. It is a melancholy and intense film. Mark Fielder, who produced both films, told me that what Charles wanted was 'a truthful, powerful telling of what had happened. Not jingoistic or solely from the British point of view, and definitely not a triumphalist celebration.'

For the BBC's live coverage of the commemorations, broadcast just yards from where Charles himself had stepped ashore fifty years before, Charles combined the role of pundit and eyewitness. John Tusa, presenting, turned to him for a few words of wisdom after the set piece reports of the day's ceremonies. Charles can be seen almost scowling from his studio armchair overlooking the beach. The BBC should have known he couldn't be counted on to serve up what was expected. 'I think what we're hearing about D-Day in these last two days is a rather sanitised history,' he growls. 'It's a sanitised production . . . There were bad mistakes, there were misjudgements, there were intelligence failures. We're hearing about all the bravery and all the good things that happened. I would like it to be a little more realistic. I think people should be a little less worried about treading on other people's feelings.' He didn't stop there. A long-standing concern for him was what happened at Caen, a city whose devastation by the Allies was something he witnessed soon after D-Day: 'Nobody is talking about the fact that somewhere between 4,000 and 10,000 people were killed in the repeated bombing and shelling of Caen. Nobody's mentioned it. And that's sad. They probably won't mention the Burma War either.'

It seems the gods of television news were listening, or at least the controller of BBC1, Alan Yentob. The following year, Charles was approached again by Mark Fielder, who had his own reasons to make sure that the neglected Far East campaign featured more prominently in the national narrative. *Burma – the Forgotten War* followed the format of the Normandy films, with the focus on three veterans, taking them back to where they had fought as young soldiers: John Hill from the 2nd Battalion of the Berkshire Regiment, Richard Rhodes James, who served with the Chindits, and Bruce Kinloch of the Gurkhas. But unlike those who had fought in Normandy, veterans of this campaign felt set aside by the people at home. In June 1944, all eyes were on D-Day and the defeat of Hitler and yet the British 14th Army (made up of Indian and other Commonwealth troops alongside the British) was just beginning to turn its fortunes around in a brutal war against the Japanese in Burma that had already lasted for more than two and a half years.

The film feels like an act of remembrance – by Charles, a veteran of Normandy; by Mark Fielder, the son of a soldier almost broken by his Japanese captors after three years as a prisoner of war following his capture at Singapore in February

1942, and from the veterans of the Burma campaign for their fallen comrades. Charles opens the film: 'Of all the British campaigns in World War Two, Burma was the worst. Not because it was the longest, though it was – nearly four years – but because here in Burma, there was so much more to fear and to endure: a fanatical enemy, the jungle, hunger, thirst, disease, dying from wounds hundreds of miles from anywhere and being taken prisoner by the Japanese. Soldiers who fought in other places knew of these things and were grateful not to be here. And so, it seems infinitely sad that for fifty years, the men who did fight here – the 14th Army – thought of themselves as forgotten.'

Charles, along with the BBC team and the veterans, flew into the Burmese capital Rangoon and then moved up-country for what was to prove a physically and emotionally exhausting journey. Nearly everyone became ill with a combination of ailments including dehydration and a mystery virus. 'It was really difficult, probably the most difficult filming trip that I have ever done, working in punishing heat of around forty-five degrees,' remembers Mark. Charles, though, remained fit. In fact, he almost embraced the difficult conditions.

Charles and the veterans revisited the locations of key battles and events, such as the early Japanese advance into central Burma, where the British Commander General Smyth blew up Sittang Bridge with thousands of troops stranded on the east side. 'I was bloody angry,' Bruce Kinloch told Charles. 'We thought we'd done our bit and then some bugger goes and blows the bridge before we can get over it.' Bruce showed him the spot where he swam 1,000 yards across the river in search of boats to bring the injured back across. He escaped to fight another day, but thousands of men were captured by the Japanese in what proved to be a major loss in the campaign.

The Japanese Army almost made it as far as India but was eventually repulsed at the Battle of Imphal in July 1944. Before then, morale was kept up by the exploits of the Chindits under the charismatic command of Major General Orde Wingate. These special military units employed guerrilla-style tactics and took the fight to the enemy in the heart of the jungle, where British troops had begun to feel the Japanese were invincible. Trudging through dense undergrowth with former Chindit officer Richard Rhodes James, Charles heard how they would be embedded behind enemy lines for weeks on end and only supplied through air drops. If the weather was too bad for the planes to fly, they could face several days without food. On one occasion, this lasted ten days. 'What did you do?' asked Charles. Richard replied that they had to resort to the pack animals. 'I do not recommend mule steak, it is impenetrable.'

By January 1945, the 14th Army had pushed the Japanese back to the mighty Irrawaddy River, which runs for 1,300 miles through Burma. The crossing would put them in striking distance of two major Japanese strongholds, Mandalay and Meiktila. Standing at the riverside next to John Hill, looking across its wide expanse to the opposite bank, Charles, sounding as much an old soldier as a BBC correspondent, remarked on the strategic failure of the Japanese in defending it properly. 'You should have been massacred,' he observed. John gave a short laugh and replied that the Japanese were taken by surprise.

Not far below the veterans' classic British sangfroid, the

emotion isn't difficult to discern. But, respectful of their reserve, Charles didn't prod too hard and often let their stories – and their silences – take their own course. This, along with his two D-Day films, feels almost as much a work of oral history as a documentary – a form that Charles would increasingly employ, especially in his many radio series on personal responses to the war, over the next ten years.

In Washington in the 1960s, Charles had admonished his colleague Gerry Priestland for sending out a camera crew unaccompanied, telling him that 'a good soldier always stays with his troops'. Charles's attitude to industrial relations at the BBC was not dissimilar. He was never active in union politics but, if asked, he lent his support. When staff went on strike again in May 1994, over the introduction of performance-related pay and conditions of service, the broadcast unions asked Charles if he would come out on the picket lines in solidarity. They wanted a high-profile supporter. He threw himself into it, especially relishing the opportunity to heckle the former Labour MP turned daytime chat show host Robert Kilroy-Silk. 'Shame on you!' Charles shouted as Kilroy-Silk crossed the line.

Charles was disappointed that so many senior BBC journalists had gone into work during the strike – so much so that he wrote to the *Guardian*: 'I would ask them to think back to the days when their professional lives were more of a struggle and consider where they would have stood on these issues when they were in their twenties and thirties. One of the reasons why I have stayed with the BBC for nearly fifty years is that I have always felt I could argue with and even make an enemy of my immediate boss, without risking my career... The trouble with performance-related pay is that it tends to reward obedience, discourage non-conformism, and to put too much power into the hands of programme editors and middle managers.'

Making enemies of managers was obviously easier when you had a long and successful career and a number of awards to your name. But protected status or not, conformism and deference were not really in his DNA. As John Simpson once told an interviewer, 'In most institutions, there's a lot of forelock tugging. Charles must have had that forelock removed at birth.'

Then, when the BBC announced its decision to launch a rolling news channel in 1997, Charles became one of the louder detractors of the idea. His perennial concern was quality, the nub of his argument being that 'the mania for live reporting', as he called it, for innumerable outlets, would make the job of the foreign correspondent impossible, depriving them of the time they needed to actually get the news. Some definitely saw Charles as a bit of a Luddite, though no less a figure than Mark Thompson, a later director general of the BBC, believes that to some extent Charles's concerns about quality were pretty astute. He told me, 'Rolling news was probably inevitable. Audiences insisted on it for the biggest breaking stories and no serious news organisation could afford to ignore that public demand. But the pressure to be constantly on air meant that reporting did sometimes suffer, while on slow days the need to fill hours of broadcast with chat could leave services looking desperately thin.'

Rolling news was simply the way the wind was blowing.

In fact, the new channel – News 24 – would also provide

the space for Charles to present a new programme: a Sunday morning discussion with foreign correspondents based in London about the weekly news in Britain, 'as others see us'. The programme was Charles's own idea, enthusiastically made into reality by Nick Guthrie, who proposed the title *Wheeler's Week*. Charles's response might have been anticipated: 'Sorry to be difficult, but may I enter an objection?' he wrote to the controller of News 24. 'It won't be my week but the contributors' – certainly it won't be about me, or stories I have done.' The programme would instead be called *Dateline London* and run for twenty-five years on BBC News and BBC World, coming to an end only in late 2022 as one of the BBC's most internationally respected news programmes.

In 2000 – having ditched *Dateline London* in favour of more time in the garden on a Sunday morning – Charles was at it again, with a string of soundbites that the media pages of the UK's major broadsheets lapped up. 'The BBC has lost its way in news,' he was widely quoted as saying. He lambasted the cult of personality in television, accusing the corporation of dumbing down, and delivered what was perhaps the unkindest cut of all to the BBC, when he said that he had now switched to watching Channel 4 news.

Charles also strongly objected to the prominence of his name when the title of the five-part *Wheeler on America* series was put to him in 1995, but on this occasion he lost that battle. The idea, commissioned by the BBC's then head of news, Tony Hall, was to put Charles at the centre of the reports – to revisit the big stories he had reported on in the US with the benefit of hindsight. They would tackle the big themes of race and civil rights, the legacy of Lyndon Johnson and his vision of the Great Society derailed by Vietnam. Initially, Charles was unsure. 'I don't just want to look back at what I did in the past,' he told producer David Coxon Taylor. 'We need to find out something new.'

'This was typical of Charles,' David told me. 'He wanted to uncover something different, take the story forward.'

And they did. With the release of the first set of tapes from the Johnson archive on Vietnam, interviews with Lady Bird Johnson (who charmed Charles and David in equal measure) and members of Johnson's inner circle keen to unburden themselves of the sins of the past, Charles and David were able to cast new light on the extent to which the Johnson administration had hidden their doubts about the Vietnam War from the American people, revealing Richard Nixon's role in sabotaging talks to end the war in Vietnam. And they reminded the audience that, despite the painful struggle that Charles had reported on in the 1960s against racism and for civil rights, the battle was far from over.

One of the programmes also covered the legacy of Ronald Reagan, whom Charles had first encountered when he was elected governor of California. At the time, he had dismissed him as lightweight, essentially shallow. That view of an intellectually ill-equipped president did not shift but he came to see Reagan as a more complex figure and his tenure as an outlet for fervent anti-communism and opposition to arms control, especially when it came to the murky dealings around the Iran–Contra affair: 'There was nothing wide-eyed about

Reagan,' Charles asserted. 'His greatest asset was his friendly and eager demeanour. I covered that [1980 election] race and, like most people, I underestimated him. He had firm beliefs and a hard, cutting edge.'

Wheeler on America took Charles and David two years to make. They would spend, as David put it, 'the whole day and half the night' talking through the structure of a film. Charles always had inbuilt reservations about the producer–reporter relationship. As he said in a radio interview around this time, 'I go to America to do a death penalty story, then I try to find out the twists and turns. This often leads to tension with the producer, who has already been researching the film for three weeks. By the time the reporter arrives on the ground, the film has been mapped out.'

When David and Charles were not physically together, they were still in almost constant daily contact, by telephone and fax, shuttling tapes of rushes, archiving, sending recorded commentaries back and forth. The customary call from David, just as Charles was settling down to supper, became a family joke. They had become, as Charles put it, 'ideological twins'. They would spend hours talking about what they were working on, but with no arguments. 'We are professionally married to each other. It's a wonderful situation but it takes years to get there.'

Charles once joked that the producer–reporter relationship was even harder to get right than that of husband and wife. 'Perhaps for him,' Dip might have scoffed. But she took most of the challenges in her stride. Dip had counselled a number of foreign correspondents and their unhappy spouses over the years – some through break-up and divorce. Her own relationship with Charles was tested at times by loneliness and isolation, especially in the Brussels years when he often seemed to be looking for stories outside the city. But she had learnt to live with those separations because she loved him fiercely and had what some today might see as an old-fashioned, if not unwavering, belief in loyalty.

The disproportionate impact of the justice system on what Charles called the 'little people' and on the Black community was a theme he was circling back to. With President Reagan's famous 'war on drugs' in the 1980s as the starting point, in the fourth film of *Wheeler on America* Charles and David Coxon Taylor examined how sentencing laws and mandatory minimum sentences were leading to mass incarceration. This was at a time when the issue was being hotly debated in the US and in Britain too: 'During the eighties, Congress got carried away in the rush to punish. It passed more than sixty mandatory sentencing laws. Most of them are harsh. The average drug-related sentence is longer than the average penalties for manslaughter, armed robbery and rape. The new laws put marijuana on a par with LSD and heroin. Trafficking in marijuana can get you life,' Charles reported.

In Georgia, Charles learnt an 'astonishing statistic' from the Department of Correction. Of the 423 men and women serving life for drug offences, 419 were Black and four white. When Charles presented the statistic to a Georgia state appeals court judge, he was shocked. Charles suggested he look into it and do something about it.

At the state's main prison for women – Metro – Charles talked to twenty-one-year-old LaTonya Wilkes. For selling $30 of crack to feed her own addiction she was serving three life sentences. It was her second offence. She'd been studying at the prison and had just got a B in English. 'You're a cheerful person, aren't you?' remarked Charles. 'I try to stay positive,' she replied, but she knew she had been unfairly treated: 'I am a drug user. The law was designed to get drug kingpins – but instead of getting them, they're getting drug users like me.'

Charles also met Donnie Clark and his son Dwayne, serving time at a federal prison. Alongside twenty-eight other local Florida farmers, they were both convicted for growing marijuana on their land. Donnie already had a record and, although he'd switched from growing pot to watermelons, he was found guilty of 'conspiracy to grow' and sentenced to life without the possibility of parole. It was Dwayne's first offence. He got ten years.

Watching that interview was a viewer in the north of England who sent a VHS copy of the item to the First Lady, Hillary Clinton, asking how such a perversion of justice could happen in the United States. On his last day in office, Bill Clinton granted 150 presidential pardons. On that list was Donnie Clark.

Charles always seemed to have any number of insults up his sleeve for American presidents. But he maintained if he was rude about them then it was because he loved the country and felt it was consistently let down by its leaders. He nursed a special disdain for Bill Clinton. It wasn't that he didn't see Clinton's strengths – especially as a communicator. He had seen him at close quarters, following the 1992 campaign for *Newsnight* up to the eve of the election when he reported that, 'In these last few days, Bill Clinton has become more presidential than the president. That's difficult for a challenger to do. As Bush has lost credibility as a leader, Clinton quite suddenly has acquired it. His crowds now sense this and they're turning his rallies into celebrations.'

But Charles's personal opinion of Clinton – when invited to express it, outside his reporting – was unusually harsh. He accused him of giving up on 'the poor' and being 'useless' and without a moral compass – 'his whole career, dashing from one side to the other'. In 1998, when Clinton was facing impeachment over the Lewinsky affair, Charles was invited to express his views for the *Sunday Mirror*, which he did with some relish: 'I have covered every president since Kennedy, and I give Clinton very low marks indeed. He is without principles – a political chameleon. This case shows his judgement is appalling. If I were an American voter, I would not trust him in a crisis.'

It wasn't Clinton's private life that had earned Charles's enduring hostility. As governor of Arkansas in 1992, Clinton had left the presidential campaign trail to sign off on the execution of Ricky Ray Rector, a mentally challenged Black man on death row. Rector had shot two people, including a policeman, and then tried, and failed, to kill himself. Charles saw in Clinton's haste to get back to the photo ops in Arkansas a cynical aim to secure the nomination and reverse the image of the Democrats being soft on crime by 'stealing the Republicans' clothes'.

Charles was implacably opposed to the death penalty. Morally, he found it abhorrent, and the disproportionate number of Black men on death row was a theme in many of his reports and where he came the closest to campaigning journalism. He was an active supporter of the charity Reprieve, set up by the dual UK–US national Clive Stafford Smith, a lawyer, and filmmaker Paul Hamann to campaign for prisoners on death row in the US. It was perhaps no coincidence either that Dip had moved from the Middle East team at Amnesty International to its anti-death penalty campaign, where she and her colleagues were pushing for the global abolition of capital punishment.

In April 1992, Charles and David took time from the presidential campaign trail to interview former coal miner Roger Coleman from the Appalachian Mountains, where, ten years before, in the small town of Grundy, he was sentenced to death for brutally murdering and sexually assaulting his nineteen-year-old sister-in-law Wanda McCoy. Coleman had already served three years for attempted rape of a primary school teacher. But there were serious doubts about the trial and the police evidence against him for Wanda McCoy's murder. 'I didn't commit this crime. And I'm not going to let them murder me without putting up a fight,' Coleman told Charles at Mecklenburg Penitentiary, a plate-glass window between them. Charles and David found Coleman and his legal team highly convincing, but his appeals failed and Coleman was executed by electric chair, after ten years on death row. 'America is now executing juvenile defenders, mentally retarded people, and it is executing people whose guilt is seriously in doubt, as this case shows,' Charles reported, producing a film with David for *Newsnight* that essentially argued that an innocent man may well have been put to death after questionable evidence and an inadequate defence. Roger Coleman's lawyers were still determined to prove his innocence, petitioning for a DNA test although their client had already been executed. When the judge finally granted the request, the test proved almost beyond doubt that Coleman was in fact guilty of the horrific crime of which he had been accused. David rang from Washington to give him the news. Charles was stunned. 'How could he have taken us in?' he asked. But Coleman, with his owlish, oversized glasses and articulate, softly spoken manner, had taken in many members of the media, appearing on the cover of *Time* magazine and being interviewed from death row on TV by Larry King. The experience might have made Charles question his instinctive and normally cast-iron judgement, but it didn't dim his opposition to the death penalty in the least. He would remain a patron of Clive Stafford Smith's Reprieve until the end of his life.

The failures of Britain's own police and justice system were laid bare in the 1999 Macpherson report into the investigation of the murder of the Black teenager Stephen Lawrence. Sir William Macpherson, a retired judge, concluded that institutional racism in the Metropolitan Police contributed to its failure to adequately investigate Stephen's death and he recommended sweeping changes to policing and wider public policy. Ten days before the report's publication, the documentary *Why Stephen?*, with Charles as presenter, ran as a special on the current affairs series *Black Britain* on BBC2. The series set out to further expose the inadequacy of the investigation into Stephen's murder, speaking to victims' families, lawyers, journalists and campaigners. But it also looked beyond the Lawrence case by attempting to grapple with the complex issue of what it takes for white society to get interested in a Black victim of crime, let alone to get justice.

Why Stephen? had more than just the police in its sights – the media and white society in general were in the spotlight too. Supported by a sophisticated campaign and legal advice, Doreen Lawrence's eloquence in advocating for her son had ensured wide press coverage. But that level of attention wasn't given to racist attacks against young men like Jakir Hussain from the Bengali community in Tower Hamlets, which had gone virtually uninvestigated by the police and barely noticed by the press. Or the murder of fifteen-year-old Rolan Adams, stabbed at a bus stop on his way home by a gang of white teenagers twenty months before Stephen. The overtly political campaign around his death had commanded a fraction of the media attention given to Stephen's murder.

Pat Younge, who was the executive producer of the programme, told me: 'For *Black Britain* to have a white host was quite a radical decision, counter-intuitive really. But Charles was a legend, and he had a long track record of covering civil rights and race stories in the US with understanding and empathy. And we needed something to break through the noise and to get people to engage with this story. We knew Charles wouldn't just take the police's word for it. We knew he would understand the relationship between conflict and narrative, and why stories don't always present themselves in a neat and tidy way.'

Charles brought his powerful scepticism to the project in

every sense. The team, all in their twenties and early thirties, valued his experience. He also valued theirs – and their perspective on an issue that he had not encountered before among the predominantly white teams working on *Newsnight* or *Panorama*. As producer on the story, Maxine Watson worked closely with Charles, dissecting and talking through each interview: 'I had sheer admiration for his body of work. At the same time, it was a real two-way relationship. He listened to us. He never presumed to know emotionally or culturally what he didn't know.' But Charles was not afraid to challenge the team to make sure the narrative held water and maintained a rigorous approach. 'I'm a Black person and this was a very emotional story for me,' she said. 'It was important to be journalistic, not too emotional. But in the end, we were all discovering something together about our institutions.'

There were many animated discussions. Pat Younge had been brought up in the Birtian school of television at ITV's *Weekend World*, where, as he said, you knew pretty much what you were doing frame by frame before you left the building. Applying that approach was never going to work with Charles. 'We sort of gave him a ready meal and he took it right back to the basic ingredients – and elevated it with his writing,' Pat recalled.

Charles's starting point, as the opening commentary shows, was stark: 'There's a word for this that doesn't often habitually crop up in Britain. Rolan and Stephen were *lynched*, and nothing can prepare mothers or fathers for that.' The racist murders of the two teenagers in south London had terrible similarities but the film also drew out the media's very different responses to them. 'Charles really got that, and it fascinated him too, having to turn his journalistic gaze inwards and question how the "white" media picks and chooses its victims, heroes and villains. When the story is about race, every victim has to be more than worthy,' Maxine said.

Of Rolan's attackers, one was convicted of murder, four were found guilty of public order offences with community service as their punishment. It would take many more years – well after the programme was aired – before anyone was convicted of Stephen's murder. Prejudice and unfounded assumptions ensured that Stephen had been made a 'suspect in his own death', as Charles put it, and he likened the experience of Doreen and Neville Lawrence after their son's murder to a racial assault. Macpherson unearthed police incompetence and racism but also confirmed something far deeper and more toxic: 'After the Macpherson inquiry, it is hard to dismiss what the Adams and Lawrence families have said about the relative value to society of white and Black lives,' said Charles.

Four years after Macpherson came the establishment of the Independent Police Complaints Commission. When the new institution advertised for recruits to its board, Charles put in an application. Arriving home after completing the recruitment tests, he was rather glum. He hadn't been invited for the second round. Interestingly, the tests included a maths section and Charles always assumed it was his shaky grasp of the subject that let him down. But it may well be that the recruiters at the Home Office baulked at the idea of Wheeler on a mission causing trouble in their midst.

*

WITNESS TO THE TWENTIETH CENTURY

At the start of the 1990s, Charles had reported on the aftermath of the first Gulf War. A decade later, in the wake of the attacks on the World Trade Center and the Pentagon on 9/11 he would report on a very different kind of war involving America – the 'War on Terror' declared by the Bush government to be carried out at home as well as abroad.

Our own family had felt the backlash directly in the fevered days after the destruction of the Twin Towers. Dip's young nephew Karambir, bound for the University of Chicago, was on a plane flying towards US airspace when the attacks were happening. The plane was diverted to Canada, from where he had to travel by bus. At a Greyhound bus stop just over the US border, this young turbaned Sikh was subject to a violent torrent of racial abuse. As it threatened to escalate, the police were called, but this was only the first of several such incidents where it was assumed he was a Muslim and fair game.

The fear engendered by the 9/11 attacks and its impact on the American home front now became the focus of Charles's reports. In September 2002, to mark the first anniversary, he returned to the US for *Newsnight* for a series of short reports on the views of young Americans on war and peace. On the campus of the University of Virginia, Charles spoke to a group of history students, who offered a reassuringly wide range of opinions on the threat to civil liberties posed by the Patriot Act, hastily introduced in the frightening weeks after the 9/11 attacks. Aimed at preventing further terrorist attacks, the Act substantially expanded the surveillance powers of agencies like the FBI and CIA while reducing judicial oversight.

Charles also spoke to an old acquaintance from the 1960s,

Julian Bond, a civil rights activist, leader of the Student Nonviolent Coordinating Committee, and now a history professor at the university. He told Charles, 'When a nation perceives itself to be under siege it can drop the protections that it adopted at a time when we were at peace. That's the situation we are operating under right now. And many of us – not all of us by any means – are worried that these threaten to become permanent.'

In Julian Bond, who had campaigned alongside Martin Luther King decades before, Charles found the dissident voice, chiming in with an unpopular refrain at a time when national debate felt constricted and monitored. Charles was looking for the challenging, off-centre viewpoint and he found it here on the campus of the University of Virginia. He asked Bond what he felt he could not say in the current climate. His rather unusual question got an interesting reply. At the time of 9/11, the heroes of the hour were the first responders, the fire crews and police who risked and, in many cases, lost their lives. But looking through the pictures of those victims of 9/11 in the *New York Times*, Julian Bond was troubled by something he saw in the images: 'You look at the pictures of the firemen and the policemen and they're all white. And it tells you that the New York Police Department and the New York Fire Department are discriminatory agencies. This is a guild, a racially restrictive guild, in which jobs are passed down from father to son, and Black people are not admitted. And my sympathy for the victims has gagged me and prevented me from saying one of the lessons we learnt from this horrible tragedy is how discriminatory our country is. And that's a lesson we shouldn't have to learn in that way.'

If Julian Bond provided a reminder that, in the wake of 9/11, the struggle for civil liberties was still ongoing and even confronted with new threats, Charles also saw in the build-up to another war in the Gulf mistakes from history being repeated. In his reports that autumn from the US, he recalled an interview he did with one of the chief architects of the Vietnam War, Robert McNamara, who had said: 'We thought we were fighting communism; we were wrong, we were fighting nationalism.' Charles wondered if ignorance was once again leading to war: 'This time the enemy is terrorism and whatever is deemed evil. And this time, the rest of the world is expected to follow.'

Charles had witnessed many of the defining events of the previous seven decades in close-up. Surveying the world as he approached his eightieth year, history was never something that was past: it might always be brought to bear upon the present and shine a torch into the future. And Charles was definitely not about to retire from the job of pointing that out.

10.
NEW HORIZONS

I just want to keep doing what I've always done, what I've been trained to do, right to the very end.
Charles to his friend Jack Altman 2005.

Whereas many politicians age prematurely, it seems that journalism keeps old reporters young. That was certainly the case with Charles. In perpetual motion, always onto the next thing, but Janus-like, with one eye on the past, the other firmly trained on the future. As the end of his eighth decade approached, Charles was being asked by numerous publishers to write his memoirs. He was never really tempted. 'I am having too much fun,' was his reply to one. In Charles's view, journalism was the 'best job in the world', and he wanted to keep doing it without sitting at a desk, hunched over a computer, any longer than strictly necessary – especially if it meant going on about himself. Charles's crisp and elegant style was the product of much agonising, poring over every word. He often said that he actually hated writing and the idea of authoring a whole book was overwhelming. Perhaps the idea of a memoir smacked too much of endings. Charles also had reservations about journalists writing books about themselves, almost as a matter of principle. David Coxon Taylor used to joke that if Charles ever wrote his memoirs, he would almost certainly find a way of writing himself out of them.

In any case, Charles really was having too much fun. He had been keeping up a productive sideline in writing insightful and acerbic book reviews for publications such as the *Times Literary Supplement* (*TLS*), the *Telegraph* and the *Oldie*. The books he reviewed were frequently biographies of prominent US politicians and journalists, the pieces making up in themselves a coherent body of work analysing recent American history. And he was busily forging an almost fresh broadcasting career with a series of documentaries for Radio 4. This was the medium in which he had started his career and, by immersing himself in the intimacy of radio, he found a chance to revisit some of the buried experiences of a nation. The programmes produced over the course of several years – *Evacuation*, *The Peacetime Conscripts*, *The Child Migrants*, *Coming Home* – were based around stories told to Charles by men and women who had lived them. They shared their experiences, dredging up sometimes traumatic memories that, in many cases, they had rarely if ever spoken about before.

David Prest, the producer who worked with Charles on most of these programmes, recalls how Charles was first sceptical, then excited, when confronted with new production techniques in the studio that major developments in sound technology had made possible. The production team could mix layered sound collages interwoven with music and review, and re-edit with ease. But at the core of the programmes were the powerful individual testimonies, bringing history into the present. Their first series together, on child evacuees in the war, broadcast in August 1999, struck an emotional chord with many listeners. Charles was quite taken aback by the reaction to the reports and the overflowing 'mailbag' that followed.

'He said to me that, when he boarded the train from Horsham to London, people had been coming up to him telling him how much they liked the series,' David told me. '"People have actually heard it," he said, and seemed quite surprised.' And when David informed him that audience figures had hit 2.5 million listeners for the morning broadcast and 1.5 million for the afternoon, Charles was astounded. There was silence as he took it in – 'I'm never going to do TV again.'

After the success of the *Evacuation* series, Charles and David Prest embarked on a series called *The Peacetime Conscripts*, about the story of post-war national service in Britain, as told by the former servicemen themselves. And then, in autumn 2003, came the five-part series, *The Child Migrants*. This turned an enquiring eye on the forced migration to Australia and other countries in the British Empire of tens of thousands of mainly poor children from deprived parts of Britain with the intention of 'seeding the colonies' – that is, supplying children who would, it was hoped, grow into loyal and productive colonial subjects. Beginning at the start of the twentieth century, the policy, with its promise of a life of greater opportunity for the children, was maintained until just after the Second World War. Charles and David travelled to Australia to interview almost a hundred of these former child migrants, now men and women mostly in their sixties and seventies. They heard traumatic tales of forced separation, neglect and abuse. They discovered a tragic betrayal of young people, all the more shocking perhaps as it was part of a programme run by such respected children's charities as Barnardo's and the National Children's Homes, along with the British and Australian governments.

'I am incognito. I don't know who I am or what I am. Surely a man has the right to know his true identity?' Laurie Humphries told Charles in the fourth report of the series. Laurie was migrated to Australia in 1948 when he was fourteen and had always been told his parents were dead. And then he found a document saying that in fact his father had died in 1976 in Britain. In the recording, Laurie breaks down, weeping as he tells the story.

The child migration programme came to an end in the 1950s. But many of the adults Charles and David spoke to, like Laurie, still carried the pain and trauma of what had been done to them. They found themselves in a bureaucratic fog, ignorant of where they came from and even whether they still had family in Britain. In Charles's commentary, you can hear the scarcely disguised anger at the injustice done to these children, not lessened by it being nearly five decades ago.

Charles turned eighty on 26 March 2003. The BBC wanted to mark the occasion with a special programme celebrating the life and career of their longest-serving foreign correspondent, to be called *Wheeler at 80*. 'He absolutely refused at first, but we pushed him and eventually he said he would do it if the person interviewing him would challenge him,' David Prest, who produced the programme for Radio 4, told me. The ever-forthright Jeremy Paxman agreed to do the job and Charles relented, knowing that, even though Jeremy was a friend and a former colleague on *Newsnight*, he was not going to give him an easy ride. Listening to the interview now – the mix of lively anecdote, good conversation and, at times, sheer spikiness on display when Paxman actually gives him a tough ride – I feel as close to being in my father's company over a late-night glass of whisky as it is possible to get.

To start things off, Paxman bowled an easy question at him: 'Charles – how old *are* you?'

'Eighty-one,' he growled. 'I wasn't sure – I thought I was eighty-two but then I counted backwards.'

In fact, the interview was recorded a couple of weeks before his eightieth birthday. It wasn't for nothing that he had earned his family nickname of 'absent-minded professor'. In contradiction to the image of a highly organised man of almost military precision, his eight decades had included plenty of last-minute frantic searches for lost keys and passports, misplaced bankcards and wayward spectacles.

Then Jeremy began to up the pace. When Charles said that he believed successive American presidents had let the American public down, and cited then-president George W. Bush and his 'gang' as an example of the 'really awful people' the system throws up, Paxman demanded, 'Who are you to say that? You're a reporter. That's all you are.'

'A reporter should be able to say what he thinks,' replied Charles.

'What he thinks or what he sees?' Jeremy pushed, getting into full Paxman attack mode. 'There's a big difference and people say you've crossed this line.'

'What line did I cross?' Charles challenged. 'Did I see too much or did I think too much?'

A silence followed.

'Don't get clever,' laughed Jeremy, stumped.

The interview was feisty and wide-ranging, although the Paxman probing was often at risk of being deflected by Charles downplaying the influence of his reporting and his natural squeamishness at talking about himself. Jeremy remarked that Charles's report on the terrible situation of the Kurds trapped in the mountains of Iraq after the Gulf War in 1991 was an 'amazing piece', which impacted government policy. But Charles wouldn't claim any personal glory for it: 'If you are there at the right time as a journalist you are lucky. There's nothing clever about it.'

Charles's stamina was always quite remarkable, but by his eighth decade it had acquired legendary status among his younger colleagues. Jeremy asked him why he was still working, still 'doing the legwork'. Charles didn't hesitate in his answer: 'Fear of stopping... because I think you die sooner.' He pointed out how 'enormously refreshing' it was to be able to work with younger journalists, 'and if you retire, that's gone'. When the subject turned to his beloved garden, Charles revealed that even the Garden Cottage, which he had spent so much time and energy creating, wasn't enough for him, even at eighty years old: 'I thought that when I was sixty or seventy, I would retire and spend my life in the garden. But when you're my age you don't really get such a kick out of gardening for eight hours a day.' Quite simply, Charles was never a subscriber to the philosophy that as we age, we must cultivate our garden and let the world go on its way.

Charles was asked to join the BBC team as veteran-cum-commentator at Ouistreham – Sword Beach – in Normandy for the commemorative sixtieth D-Day anniversary live broadcasts. Dip and my own family decided to go too, opting to get to Ouistreham by road and ferry. True to form, though, Charles made the journey with a bit more dash. At the invitation of his goddaughter Phyl and her ex-Gurkha husband Phil, eighty-one-year-old Charles set off from Brighton to cross the Channel in their sea-going Dutch barge, the *Zingara*. Phil focused on the navigation and keeping an eye out for passing ships. His son Stewart and Charles took turns at the helm. Charles was in his element, deep in thought on the fly bridge, Phil told me. Perhaps he was remembering his friend Peter Haynes, who had taken him across to Sword Beach in his landing craft on D-Day to 'have a look', and who was killed on board the vessel a few weeks later. Or perhaps he was remembering his brother, John, who had died aged nineteen in a Luftwaffe raid on RAF Andover. The sea was not rough, just a slight swell – a perfect crossing. There was time to think.

Twelve and a half hours after leaving Brighton, the barge passed through the locks at Ouistreham and moored on the town quay. The world's press was already assembling and, that evening, CNN's Christiane Amanpour came for dinner aboard the *Zingara*. She still remembers Charles's expansive mood over dinner, how he was full of stories from the past. In fact, Christiane had known Charles since her brief time at the BBC as a twenty-three-year-old intern in 1981, working on Radio 4's *The World Tonight*. She credits Charles with giving her the opportunity during the riots in Brixton to appear on air and then, over the years, for taking an interest in her.

'We had a sort of back-and-forth mentorship,' she explained to me. 'I never thought of Charles as being old . . . He had so much vitality, so much enthusiasm for the job. Watching his stuff, I guess I learnt by osmosis, and by talking to him and understanding his approach. He also paid attention to what I was doing. He would comment on a piece I had done, a live shot . . . I learnt the fundamentals from Charles. That endless curiosity and that endless willingness to learn. He was a repository of all that was right about fact-based journalism, and he kept doing it right to the end. He had so much integrity and he never compromised on that.'

We spent two days with Charles in Ouistreham, which was packed with veterans and visited by a stream of dignitaries, including Prince Charles and the French president, Jacques Chirac. This gave Charles the opportunity to meet old friends and join in some of the official commemorations, but his broadcasting duties also kept him at a slight distance from the main event, which is how he wanted it, as he was always keen to make clear that he was not part of that first wave who fought on the beaches that day, and that those men, not he, were the heroes of the hour. Charles did live two-ways for BBC *Breakfast News* and News 24 but decided to attend the ceremony at the Royal Marines memorial in Ouistreham as a veteran. When he came over to join us in the crowd, he pointed out a tall, imposing-looking man. 'That's the beachmaster,' he told me – the very same who, on 6 June 1944, had told Charles and Peter Haynes that he would not allow them to stay on the beach.

After the ceremony was over, we all went down to Sword Beach itself. Charles took my six-year-old daughter's small Tupperware snack box and filled it with sand, then gave it to her as a keepsake. 'I hope I can get back for the seventieth anniversary and give a hand with the old codgers,' he said to me. 'Some of them are really getting quite decrepit.' It was typical of him that he felt he would go on forever.

The last of Charles's set of historical series for BBC Radio 4 was called *Coming Home* and was broadcast to coincide with the sixtieth anniversary of VE Day in May 2005. The series focused on the vast changes confronting the people of post-war Britain as the country transitioned from a military to a civil society once again. Like his previous radio documentaries, it was above all a work of oral history, recording the memories of veterans and civilians of the great expectations and profound challenges facing them in 1945, as they voted in a Labour government committed to creating the Welfare State. As always, Charles was sensitive to the impact and significance of the more personal and low-key stories and, across the five programmes, constructed a complex narrative of a population dealing with loss and bereavement, the problems of demobilisation and marriage break-ups after long absences, and the role of women and work in a new era. Again, the programmes sparked a particularly emotional reaction from some listeners, who wrote to say how moved they had been by some of the stories they had heard. The head of BBC Radio, Mark Damazer, said at the time, 'If this series is bettered in my lifetime I will be surprised . . . Above all, authenticity to the human experience . . . The end of war – as acute and intense an experience as war itself. So rich with evidence and anecdote and turmoil.'

This was, of course, a subject that was personal to Charles, as it touched on something he'd had to confront himself when he returned from the war in 1946. I came across an intriguing insight into his own thoughts at that time while reading through his personal archive. From the 1990s, newsletters from the 30AU veterans' association and letters from old comrades begin to appear. Charles started up a regular correspondence with his former Marine driver Ron Knight, with whom he had criss-crossed a devastated Germany immediately after the war and encountered the Red Army in Leipzig. The letters were obviously cherished, as was the friendship. In one letter, sent in 2005, Ron touches on the topic of coming home and the sense of uncertainty they had both felt about it. 'I remember so clearly what your conversation was to me one day when we were going to get that German naval officer from that lovely mountainside home he had in the south of Germany. You asked me what I'd do in getting a job after the war was over and I replied I had no idea whatever, then you told me you had no intention of sitting in an insurance office, no way that would ever happen. And of course, it never did, Charles.'

*

WITNESS TO THE TWENTIETH CENTURY

Since the early 1950s, a constant companion to Charles had been the small portrait of an aristocratic lady with rings on her fingers petting a little dog, that had been given to him as a present by an East German farmer who used to visit the BBC office in Berlin. It had travelled with him across two more continents and sat on various mantelpieces and bookshelves for more than five decades, finally coming to rest near a photo of his brother John in the sitting room of the Garden Cottage. To me, she'd been a permanent feature of my parents' homes throughout my life and was a part of the family.

In one of the *Coming Home* programmes, Charles had touched on the subject of the huge amount of art looted during the war and the task of recovering it, which began with the war's end. The topic caught his imagination and, in 2006, he and Mark Burman, the producer, made a two-part programme called *Looted Art*, focusing on both the Nazis' widescale theft of paintings, sculptures and other works of art across Europe, and Stalin's specialist trophy brigades, which hoovered up many of the very same artworks after Germany's defeat in 1945. For an expert voice, they brought in Anne Webber from the Commission for Looted Art. It was while they were making the programme that Charles thought he'd ask her what she made of his miniature painting of the lady with the lapdog. He would get a lot more than he'd bargained for as a result.

The picture turned out to be a sixteenth-century portrait of Eleonora, wife of Cosimo Medici, the Grand Duke of Florence, and attributed to Alessandro Allori, a pupil of the Medicis' court painter, Agnolo Bronzino. It had gone missing from Berlin's Kaiser Friedrich Museum, now called the Gemäldegalerie, in

1944. Charles immediately said he wanted to give the painting back and Anne Webber facilitated the handover. On 1 June 2006, they travelled to Berlin to attend a small ceremony at the gallery, where they were informed that this was the very first of the 441 artworks looted from the Gemäldegalerie more than sixty years earlier to have been returned to its rightful home. Eleanora resides there now, in a discreet corner, on a green wall, with her little dog, staring out as serenely as ever.

But Charles wasn't quite finished with her yet. He began work on a programme for BBC Radio 4 in the *It's My Story* series, in which he related his own part in the painting's colourful history. But he was not able to piece together exactly how it came to be in the possession of the Russian soldier who traded it for a sack of potatoes with the East German farmer who gave it to him – the painting had gone missing from the gallery a year before the Russians conquered Berlin.

The story that Charles had a Renaissance painting on his shelf for half a century without knowing it drew considerable media attention around the world – especially in the UK and Germany. At the urging of the BBC publicity department, Charles wrote an article for the *Daily Mail*. He described the painting as a 'piece of wartime loot', but a *Daily Mail* sub-editor inserted the phrase 'and possibly Nazi' before the word 'loot'. Charles hit the roof. He fired off a letter to the editor pointing out that, given the painting was catalogued and maintained by the curators under the Nazi regime, it absolutely couldn't be called Nazi loot. 'The way your paper mistreated my copy . . . strikes me as exceptionally shoddy journalism,' Charles told him, concluding, 'I don't share the enduring obsession of some

London papers with all things Nazi, and I am ashamed that your readers will think I do.' A suitably apologetic response followed. The article remains in the *Daily Mail* online archive minus those three offending words.

When he got the letter in 2006 telling him the Queen intended to offer him a knighthood, Charles didn't hesitate in composing a polite note of refusal. He had turned one down before, as to him this did not seem quite the thing for a working journalist, especially one who had partly made his name by challenging the Establishment. But Dip asked him to reflect before he posted it, and to find out what Marina and I thought. I felt that perhaps knowing the views of some fellow journalists, especially the under-fifties who looked up to him, might help him make a decision. I told him I'd canvass opinion in the BBC Brussels office, where I was working at the time. Would they feel he was selling out? I asked. My always straight-talking colleague Oana Lungescu, Europe editor for BBC World Service, summed up the feeling of the bureau: 'Of course he should accept. It's a reflection of the store that our society places on good and truthful journalism.' I relayed the results of my straw poll, with which – to Charles's surprise – I also concurred wholeheartedly.

Dip, Marina and I accompanied Charles to Buckingham Palace for the knighthood ceremony in December 2006. Although it was more than four decades since he'd been declared persona non grata by the Palace after his exasperated comments about the Queen during her Royal Tour of India, he was, he confessed to us, feeling a little awkward about the encounter.

We took our place in the Grand Ballroom and watched as the Queen and Charles exchanged a few words after she'd tapped his shoulders with the knighting sword. 'What did she say?' we asked him as we filed out. 'She remarked on how long I'd been at the job,' he told us. If Her Majesty was ever even aware of Charles's run-in with her courtiers back in Nepal in the 1960s, she was certainly too discreet to mention it. And Charles, being on his best behaviour this time, refrained from pointing out that he might in return have remarked on the equally impressive length of her career.

The dread, if there was any, Charles told Dr Raj Persaud, BBC Radio 4's presenter-psychiatrist for a special programme on ageing, was always about parts of the memory disappearing. His long memory – of growing up in Nazi Germany, of his experiences in the war, of reporting from close quarters the tumult of the twentieth century – informed his work to a profound degree. Memory was at the heart of his programmes about the Forgotten Army and D-Day, about evacuees, child migrants and peacetime conscripts. Charles was always fully aware that oral history was above all the act of recording memories. Perhaps it was the thought of dementia that led him to ask me only half-jokingly to promise to just 'put a pillow over my head' if it ever got to that.

Thankfully, it never did. But in March 2008, Charles was diagnosed with cancer, at an advanced stage. He was adamant that he wanted no debilitating treatments. He would stay at the Garden Cottage and face the thing down, and we would be there to care for him with the help of St Catherine's Hospice.

A few weeks after the diagnosis, we gathered there to celebrate his eighty-fifth birthday. Charles and Dip's birthdays always had a national holiday feel in our house. Charles's birthdays especially prompted a flurry of stories and memories – for his eightieth, we'd travelled to Thurlestone Manor in Somerset, the site of his officer training course for the Royal Marines in 1943. This time was to be the last birthday celebration with him but, far from being a gloomy affair, Charles was full of stories and even pulled one out of the hat that I'd never heard before.

Back in the 1980s, he and Dip were driving back to England after a trip to see their friends, Hywel and Morwenna Jones, at their house near the vineyards of Burgundy. At Calais, Charles took out his passport to show to the customs officer and a stack of francs he'd left in it for safekeeping fell out. The officer was outraged and virtually accused Charles of trying to bribe him, informing him he would now have to search the car and ordering Charles to take everything out of it. Barely controlling his temper, Charles complied but, as he drove off, he muttered to Dip, 'And to think I saved half of Calais from destruction.' And this is how he did it:

In September 1944, Charles had been 'lent' to the short-lived Mobile Port Reconnaissance Unit, which was moving in behind the 3rd Canadian Infantry Division during the liberation of coastal ports such as Boulogne and Calais. After the liberation of Calais at the end of September, Charles was on hand for the interrogation of captured naval personnel. He was, he said, questioning one prisoner of war, a German naval commander, when the man revealed there was a booby-trap mine near the harbour. 'I know how to take out the fuse –

I'll do it if you like,' he offered. So he and Charles went off to sort out the bomb. It was gigantic, according to Charles – big enough to blow up a lot of central Calais around the port area. The Germans had already tried to set it off by lighting papers around it, hoping the fire would build up enough to cause it to explode after they'd escaped. With the papers still smouldering, the German officer duly took out the fuse and Charles stood by him to make sure he carried out the task. And so it was that Charles Wheeler saved half of Calais.

At his home outside Paris in the summer of 2022, my godfather Jack Altman told me that in the last conversation they had, Charles had said to him, 'I just want to keep doing what I've always done, what I've been trained to do, right to the very end.'

There were many people who helped ensure that Charles was doing exactly what he wanted to at the very end. His last piece of work was a documentary for Radio 4 called *The Flight of the Dalai Lama*, intended to revisit Charles's own coverage of the arrival of the exiled leader in India fifty years earlier, in 1958. Eleanor Thomas, its producer, who was twenty-five years old at the time, told me, 'Meeting, working and becoming friends with Charles was one of the great privileges of my life. I have only met a few others, what I think of as genuine, "free thinkers". He was so inspiring and so honest – a real hero. I loved him very much. There are so many different types of love but the one for a mentor or teacher is for me a strong one.'

As Charles prepared the script for his final broadcast, he was battling the effects of morphine and was afraid he might lose his way in the studio discussion with old colleagues, including Prem Prakash from Visnews, Peter Jackson and Adrienne Farrell of Reuters, and Peter Woon of the *Daily Express*, who had all covered the story of the Dalai Lama half a century before. Years earlier, back in Brussels, twelve years old, lounging on the sofa in his small study, I had played the sounding board to Charles's scripts before he phoned them over to London. In the last weeks of his life, we replayed another version of the scene in his study in Sussex. By this time, I'd learnt enough of the craft to help him with a structure and some scripting for the studio discussion. We worked late, mapping out the flow – the cues and Charles's own memories of the day when the bespectacled young man they called the 'God King' came down from the hills to the waiting throngs of the international press. Dip poked her head around the door a few times, worried that he was getting tired. But that night we worked for hours, and I felt that my own journalism was being put to use, for my wonderful father and a great journalist.

A few days later, my sister Marina accompanied him to Broadcasting House, occasionally passing him oxygen as they recorded the discussion. Over the next few hours, friends and old colleagues filed in, popping into the studio to say hello – and goodbye.

Spring turned to summer. We spent as many hours outside with Charles as the weather would allow us. Under his instruction, I planted a new tree in the orchard – a purple acer – and took notes from him on the names of the shrubs, when and how hard to prune. Playing with his hair in the garden, his grandchildren wrapped his thick white locks into hair bungees, as Marina and I had done four decades before – and then went at it with pink and blue food colouring. He didn't seem to mind, happy to indulge them.

One night, near the end, Charles had a morphine-induced waking dream. He told me he was anxious he would be late for an interview with none other than Dr Henry Kissinger, President Nixon's special advisor. It was agonising to witness my father endure such suffering but, at the same time, it was a reminder that Charles was a newsman to his very core. This cast of brilliant, flawed, charismatic and manipulative characters he had met and reported on were stalking his brain, as if on a Shakespearean stage.

This is perhaps the strongest memory from my childhood and of my bond with my father. We are in a big pool at one of Washington's international hotels. It's a favourite place on the weekends when Charles isn't travelling. He dives – 'Hold on!' he says, and I do, onto his back, my small fingers curved into the hollow of his collar bone. This is our thing. He's my turtle father. We swim under into the silent world. When I can't hold my breath any more, I grab a handful of his hair and tug gently and he comes up. I thought of this towards the end of his illness, as I held the mask attached to the portable canister for him. He gulped the oxygen, and I rested my hand on his back . . .

Charles died at home on 4 July 2008, American Independence Day. The scent of the roses in his garden was so intense that morning. I rang Mark Damazer at the BBC to tell him the news. Within minutes it was on the radio bulletin – Radio 4 was always permanently switched on in our household. Hearing the tributes so soon felt strange and yet fitting.

Six months later, on 20 January 2009, a memorial for Charles was held in Westminster Abbey. On the same day, Barack Obama, America's first Black president, was inaugurated. I don't doubt that most of Charles's friends and former colleagues in the abbey felt the significance of the day as the choir sang 'We Shall Overcome', the anthem of the civil rights movement, which Charles had first reported on when he arrived in the United States in 1965, and which had informed so much of his reporting in the years that followed.

Ahead of the memorial, during our meetings with the BBC and the team at the abbey to plan the occasion, it had felt like it was fast turning into something on the scale of a BBC outside broadcast, minus the cameras. Marina and I were determined to keep a handle on what we could. Dip had mainly left it to us, and in fact soon fell ill and did not make it to the memorial itself. She felt the loss of Charles keenly, and, while she'd been extraordinarily strong during his illness, she found it hard to find joy or meaning after his death. The dean's team at the abbey told us they would organise the flowers at the altar. But we were adamant that Charles's six grandchildren, then aged from five to fifteen, would bring flowers from his garden in Sussex for the ceremony.

'It's January. There won't be anything in bloom,' said the curate. 'Let us handle it for you.'

'You'll be surprised. This is my father's garden,' I told them.

Sure enough, Charles, like every good gardener, had planted for colour all year round. In late January, there was the yellow mahonia with its holly-shaped leaves, the winter jasmine, pink viburnums and the glamorous orange-red of the Japanese quince. On the morning of the memorial, before we set off for London, each of the children emerged from the garden with armfuls of the flowering branches and blooms. They carried them up to the altar at the abbey later that day and laid them down in memory of their grandfather.

Charles reported much of the twentieth century using a set of broadcasting tools that evolved hugely during his own lifetime: from sending a dispatch by Morse code from northern India to deploying one of the first ever transatlantic satellites from the Washington studio. His successors are now making sense of the current century in a very different environment. They can get to places faster and make and send their dispatches in minutes if needed. There is more noise, more competition, more outlets to serve and audiences to please and placate. But whether they are covering the impact of war, or the struggle of the marginalised to be heard, or analysing complex political stories, some constants remain. Many have found those constants in Charles's reporting.

Lindsey Hilsum, Channel 4's highly respected international editor, told me that what stood out for her when she was starting out was the power of what she called Charles's 'restrained fury'. After watching his reporting on the 1992 Rodney King verdict, she went back to his earlier pieces from the Watts Riots in LA and was struck by the contrast between the mild, clipped tones in which he spoke and the anger against the injustice he saw meted out to the Black population.

'A lesser broadcaster would have shown emotion; he didn't need to because it was all in the script and the storytelling. The passion was there beneath the surface. I thought his was a tradition I'd like to follow. Some TV reporters, especially at the BBC, are cold and analytical, while others dial up the emotion and it feels inauthentic. But I wanted to be like Charles – there in the thick of it, able to take a step back while conveying the emotion of the moment,' Lindsey explained.

More than twenty years ago, Katya Adler, the BBC's Europe editor, approached Charles for guidance, 'feeling lost', in her words, and unsure how to pursue her passion for reporting. 'I went for career advice and I found a soulmate,' she said. 'Charles for me is one of the greats – he is the journalist that I would aspire to be in his integrity, in his people-first approach, in his lack of ego and in his telling of truth to power. He put the story first – people first, not politicians or titles first. And I hold onto someone like that.'

All around the Garden Cottage, yellow poppies from Charles's own father's garden have seeded themselves. From late spring to autumn they bloom, irreverently spilling out of the flowerbeds onto paths, under shrubs, woven into the wild, grassy undergrowth behind the apple trees. I have a strong sense, looking at these bright spots and flashes of colour, of Charles himself, but also of his own legacy.

His is a layered inheritance touching several generations of journalists – energising and challenging the young reporters and producers who worked alongside him, many themselves now considered the veterans of their trade; inspiring and encouraging others with an approach that was always fresh and often surprising. Perhaps for those young journalists working today, who may never have met or even heard of him, there is a tradition to draw on that Charles went a long way to creating and shaping. It is about values and approach as much as it is style; and is perhaps more relevant than ever in an age where truth is sometimes dismissed as relative, and impartiality pursued as a holy grail.

Today, the relevance of his work may also lie in the deceptively uncomplicated approach that he advocated and practised. When asked once what kind of advice he would give to aspiring journalists, he boiled it down simply to this:

'You stand for telling what you believe to be the truth about the situation you're covering. That is your basic position; it's the only guideline that you need. Are you telling the truth?'

ACKNOWLEDGEMENTS

Charles never really wanted to write his memoir.

He was bombarded by a succession of agents and publishers over the years, but his replies were inevitably all various versions of 'no'.

'I'm having too much fun,' one went. Another wondered 'who would want to read about me?'. He even claimed his writing skills weren't up to it: 'I'm no Robert Harris…' He shelved the idea but, as I was to discover, without ever entirely ruling it out.

A few years ago, I was looking through his papers when I came across a copy of another of one of those 'rejection' letters. It was less resolutely negative than the others. 'I enjoyed our lunch and if I do decide to publish my memoir I promise it will be with you'.

So I tracked down that lunch companion of his from twenty

years ago: Kate Parkin. What prompted me was something that had become a regular refrain from friends and family: 'What would Charles have thought about this?' – about Britain's exit from the EU, the Trump Presidency, the rise of Narendra Modi in India, parts of the media under attack and in crisis. I became convinced that his journalism and the way he engaged with the events he witnessed and the people at the centre of them had something important to tell us today. Kate, it turned out, was now at Bonnier Books. I suggested we might pick up where she left off with Charles and she didn't hesitate. Her encouragement has been unstinting since then. Heartfelt thanks to her and the wonderful team at Bonnier, especially Justine Taylor, Margaret Stead and Liz Marvin for all their support and sensitive editing.

Charles's own archive at home delivered many surprises: at the top of a broom cupboard I discovered a sheath of typewritten dispatches from his first stint in Berlin for the BBC in the early 1950s on the tightening grip of the Russian backed East German regime, and then a green plastic folder labelled 'Kate Parkin Project'. Charles seemed to have started mapping out a possible book, jotting down the names of stories he'd reported on. I knew I had gone to the right person to bring this idea to fruition. These sketchy notes proved a useful guide, with the occasional detour. In a list that included 'East German Rising' and 'Hungary', the addition of 'Heliotrope the Frog' was baffling. My sleuthing took me to the Times archive – and a tongue-in-cheek letter from Charles to the newspaper in 1948, praising a frog called Heliotrope whose leaps had broken all frog jumping records in the year of the London Olympics. It may have been the first time his name appeared in print, but why he included it in his notes and its precise status in Charles's career remains a mystery to me. My editors were equally bemused and it hasn't been included in the final cut.

The book is built around Charles's journalism. I could not have managed it without the fantastic access I had to the BBC archive. The patience and helpfulness of the team at the digital collection has been boundless, especially from Emma Gibbs. Thanks too to Peter Rippon, Mark Macey and Hannah Spinks at the Written Archive in Caversham; and to the BBC's Head of History Robert Seatter. Being able to read, listen and watch Charles over these past couple of years has also been a wonderful part of writing this book.

My colleagues at work, without exception, have given me leeway, time and encouragement. I'm very grateful to them all, especially to Matteo Maggiore and Dirk Heilmann.

Charles's wartime service helped shape him as a journalist. It is largely thanks to the assiduous diary writing of Dan Colwell, my husband, that I've been able to paint such a vivid picture of that time. Over late-night whiskys, lunchtime conversations in the garden in Sussex, on family holidays to Brittany, Copenhagen and Hamburg, Charles sometimes would expand on these experiences of his early twenties. Meanwhile, Dan was busily capturing most of these anecdotes in his diary, which he's been writing every day for more than 30 years. But my deep thanks to him goes much further. He has supported me in every way possible, with honest feedback, clear-eyed editing, research, fact-checking and excellent pasta suppers. All of it, invaluable.

Underpinning this story is a happy and loving childhood, shared with my sister Marina. As she knows already, writing about a parent has its own challenges and I am so grateful for her love, support and generosity. Together we tend Charles's garden – and his memory.

Our mother Dip watched, listened and read every piece of journalism Charles ever made. Above all other critics, it was her acute opinion that he valued most. Her love and support was an essential ingredient to his success and should be acknowledged here.

Many of Charles's former colleagues and friends have given me their time and support, sharing their recollections and insights generously. My special thanks go to Christiane Amanpour, John Humphrys, Martin Bell, John Simpson, Lindsey Hilsum, Jim Gray, John Osman, Malcolm Downing, Mark Thompson, John Birt, Mark Fielder, George Carey, Katya Adler, Pat Younge, Maxine Watson, Eamonn Matthews, Eric Thirer, Witold Stok, Eleanor Thomas, Tim Gardam and Rona Christie. Thank you for helping me to pinpoint what mattered about Charles's journalism.

Speaking about himself didn't come naturally to Charles – especially in public. But one interview about his journalism and his life that stands out is with his former colleague on *Newsnight*, Jeremy Paxman for BBC Radio 4's *Archive Hour*. It's the most unguarded I've ever heard Charles speaking publicly. I'm so grateful to Jeremy for applying his skill as an interviewer to his friend and to the producer David Prest from Whistledown for leaving us this wonderful record.

In fact, David Prest was one of two Davids in Charles's life.

Untangling Tonkin and the Johnson years without having David Coxon Taylor's encyclopaedic knowledge on tap would have been a lot harder. Charles was lucky to have them as friends and colleagues and I've been very fortunate in benefitting from their support and their memories of working with Charles as well.

Thanks also to the inspiring Gareth Peirce for sharing her take on the miscarriage of justice and improper policing cases she worked on with Charles, and to Hania Mufti for her insights and her sage advice on the Kuwait and Kurdish stories. Melanie McFadyean, sadly no longer with us, shared her own memories of her father Colin and Charles's time together in the top secret Combined Services Detailed Interrogation Centre. Thanks too to the team at *The Oldie* for trawling their archive for Charles's book reviews.

Warm thanks to Jenonne Walker and Adam and Caroline Raphael for sharing their memories with me from the Washington days; and Phyl and Phyllis for Zingara anecdotes when we gathered with Charles at Ouistreham for the 60th anniversary of D-Day. A huge hug of gratitude to Jack Altman, writer, journalist, godfather, for your hilarious Berlin and Chicago stories and for your love and encouragement.

Charles had something about him that made you feel understood. I know every one of his six grandchildren felt this. And so did members of our family in India too, almost every niece or nephew, their partners and their children who knew him. Thanks to them for sharing their memories, encouragement and suggestions especially on his time in India when he met and married the beautiful Dip. They tell me they found a natural curiosity, instinctive compassion and respect in Charles that was, I think, reflected in his reporting of other cultures, across continents.

Maya and Nina, my darling daughters, have helped keep me calm. Maya saved me from IT hell, read the first drafts and performed wonders with Excel. For making me believe I could do this, all along the way, I have them both to thank.

Charles has been a wonderful subject for a book, a man who sailed close to the wind, to use one of his favourite phrases, setting his course by what he believed to be true. It's been a joy to be in his company again for these last two years. We were so lucky to have him in our lives.

BIBLIOGRAPHY

Appelbaum, Anne, *Iron Curtain: The Crushing of Eastern Europe 1944–1956* (London: Penguin Books, 2013)

Blake, George, *No Other Choice* (London: Jonathan Cape, 1990)

Brandt, Willy, *People & Politics* (London: Collins, 1978)

Brant, Stefan, *The East German Rising*, translated and adapted by Charles Wheeler, (London: Thames and Hudson, 1955)

Brown, Judith, *Nehru: A Political Life* (New Haven: Yale University Press, 2003)

Cabell, Craig, *The History of 30 Assault Unit: Ian Fleming's Red Indians* (Barnsley: Pen & Sword Books, 2009)

Crawshaw, Steve, *Easier Fatherland: Germany and the Twenty-First Century* (Continuum Books, 2004)

Crouse, Timothy, *The Boys on the Bus* (New York: Random House, 1973)

Dallek, Robert, *John F Kennedy: An Unfinished Life* (London: Penguin Books, 2003)

Dalzel-Job, Patrick, *Arctic Snow to Dust of Normandy* (Barnsley: Pen & Sword Books, 2005)

Dorril, Stephen, *MI6: Fifty Years of Special Operations* (London: Fourth Estate, 2000)

Fry, Helen, *The Walls Have Ears* (New Haven: Yale University Press, 2019)

Hermiston, Roger, *The Greatest Traitor: The Secret Lives of Agent George Blake* (London: Aurum Press, 2013)

Higgins, Charlotte, *This New Noise: The Extraordinary Birth and Troubled Life of the BBC* (London: Faber & Faber, 2015)

Hugill, J.A.C., *The Hazard Mesh* (London: Faber & Faber, 2011)

Hugill, J.A.C., unpublished diaries, held at Churchill Archive Centre, Churchill College, Cambridge, GBR/0014/HUGL4

Humphrys, John, *A Day Like Today* (London: William Collins, 2019)

Lindley, Richard, *Panorama: Fifty Years of Pride and Paranoia* (London: Politico's Publishing, 2002)

Maddrell, Paul, *Spying on Science: Western Intelligence in Divided Germany 1945–1961* (Oxford: Oxford University Press, 2006)

Mailer, Norman, *Miami and the Siege of Chicago* (New York: World Publishing Company, 1968)

McLachlan, Donald, *Room 39: Naval Intelligence in Action 1939–45* (London: Weidenfeld & Nicolson, 1968)

Nelson, Michael, *War of the Black Heavens: The Battles of Western Broadcasting in the Cold War* (London: Brassey's, 1997)

Nixon, Richard, *Memoirs* (New York: Grosset & Dunlap, 1978)

Nutting, David (ed,), *Attain by Surprise: Capturing Top Secret Intelligence in WWII* (Chichester: David Colver Publishing, 1997)

Priestland, Gerald, *Something Understood* (London: Arrow Books, 1988)

Purvis, Stewart & Hulbert, Jeff, *When Reporters Cross the Line* (Hull: Biteback, 2013)

Rankin, Nicholas, *Ian Fleming's Commandos: The Story of 30 Assault Unit in WWII* (London: Faber & Faber, 2011)

Seaton, Jean, *'Pinkoes and Traitors': The BBC and the Nation, 1974–1987* (London: Profile Books, 2015)

Simpson, John, *Strange Places, Questionable People* (London: Macmillan, 1998)

Smith, Arthur L, *Kidnap City: Cold War Berlin* (Westport: Greenwood Press, 2002)

Summers, Anthony, *The Arrogance of Power: The Secret World of Richard Nixon* (London: Weidenfeld & Nicolson, 2000)

Wall, Stephen, *Reluctant European: Britain and the European Union from 1945 to Brexit* (Oxford: Oxford University Press, 2020)

Webb, Alban, *London Calling: Britain, the BBC World Service and the Cold War*, Bloomsbury Publishing, 2015,

Wheeler, Marina, *The Lost Homestead: My Mother, Partition and the Punjab* (London Hodder and Stoughton, 2020)

Wittman, Rebecca, *Beyond Justice: The Auschwitz Trial* (Cambridge: Harvard University Press, 2005)

NOTES

Please note that all references to Charles's reports for BBC radio and television are courtesy of BBC Archive, which holds the digital recordings.

BBC related scripts, letters and documents are held by the BBC Written Archives Centre, Caversham, referred to here as 'WAC' and reproduced with their permission.

Charles's own personal archive, kept at home, also contains many documents as well as the 1952-54 Berlin scripts.

The programme *From Our Own Correspondent* on BBC Radio is abbreviated to 'FOOC,'; Charles Wheeler's files in WAC are shortened to 'CW file'.

Dan Colwell, the author's husband, recorded a number of anecdotes told by Charles in his unpublished diaries referred to here as 'DC diaries'.

Chapter 1
5 'Selwyn had quite a good birthday': undated letter from John Wheeler, CW personal archive.
8 'One day I was up for over six hours': letter from JW, 5/4/1941, CW personal archive.
8 'We all went to the windows': letter from JW, 26/3/1941, CW personal archive
8 'Immediately the bombs started falling': letter from Peter Smith, 1/7/1941 CW personal archive.
9 'I remember the shock of him being killed': *The Oldie*, June 1996.
10 'Walking around with a trilby': CW interview, *The Press and Journal*, 19 November 1977.
12 'assert his personality': National Archive, Kew, ADM 223/475.
13 'The only civilian occupation': ibid.
14 'never, probably, have intelligence officers': Donald McLachlan, *Room 39: Naval Intelligence in Action 1939–45*, Weidenfeld & Nicolson, 1968, 172.
17 'And there he was, having a shave': BBC Television Feature Service, May 1994.
18 'I told him that': CW interview, *The Oldie*, November 2006.
19 'I remember one evening early in July': unpublished manuscript, CW personal archive.
19 'As a military operation': ibid.

20	'I was joined by a lively young officer': Patrick Dalzel-Job, *Arctic Snow to Dust of Normandy*, Pen & Sword Books, 2005, 130.
20	'Marvellously well-equipped…': CW's foreword to *Arctic Snow to Dust of Normandy*, 6.
21	'It was a pretty undisciplined freelance outfit': *The Oldie*, November 2006.
22	'Largely on account of the boisterous manner': National Archive, HW 8/104.
23	'The antics of Ginette de St Sauveur': J.A.C. Hugill, unpublished diaries, Churchill Archive Centre, Churchill College, Cambridge, GBR/0014/HUGL4.
25	'It was because Charles… gleaned so much': *Arctic Snow to Dust of Normandy*, p. 161.
26	'I slowly discovered that': CW's foreword to *Arctic Snow to Dust of Normandy*, p. 7.
26	'Ils sont partout!': J.A.C. Hugill, *The Hazard Mesh*, Faber & Faber, 2011, pp. 79–80.
27	'We took some prisoners in Brittany': BBC Television Feature Service, May 1994.
27	'I've heard they are killing German prisoners': DC diaries.
29	'I urge you not to continue questioning': Craig Cabell, *The History of 30 Assault Unit*, Pen & Sword Books, 2009, pp. 129–130.
29	'to surrender it': letter from John Hickey, CW personal archive, dated 18/9/1968.
30	'Mais, Capitaine Charles Wheeler': *Attain by Surprise*, David Colver Publishing, 1997, p. 275.
30	'lived in the Viscount's barn': from Charles's notes for an address at Ralph Izzard's funeral in 1992, in CW archive.
30	'It was when we crossed the Dutch frontier': from CW's foreword to *Germany 1944: The British Soldier's Handbook*, The National Archive, 2006, p. iv.
32	'It had rained for three days': ibid, p. v.
32	'There was a huge flurry of activity': National Geographic Channel, *The Hunt for Hitler's Scientists*, Windfall Films, 2005.
34	'You are my prisoner, he told Charles': DC diaries. CW's official report held in Churchill Archive Centre, GBR/0014/MISC 31.
35	'Oh, to hell with him, Wheeler': *Attain by Surprise*, p. 278.
36	'You will come here tomorrow at nine': DC diaries.
37	'subterranean shambles': BBC Written Archive Centre, Caversham (WAC), FOOC, Brandenburg Gate Anniversary, February 1963.
37	'personal friends, many of whom were': George Blake, *No Other Choice*, Jonathan Cape, 1990, p. 103.
38	'We drove her through two Russian checkpoints': *The Hunt for Hitler's Scientists*.
38	'People had to be pretty careful', ibid.
39	'He served in the German campaign': WAC, Letter from Admiral Rushbrooke, CW file L1/2077/3, 15/8/1946.
40	'They'll take anyone on': *The Journalist's Handbook*, Carrick, April 2000, No 61, p. 17.

Chapter 2

41	'terribly orthodox': *The Journalist's Handbook*, p. 17.
41	'Never, ever, speak a foreign language': ibid.
42	'What you had to do was': BBC Radio London, interview with Roger Clark, 10/8/1988.
43	'I'm writing to you from the living room': letter from René Dubois, CW personal archive, November 1948.
44	'Undertake an interrogating job': letter from Commander Malcolm Saunders, CW personal archive, 10/7/1948.
45	'Deepish baritone': WAC, voice test report, CW file L1/2077/3, 5/10/1950.

45	'engaged on work of national importance': WAC, letter to BBC from Commander A.T. Courtney, Chief of Naval Intelligence Staff, Germany, CW file L1/2077/3, 30/12/1948.
45	'pleasant personality': ibid.
46	'occasionally necessary to remind him': WAC, BBC report, CW file L1/2077/3, 3/9/1951.
46	'enable the Corporation': Michael Nelson, *War of the Black Heavens: The Battles of Western Broadcasting in the Cold War*. Brassey's,1997, p. 12.
46	'I knew that the stuff I was sending back': CW interview, *Independent*, 1997.
47	'more vigorous reply': Nelson, p. 14.
48	'I take this opportunity of asking you': letter from Geoffrey Bourne, CW personal archive, 5/5/1951.
49	'The domestic service had nothing to do with': *The Times*, 20/10/1997.
49	'People behaved in the same way…': *The Oldie*, June 1996.
49	'Charles Wheeler had hardly concealed': Patrick Major, 'Listening Behind the Curtain: BBC Broadcasting to East Germany and its Cold War Echo', in *Cold War History*, Vol.13 no. 2, 2013, p. 259.
51	'West Berlin remained a place of refuge': dispatch, BBC German Service, CW personal archive, 20/2/1953.
52	'He smiled a lot': BBC1, *Inside Story*, 'The Confession',19/9/1990.
53	'He spun round': *The Listener*, 4/5/1989.
53	'A Cold War kind of job': *The Oldie*, November 2006.
54	'It was all done on an old boys' basis': CW interview, *Independent*, 1997.
54	'He was in fact an enemy agent': *Daily Telegraph & Morning Post*,11/9/1952, p.8.
55	'A few days ago a friend and I': dispatch, 'Life in Berlin', BBC European Service, CW personal archive, 3/6/1952.
55	'It was intended as a justification': dispatch, 'Berlin's Eastern Barriers', BBC European Service, CW personal archive, 23/2/1953.
56	'in the name of the people': dispatch, 'Changes in Eastern Germany', BBC European Service, CW personal archive, 14/8/52.
56	'Thousands of young voices': dispatch, 'East German Situation', BBC European Service, CW personal archive, 26/6/52.
57	'Our national armed forces': dispatch, 'Changes in Eastern Germany', ibid
57	'mount a defence of their anti-Jewish policies': news dispatch, BBC European Service, CW personal archive, 26/1/1953.
58	'For the past week refugees': dispatch, 'Refugees from East Germany', BBC European Service, CW personal archive, 26/1/53.
58	'They are finding it daily more difficult': dispatch, 'Report on Eastern Germany', BBC European Service, CW personal archive, 5/2/1953.
59	'Until Thursday it was a rather depressing week': dispatch, 'Berlin Letter', BBC European Service, CW personal archive, 13/6/1953.
60	'I think you should, Peter replied': undated draft script, CW personal archive, circa 1980.
60	'Their own delighted surprise': dispatch, 'Two Days in Berlin', BBC European Service, CW personal archive, 18/6/1953.
61	'Happily disposing of the outward signs': International Survey, BBC Overseas Service, CW personal archive, 2/11/1953.
61	'We heard shouting in chorus': transcript of news report, BBC European Service, CW personal archive,18/6/1953.
61	'Violence began when police': Dispatch, 'Two Days in Berlin'.

62	'It was rapidly becoming a hopeless cause': ibid.
62	'Every exit to West Berlin is guarded': ibid.
62	'In spite of the casualties, I believe': ibid.
64	'Nothing can wipe out the East German people's...': dispatch, 'Changes in Eastern Germany', BBC European Service, CW personal archive, 25/6/1953.
64	'Powerful deterrent to a Third World War': *London Review of Books*, Volume 18, 19/9/1996.
64	'It is not through his vivid reporting alone': WAC, letter from 'Sixtus 2' to BBC German Service (translated from German original), CW file L1/2077/3, 10/9/1953.
66	'Don't let him drink': DC diaries.
68	'We dumped it in a ditch': *London Review of Books*, Volume 18, 19/9/1996.
68	'At Sopron University students...': BBC News Online, 'BBC's dilemmas over revolution' article, 23/10/2006.
68	'We hope that our country will be entirely free': BBC1, *Panorama*, 5/11/1956.
69	'We heard the news in the cutting room at Lime Grove': BBC News Online, ibid.
70	'Our boys are dying...': *London Review of Books*, ibid.
70	'He told us that by intervening at Suez': CW interview, National Security Archive at George Washington University, 13/5/1996.

Chapter 3

73	'Last week showed how near Cyprus': BBC News, Cyprus report, 16/6/1958.
74	'His country is on the verge of bloody revolution': WAC: *From Our Own Correspondent*, (FOOC,) 'King Hussein of Jordan', 2/8/1958.
78	'Two men took over': WAC, FOOC, 'Pakistan's Revolution', 11/10/1958.
79	'For those people who understand': *Dawn* newspaper, 'No Forsaking of Democracy' Nasim Ahmad, 10/10/1958.
79	'Both of them strike one as relaxed': WAC, FOOC, 'Democracy in Pakistan and India', 18/10/1958.
80	'Is there not a danger that the army': ibid.
80	'Independent India has a record': ibid.
81	'The fate of the Dalai Lama is unknown': WAC, FOOC, 'Tibet Round Up', 28/3/1959.
81	'What I remember so vividly': BBC R4, *In Pursuit of the Dalai Lama*, Loftus Production Company, 13/7/2008.
82	'The competition was sharpest': ibid.
85	'The Indian people': BBC TV News, CW Interview with Dalai Lama, 16/9/1959.
85	'all that is Tibetan': WAC, FOOC, 'Tibet, a Year After', 4/6/1960.
85	'They didn't want to upset the Chinese': BBC R4, *In Pursuit of the Dalai Lama*, ibid.
86	'Very gradually, the facts': WAC, FOOC, 'China and India', 15/8/1959.
87	'The night clerk at the tiny, sleepy post office': CW foreword to *The Best of From Our Own Correspondent*, Vol. 3, ed. Mike Popham and Geoff Spink, Broadside Books, 1992, p. 7.
87	'If the Indian government does have a policy': WAC, FOOC, 'Sikkim and Bhutan', 28/8/1959.
87	'Members of Parliament are getting': WAC, FOOC, 'Nehru's Trials', 5/9/1959.
88	'It was the first glimpse': ibid.
89	'It's doubtful if a month ago': ibid.
89	'In some respects, Ceylon last week': WAC, FOOC, 'Censorship in Ceylon' 10/10/1959.
90	'The BBC had descended': *Times of Ceylon*, 19/10/1959.
90	'The broadcast contained unwarranted criticisms': *Ceylon Observer*, 21/10/1959.

WITNESS TO THE TWENTIETH CENTURY

91	'Grossly improper...': undated newspaper cutting, CW personal archive, October 1959.
91	'My piece was a distillation': undated notes for telex to BBC, CW personal archive.
91	'I know that you will fully understand': letter from CW, CW personal archive, October 1959.
92	'In spite of this, "wheel-again Wheeler"': *Ceylon Observer*, 24/10/1959.
92	'The BBC has already apologised twice': *Daily Telegraph*, 22/10/1959.
92	'I am sorry to have caused this incident': letter from CW, CW personal archive, 19/10/1959.
93	'He didn't allow himself to be thrown': WAC, Annual Report 1960, CW file L1/2077/3.
93	'Charles, the thing to do': *Journalist's Handbook*, p. 22.
94	'His recent speeches...': WAC, FOOC, 'India Before Parliament Meeting', 14/11/1959.
94	'Angry, indignant and excited': BBC TV News, interview with Indira Gandhi, 17/11/1959.
95	'Perhaps India provided the ideal background': WAC, FOOC, 'Ike and India', 19/12/1959.
96	'A much more militant communism': WAC, FOOC, 'Kerala Situation', 1/8/1959.
97	'If only they weren't Communists': WAC, FOOC, 'Portrait of Kerala', 10/1/1959.
97	'There is nothing of the police state': ibid.
97	'Congress, in power everywhere': WAC, FOOC, 'The Situation in Kerala', 20/6/1959.
98	'The government of Kerala is the only Communist government': WAC, FOOC, 'Kerala Situation'.
98	'Tied to an inflexible dogma': WAC, FOOC, 'Portrait of Kerala'.
98	'The head of a great and friendly state': WAC, FOOC, 'Trivandrum', 6/2/1960.
99	'Both sides expected too much': WAC, FOOC, 'Indian Reaction to Khrushchev's Visit', 5/3/1960.
99	'Even one's Communist acquaintances': ibid.
101	'Sallies that provoked gales of sycophantic': WAC, FOOC, 'Stocktaking After the Delhi Talks', 30/4/1960.
103	'He admired the view': WAC, FOOC, 'Nehru and Ayub', 22/7/1961.
105	'A cross between St Paul's': WAC, FOOC, 'Preparations for the Royal Tour', 17/12/1961.
106	'Which works quickly': WAC, FOOC, 'Swat', 3/1/1959.
107	'suitably cosmopolitan': WAC, FOOC, 'Nepal Impressions', 22/8/1959.
109	'young and energetic': WAC, FOOC, Koirala 'Man of the Year', 24/12/1960.
109	'The effect of the Queen's personality': WAC, FOOC, 'Queen's Tour Sum Up', 4/3/1961.
110	'All too many people are saying that': ibid.
111	'Everybody is in position now': BBC Radio News dispatch, 'Royal Tour: India, Pakistan and Nepal', 1/1/1961.
112	'Persona non grata at the palace': *Television*, (RTS magazine), November 2006, p. 30.
114	'my country right or wrong': Marina Wheeler, *The Lost Homestead*, Hodder and Stoughton, 2020, p. 128.
114	'There is absolutely no disposition in Pakistan': WAC, FOOC, 'Ike and Pakistan', 19/12/1959.
114	'It is being said in Delhi': WAC, FOOC, 'Nehru and Ayub', 22/7/1961.
114	'It is the sharpest attack Mr Nehru had ever made': ibid.
115	'Mr Menon has been attacked': WAC, FOOC, 'India and the United States', 4/11/1961.
116	'While the weapon had survived': WAC, FOOC, 'The Golden Temple Fast', 26/8/1961.
117	'If it was a war': WAC, FOOC, 'Goa', 24/12/1961.
117	'To a country like India': WAC, FOOC, 'Goa', 9/12/1961.
118	'PIDE [the Salazar regime's secret police]': diplomatic cable, Arquivo Histórico-Diplomático, MNE, Lisbon (Portuguese Foreign Office archive), 14/12/1961.
118	'The Indian army had reason to be pleased': WAC, FOOC, 'Goa', 24/12/1961.
119	'Mr Nehru is amassing a crushing inheritance': WAC, FOOC, 'After Nehru', 26/8/1961.

120 'grown in stature': WAC, Annual Report 1962, CW file L1/2077/3.
120 'This has been a week to long for home': WAC, FOOC, 'On Leaving India', 2/6/1962.
121 'India is a country in which events': ibid.

Chapter 4

124 'The case of Fechter': WAC, FOOC, 'Morale Sags in Berlin', 25/8/1962.
125 'It took him about forty minutes to die': BBC R4 *Archive Hour*: 'Wheeler at 80'
126 'There was a lot of resentment from the West Berliners': ibid.
126 'What was unusual' WAC: 'Morale Sags in Berlin': ibid.
126 'I got a telephone call': BBC Radio London with Roger Clark, 10/8/1988.
127 'There was nothing they could do': ibid.
128 'We really went for those two interrogators': ibid.
129 'cold-blooded killings': WAC: BBC Radio Bulletins, 'Berlin Notes', 24/8/1964.
129 'The average West Berliner is not the optimist': WAC, 'Morale Sags in Berlin', ibid.
129 'The important thing now is': BBC News bulletins, 31/8/1962.
130 'The shadow of an all-out nuclear war': WAC, FOOC, by Douglas Stuart, 27/10/1962.
130 'I was thousands of miles from Cuba': BBC2, *Explorer*: 'Charles Wheeler's Cold War', 7/10/1998.
133 'Often I have gazed at a map': 'Day Trip to the East', WAC, FOOC, 6/6/1963, published in *From Our Own Correspondent: The First Forty Years*, ed. Tony Grant, Pan Books, 1995, pp. 41–43
135 'He made the kind of speech': CW interview for National Security Archive at George Washington University.
136 'Ich bin ein Berliner': DC diaries.
137 'The crowd roared its approval': Willy Brandt, *People and Politics*, Collins, 1978, p 73.
138 'The oppressive number of': Richard Nixon, *Memoirs*, Grosset & Dunlap, 1978, p. 249.
138 'From our welcome abroad': ibid, p. 248.
139 'A narrow steel tube': WAC, CW dispatch for BBC Radio News bulletins, 27/10/1963.
140 'The final stage': BBC Radio Newsreel, 7/11/1963.
140 'They've been terribly pessimistic': BBC1 Live two-way for *Panorama*, 4/11/1963.
141 'The biggest challenge': WAC, Annual Report 1963, CW file L1/2077/3.
142 'He climbed up on the top': BBC1, 'JFK: Legend and Leader', 21/11/2003.
142 'Berlin really closed down': ibid.
142 'A torchlight procession': BBC Home Service, 'The Man We Mourn', 23/11/1963.
142 'West Berlin is a lifeless city today': ibid.
144 'Actually operated the extermination machine': WAC, FOOC, 'Staff at Auschwitz', 2/4/1964.
144 'A fair cross-section of German males': ibid.
144 'Of the nineteen other defendants': WAC, FOOC, 'Auschwitz and the Germans', 18/4/1964.
144 'How can a life sentence be considered': ibid.
145 'Wishful fantasy': Franz Bauer from Rebecca Wittman, *Beyond Justice: The Auschwitz Trial*, Harvard University Press, 2012, p. 255.
145 'sorting out Jews': WAC, FOOC, 'Auschwitz pre-trial dentist', 3/5/1963.
146 'The textbook civil servant': WAC, FOOC, 'Trials in East and West Berlin', 8/7/1963.
147 'I didn't learn of the killings': WAC, FOOC, 'Justice for Some', 13/10/1963.
147 'Under Hitler he was': WAC, FOOC, 'Auschwitz pre-trial dentist', 3/5/1963.
147 'Highly commended by the late Herr Frick': ibid.

147	'He can't govern forever in a state of war': WAC, FOOC, 'Ulbricht's amnesty', 17/10/1964.
148	'Insofar as Bonn has pursued any policy': ibid.
148	'Bonn is looking for a new policy': ibid.
148	'Twelve months ago': ibid.
148	'I agree with his view': WAC, Annual Report 1963, CW file L1/2077/3.
150	'General Thimayya's remarks': original script quoted in letter from Gerald Norman, CW personal archive, 26/8/1964.
151	'We are gravely concerned': WAC, letter from Donald Edwards, News: Cyprus R28/324/1, 25/8/1964.
151	'It could be argued that the shortened form': ibid.
151	'I am in no position': letter to Gerald Norman, CW personal archive, 29/8/1964.
151	'He clearly prefers to be a correspondent abroad': WAC, Interview Report, 3/7/1964, CW file L1/2077/3.
152	'crash course in Russian': WAC, Annual Report 1964, CW file L1/2077/3.

Chapter 5

153	'The country seemed ripe for revolution': BBC1 *Wheeler on America*, series introduction, 1996.
153	'The supremacy of one race': BBC1 *Wheeler on America*, 'Part 2: America's Long March', 3/3/1996.
155	'He said that he got scared': BBC TV News, New Voting Rights Bill, 12/8/1965.
157	'Burnt buildings, looted shops…': BBC Radio News, 'Los Angeles Race Riots', 16/8/1965.
157	'To the people who did this': BBC1, *Wheeler on America*, ibid.
157	'They talk about police brutality', BBC TV News, 'Race Riots Los Angeles aftermath', 18/8/1965.
158	'The violence was justified…': BBC R4, *Archive Hour*: 'Wheeler at 80'.
158	'On some topics': WAC, Annual Report 1967, CW file L1/2077/3.
158	'"He does need to guard": WAC, Annual Report 1972, CW file l1/2077/1.
159	'It depends on the leadership': BBC TV CW interview with Martin Luther King, 30/8/1965.
163	'Was Washington big enough for the three of them?': Gerald Priestland, *Something Understood*, Arrow Books, 1988, p. 211.
164	'A good officer', Priestland, ibid.
164	'Nerves of steel': Priestland, ibid.
166	'Nobody wants to be associated with the Klan': BBC TV News, 'Beatles in Washington', 17/8/1966.
168	'Penetrating white neighbourhoods': BBC News, 'Chicago Demonstrations', 8/8/1966.
168	'I've been hit so many times': ibid.
169	'King go back to Africa': BBC R4, *Archive Hour*: 'Wheeler at 80'.
169	'Afternoon of almost uncontrolled terrorism': D.J.R. Bruckner, *Los Angeles Times*, 6/8/1966.
170	'No one who was there': BBC2, *Newsnight*, 15/6/1981.
171	'The danger to life and limb': ibid.
172	'The crisis in American cities': BBC TV News, 'Increase Crime and Race Riots in US', 22/12/1969.
172	'Poverty is as permanent': BBC TV News, 'Slums', 4/8/1967.
173	'There is something strangely inconsistent': Martin Luther King, Ebenezer Baptist Church, 30/4/1967.
175	'As I record this report': WAC, FOOC, 'MLK Assassination', 5/4/1968.

176	'No soldier fired anything more lethal than': BBC TV News, 'Violence after MLK death', 9/4/1968.
176	'Unless the conditions, which are festering grounds': ibid.
177	'But people rarely do': BBC News, 'Poor People's March', 11/5/1968.
178	'Is anybody living here?': BBC2 *Assignment Special: The Legacy of Martin Luther King*, 3/4/1993.
179	'I found him extraordinarily compelling': *The Oldie*, June 1996.
180	'It was sloppy, messy': BBC1, *Wheeler on America*, 'Part 2: America's Long March'.
182	'We are not resentful': BBC2, *Newsnight*, 5/5/1992.
183	'In making King a national hero': BBC2, *The Legacy of Martin Luther King*, ibid.
183	'America's brief infatuation': BBC1, *Wheeler on America*, ibid.

Chapter 6

188	'If anything can help to carry President Johnson': BBC TV News, 5/2/1968.
188	'They were enormously persuasive': BBC R4, *Great Lives*, 7/5/2004.
188	'It's a big, bloody, costly, risky war': BBC News, *Review of the Year*, 30/12/1965.
189	'It was one of those famous two-wayers': BBC R4, *Great Lives*, ibid.
189	'reporters should avoid': BBC1, *Wheeler on America*, 'Part 1: Lyndon Johnson's War', 18/2/1996.
190	'It really was an agonising': ibid.
190	'no evidence yet made public': undated draft for dispatch from Dominican Republic, CW personal archive, May 1965.
191	'This man is really not telling the truth': BBC R4, *Great Lives*, ibid.
193	'I had complete confidence in him': BBC R4, *Archive on 4*, 'Wheeler: The Final Word', Whistledown Productions, 13/3/2013.
194	'I spent many afternoons watching': BBC1, *Wheeler on America*, ibid
194	'We misunderstood our enemy': ibid.
195	'No, no, no': Channel 4, *Playing with the Truth*, Carey Barraclough Production, January 1999.
198	'Over 35,000 names they read': BBC TV News, 'Anti-Vietnam Protests', 29/5/1969.
199	'I thought I would say': BBC1, *Our Own Correspondent*, documentary, 24/10/1972.
200	'Marijuana is smoked quite freely': BBC TV News, 'Morningstar Ranch', 7/9/1967.
201	'Unmistakable stench of pigs': BBC TV News, 26/8/1968.
202	'Rousing stuff but more often than not': BBC TV News, Chicago Convention, 29/8/1968.
203	'At three a.m. after the convention had adjourned': BBC Radio newsreel, 29/8/1968.
203	'The wounds the party had suffered': ibid.
203	'Local politicians here call him Mr President': 1968 Nixon campaign report, BBC R4, *Archive on 4*, 'Wheeler: The Final Word'.
205	'She was in almost daily conversation': *The Oldie*, 'Tricky Dicky's Dirtiest Trick', 27/11/ 2000.
207	'The dirtiest of Nixon's lifetime of dirty tricks': *The Oldie*, ibid.
211	'Why didn't you take care…?': BBC TV News, 18/11/1970.
212	'All wars blunt people's sensitivities': BBC Four, *Timewatch Special: Charles Wheeler: Edge of Frame*, 4/4/2004.
213	'Some twenty-nine years ago': BBC TV News, 'McGovern Campaign', 30/6/1972.
214	'This Democratic primary is probably the silliest': BBC TV News, 'Primary Florida', 13/3/1972.
215	'His message is the racist message of the old days': BBC TV News, 'Florida Democratic Primaries', 10/3/1972.

215	'He's trying to bring America back to what it should be': BBC TV News, 'Wallace Campaign', 2/10/1968.
215	'Wallace is not a prepossessing figure…': ibid.
217	'He was wearing Stars and Stripes socks…': live (audio) two-way, BBC1, 'Twenty-Four Hours', 15/5/1972.
218	'The police arrangements were in fact very bad': ibid.
218	'Charles Wheeler's astonishing capacity': BBC memo, CW personal archive, 19 May 1972.
219	'northern, suburban George Wallace': BBC Radio newsreel, 27/12/1969.
222	'Charles Wheeler tried to organise': Timothy Crouse, *The Boys on the Bus*, Random House, 1973, p. 235.
222	'the Democratic candidate': BBC TV News, 3/11/1972.
223	'How is it that an incumbent candidate…': BBC2 *Friday Talk-In*, 10/11/1972.
224	'His personal insecurity and fear of defeat': *The Oldie*, 'Tricky Dicky's Dirtiest Trick', ibid.
227	'I wasn't there to make friends': BBC R4, *The World Tonight*, Interview with J. Erlichman (plus full transcript in CW personal archive), 29/6/1973.
229	'It shattered the myth': Book review of Fred Emery, *Watergate: the Corruption and Fall of Richard Nixon*, *Observer*, 5/6/1994.

Chapter 7

233	'I don't really enjoy responsibility': letter from Dick Walker, CW personal archive, 15/1/1972.
234	'the Year of Wheeler': WAC, Annual Report 1973, CW file L1/2077/1.
234	'of a calibre which requires': WAC: 5-Year Report 1972, CW file L1/2077/1.
236	'That much maligned talking shop': BBC R4, FOOC, 'Problems in the Common Market', 20/12/1973.
236	'I admit I don't go there very often': BBC R4, *Analysis*: ; 'Towards One Europe', 22/1/1976.
236	'If European industry is going to grind': WAC, FOOC, 'Britain and the Community', 21/3/1974.
237	'The press in more and more countries are beginning to say': BBC1, *Panorama*, 'Oil', 3/12/1973.
237	'In a common crisis': Open University course: 'EEC: The State of the Union', BBC radio transcript in CW personal archive, November 1974.
237	'Found oil spreading': BBC R4, 'Problems in the Common Market', ibid.
238	'There must have been moments late last Saturday night': BBC R4, FOOC, 'Common Market Summit: Copenhagen' 18/12/1973.
238	'They've been too busy running a market', ibid.
239	'There was an inevitable period': WAC, Annual Staff Report 1975, CW file L1/2077/1.
239	'It was the product of an ambition': 'Common Market Summit', ibid.
240	'Has now become a fact of community life': 'Problems in Common Market', ibid.
240	'In the community's interest': ibid.
241	'The question should Britain stay in or get out': ibid.
241	'imbued with a new enthusiasm': WAC, Annual Report 1975, ibid.
242	'Feel its way forward': WAC, FOOC, 'Britain and the Community', 21/3/1974.
242	'At present they are by no means': ibid.
242	'It is not just a question of whether': ibid.
243	'The fact is, nobody among': WAC, FOOC, 'Renegotiation Prospects', 30/3/1974.
243	'Behaved with gratuitous': Stephen Wall, *Reluctant European, Britain and the European Union from 1945 to Brexit*, Oxford University Press, 2020, p. 125.

245 'The first is familiar – do the British want to stay in Europe?': Open University: 'EEC: The State of the Union'.
245 'The real issue is sovereignty': ibid.
246 'Among the other eight a feeling has grown': BBC TV News bulletins, 'Dublin: Preparations for EEC Summit', 9/3/1975.
246 'The impression of a man who': Wall, ibid, p. 281.
247 'The country is divided, every party is divided': BBC1, *Midweek*, 11/3/1975.
248 'I think the community would have to', BBC R4, *Inside Europe: Future Uncertainties*, 28/4/74.
252 'For what is significant about Portugal': WAC, FOOC, 'Portugal: After the Revolution', 9/10/1975, published in *From Our Own Correspondent: Twenty-five Years of Foreign Reports*, ed. Roger Lazar, BBC, 1980, p. 165.
253 'The accused were not told': BBC TV News, report on Franco's Death, 20/11/1975.
254 'In an incident interpreted by many': Christopher Tulloch, 'The Influence of the International Press and Foreign Correspondents in Transitional Democracies', *Journalism Studies* Volume 18, No. 3, March 2017.
255 'Call the consulate': DC diaries.
256 'May not succeed because Franco': BBC TV News, report on Franco's Death, ibid.
256 'News, real news': BBC2, *Newsday*, 'Spanish Press', 20/5/1976.
257 'The nine member states have something to do': BBC R4,
258 *Analysis*, 'Towards One Europe', 22/1/1976.
259 'Earlier this year, Charles gave notice of his wish': WAC, Annual Report 1976, CW file L1/2077/1.

Chapter 8

261 'My cousin buys up old cottages': letter from CW, in CW personal archive, 21/4/1961.
264 'Face bigger problems of adjustment': BBC1, 'Where Do We Go from Here?', 19/9/1977.
266 'I've never seen anyone attempt to listen so hard': BBC2, *Newsnight*, 17/7/1981.
267 'The progress of Blacks here': BBC2, *Newsnight*, 16/10/1985.
269 'I think *Panorama* was better then': BBC Radio London, *Close Encounters*, 1988.
269 'Revolution I'd longed for': BBC Online, 'Newsnight 25', 21/1/2005.
272 'I hope a time will come': BBC2, *Newsnight*, 24/11/1982.
273 'The choice of Henry Kissinger': BBC2, *Newsnight*, 18/6/1985.
273 'Innocent Americans cannot become the subject of blackmail': ibid.
275 'What a scorecard': letter from John Mahoney, CW personal archive, 2/7/1985.
275 'Just like Mafia godfathers have done' BBC2, *Newsnight*, 3/12/1986.
275 'His basic personality is not sympathetic': ibid.
276 'When we talked a year ago': letter, WAC, letter to contracts manager, CW file T67/479/1, 8/12/1984.
276 'Now that the election is out of the way', WAC, BBC internal letter, CW file T67/479/1.
279 'It should be understood as a very dramatic sentence': BBC2, *Newsnight* 27/10/1981.
283 'Have you lowered your objectives': BBC2, *Newsnight*, 17/5/1988.
283 'Pliable Greeks in a world': Norman Davies, *Heart of Europe: A Short History of Poland*, Oxford University Press, 1984, p. 308.
284 'Do you think that only the existence of Solidarity': BBC2, *Newsnight*, 17/5/1988.
285 'I think we all put our views very, very frankly': BBC2, *Newsnight*, 30/3/1987.
286 'Pressure on this issue cannot harm Gorbachev': BBC2, *Newsnight*, 31/3/1987.
286 'For the first ever time she said yes': BBC Radio London, Roger Clark, ibid, 10/8/1988.

286 'That suited me…': BBC2, *Newsnight*, 31/3/1987.
287 'When I was last there in March '87': letters from CW, CW personal archive, 21/4/1988 & 3/7/1988.
288 'All rousing stuff': ibid.
289 'In this report, we are not saying that': BBC2, *Newsnight*, 7/5/1986.
290 'There is an intense feeling': ibid.
292 'The purpose of this film is not to ask': BBC2, *Inside Story: Beyond Reasonable Doubt*, 16/5/1990.
295 'It's smaller than a typewriter': letter from CW, CW personal archive, 21/4/1988.
296 'That the neurotic, humourless, insecure': draft review of 'What it Takes: The Way to the White House', CW personal archive, 1992.
297 'Suitably banal and encouragingly belligerent': BBC2, *Newsnight*, 18/8/1988.
298 'In my world, any project': undated letter, CW personal archive.
299 'Look, Charles, I've read the books': CW profile, *Observer*, March 1993.
299 'I hear younger people say': letter from Molly McEwan, CW personal archive, 29/10/1989.
301 'He sprayed gas into my mouth': BBC1, *Panorama*, 'Gorbachev: Reaping the Whirlwind 2, Bloody Sunday', 20/11/1989.
301 'Lots of us knew the hard times were coming': letter from Maya Kiasashvili, CW personal archive, 23/6/1993.
302 'The process taking place now': BBC1, 'Bloody Sunday', ibid.
303 'When you say analysis': BBC 'bootleg' recording from *Timewatch Special: Charles Wheeler: Edge of Frame*.
304 'If John Birt was the Roundheads' Roundhead': Mark Thompson, Charles Wheeler Memorial Lecture, 20/5/2009.
305 'I'm going to join the strike': *Sunday Times*, 23/4/1989.
306 'When you telephoned me': letter from CW, CW personal archive, 28/4/1989.
306 'Denials and explanations': Unpublished article for *The Listener*, CW personal archive, May 1989.
308 'I'd like to be down there': BBC2 *Newsnight* live, 3/10/1990.

Chapter 9
309 'Must go to the local graveyard': undated letter from CW; CW personal archive, March 1991.
311 'What marks out Hawalli': BBC2, *Newsnight*, 18/3/1991.
312 'Have any non-Kuwaitis been brought here for burial': ibid.
313 'There was injury': ibid
315 'I don't think Dr Ali was at a linguistic disadvantage': undated draft of letter from CW. CW personal archive, summer 1991.
316 'He's going to be hungry, he's very thin': BBC2, *Newsnight*, 12/3/199.
318 'Your son and I became good friends': copy of letter, CW personal archive, 25/3/1991.
318 'The whole family was highly worried': letter from R. Somasundaram, CW personal archive, 26/4/1991.
320 'Five million people are on this mountain': BBC2, *Newsnight*,15/4/1991.
321 'We seem to have been the first Westerners here': ibid.
322 'I am told by the Foreign Office': undated letter from Tim Gardam, CW personal archive, 1991.
323 'There is nothing but mud and water': BBC2, *Newsnight*, 18/4/1991.
324 'I got terribly wrapped up in it': BBC R4 *Archive Hour*: 'Wheeler at 80'.

325 'I can't believe how lucky I am to be here': Jeremy Paxman interview with CW, *Sunday Telegraph*, 18/2/1996.
325 'Most of us guessed quite early in 1944': BBC1, *D-Day: Turning the Tide*, 5/6/1994.
326 'I think what we're hearing about D-Day': BBC TV Live 50th Anniversary D-Day, 6/6/1994.
328 'Of all the British campaigns in World War Two': BBC1, *Burma: The Forgotten War*, 14/8/1995.
330 'I would ask them to think back to the days': CW letter to the *Guardian*, 26/5/1994.
331 'In most institutions there's a lot of forelock tugging': *Timewatch Special, Charles Wheeler: Edge of Frame*, ibid.
332 'Sorry to be difficult, but may I enter an objection': letter from CW, CW personal archive, 15/9/1997
332 'The BBC has lost its way in news': *The Times*, 21/8/2000.
334 'There was nothing wide-eyed about Reagan': BBC1, *Wheeler on America*, 'Part 5: The Reagan Legacy', 24/3/1996.
334 'I go to America to do a death-penalty story': BBC R4, *Archive Hour*: 'Wheeler at 80'.
334 'We are professionally married to each other': ibid.
335 'During the eighties, Congress got carried away in the rush to punish': BBC1, *Wheeler on America*, 'Part 4: Drugs and Punishment', 10/3/1996.
337 'In these last few days, Bill Clinton': BBC2, *Newsnight*, 2/11/1992.
337 'I have covered every President since Kennedy': *Sunday Mirror*, 13/9/1998.
338 'I didn't commit this crime': BBC2, *Newsnight*, 19/5/1992.
341 'There's a word for this that doesn't often habitually crop up in Britain': BBC2, *Black Britain* special, 'Why Stephen?',13/2/1999.
344 'When a nation perceives itself to be under siege': BBC2, *Newsnight*, 10/9/2002.

Chapter 10
350 'I am incognito. I don't know who I am': BBC R4, *The Child Migrants*, Whistledown Productions, September 2003.
351 'Charles – how old are you?': BBC R4, *Archive Hour*: 'Wheeler at 80'.
356 'If this series is bettered in my lifetime I will be surprised': email from Mark Damazer, CW personal archive, 13/5/05.
356 'I remember so clearly': undated letter from Ron Knight, CW personal archive, 2005.
358 'The way your paper mistreated my copy': letter from CW, CW personal archive, 6/6/2006.
361 'And to think I saved half of Calais': DC diaries.
368 'You stand for telling what you believe to be the truth': CW Interview for BBC College site/ referenced by Former BBC Director-General Mark Thompson, Charles Wheeler Memorial Lecture, 20/5/2009.